WITHDRAWN

FEDERAL APPLICATIONS
THAT GET RESULTS

Other books by Dr. Russ Smith

The Right SF 171 Writer: The Complete Guide to Communicating Your Qualifications to Federal Employers

Federal Jobs in Law Enforcement

FEDERAL APPLICATIONS THAT GET RESULTS

From SF 171s to Federal-Style Resumes

Russ Smith, Ph.D.

IMPACT PUBLICATIONS
Manassas Park, VA

Library of Congress Cataloguing-in-Publication Data

Smith, Russ
  Federal applications that get results : From SF 171s to federal-style resumes / Russ Smith.
     p.   cm.
  Includes bibliographical references and index.
  ISBN 1-57023-034-X : $23.95.
  1. Applications for positions. 2. Résumés (Employment) 3. Civil service positions—United States. 4. United States—Officials and employees —Recruiting. I. Title.
  JK765/S54 1995
  659.14—dc20   95-23072
                                                        CIP

For information on distribution or quantity discount rates, Tel. 703/361-7300, FAX 703/335-9486, or write to: Sales Department, IMPACT PUBLICATIONS, 9104-N Manassas Drive, Manassas Park, VA 22111-5211. Distributed to the trade by National Book Network, 4720 Boston Way, Suite A Lanham, MD 20706, Tel. 301/459-8696.

CONTENTS

CHAPTER 1
Creating a Unique and Powerful Application 1

CHAPTER 2
Myths and Realities 7
- Test Your Job Application Smarts 7
- Federal Job Applications: Myths and Realities 8

CHAPTER 3
Working For the Federal Government 15
- Position Management 15
- Occupational Groups 16
- General Schedule Jobs 16
- Wage Grade Jobs 18
- Executive Schedule and SES 19
- Example of Position Management 19
- Where Are the Jobs? 20
- Turnover 22
- Organizations in the Hiring Process 25

iii

CHAPTER 4
Position Standards 30
- X-118 Qualification Standards 32
- Status 40
- Summary 41

CHAPTER 5
The Application Packet 43
- Basic Information Requirements 44
- Description of Work 52
- SF 171-A/OF 612 Work Experience Continuation 57
- Supplemental Information Sheet 57
- KSAOs 59

CHAPTER 6
The Application Action Plan
and Career Resources 60
- List Your Assets 60
- Identify Jobs and Grades
  For Which You Are Eligible 62
- Focus on the Requirements For Target Jobs 62
- Get Current Job Announcements 63
- Begin Preparing The SF 171 Application Packet 63
- Prepare a "Mail-In" Packet 64
- Follow-Through 65
- Resources 66

Appendices
  A: Explanation of Terms 70
  B: General Schedule Occupations 76
  C: Selected Federal Pay Schedules For 1995 90
  D: Wage Grade Positions 95
  E: Federal Job Information Centers 102
  F: Sample Job Announcements 109
  G: Position Qualification Standards 119
  H: Position Classification Standards 141
  I: Sample Application Packets 150
  J: Sample Application Checklist 195
  K: Standard Forms 198

Index 235

ACKNOWLEDGEMENTS

Ron and Caryl Krannich were instrumental in bringing this book to print, for which help I cannot thank them enough. Jim reviewed a draft of this book and his recommendations, criticisms and advice strengthen the quality of the final draft. Joan H. and Linda K. were especially kind, helpful and tolerant in researching for this book; they share no blame, only kudos for their insights and help. Finally, to my long-suffering cats, I return the living room to you.

The opinions expressed here are those of the author. They are not necessarily shared by Impact Publications, the U.S. Army, the Office of Personnel Management, or anyone else with a god-like power over the author.

FEDERAL APPLICATIONS THAT GET RESULTS

1

CREATING A UNIQUE AND POWERFUL APPLICATION

The federal Office of Personnel Management made a major policy decision in 1994 when it decided to not "renew" the federal Standard Form 171 (Application for Federal Employment). Since 1 January, 1995, people could use one of several formats to apply for a federal job, including resumes, the new OF 612 (Optional Form 612—Optional Application for Federal Employment), the newly abandoned SF 171 or even computerized forms. After a twenty-seven year history as a major hurdle in the process of applying for federal jobs, this aspect of government was being reinvented to help simplify the process.

Throughout this century, the process of applying for a government job has gradually evolved toward developing methods for selecting the most qualified person. Various methods were used for helping managers find the most qualified employees. One trend has been to make "objective" or unbiased comparisons of applicants' skills in reference to job requirements. The requirements must be met or exceeded in order for an individual to be eligible for hiring. This is exactly what the SF 171 was designed to accomplish. The problem faced by many people who tried to complete the form was that it seemed extremely long and complicated.

The SF 171 was developed to help personnel specialists determine whether people were qualified for federal jobs. Personnel experts from many different agencies spent hundreds of hours identifying the kinds of information they needed

1

to evaluate people applying for federal jobs. Like many things designed by a group of people, though, parts of it seem useless to one person but are vitally important to another. The block for typing skills on the form, for example, may seem useless to someone applying for a warehouse or accountancy position, but will be critical for someone applying for any of a number of positions requiring that particular skill.

The new OF 612 form and the recommended format for resumes have simplified the application process by eliminating some of the blocks found on the SF 171. But while the forms differ from the old SF 171, they must do almost the same thing for an applicant that the SF 171 did. They must show that the applicant can do the work required by the job. In a very large sense, the new forms allow applicants more freedom in how they describe themselves. The important thing to remember about the various forms and the resume is that you still have to have a plan to methodically demonstrate that your education, skills, and work experience qualify you for the job you seek! Also, more than just the OF 612 or SF 171 or a resume is needed to apply for most federal jobs. As will be shown in later chapters, job applicants need to assemble "application packets," often two or more items, describing their qualifications. Typically, an application packet will include a "core" (the SF 171, a resume, or the OF 612), a supplemental experience statement or KSA (Knowledge, Skills and Abilities) summary, a copy of a recent performance appraisal, OPM Form 1386, Background Survey (a standard form which identifies an applicant's race, sex, and national origin), OPM Form 1170/17, List of College Courses (or a transcript), and in some cases, SF 15, Application for 10-Point Veteran Preference. A lot of paperwork may be needed to show qualifications!

*Your application must show how
you fit the requirements of the job.*

For the next year or two, many federal agencies will still accept applications on SF 171s. Most federal agencies in fact, as of January, 1995, had not developed alternatives to the SF 171 and are still accepting that form. As this book shows in later chapters, **the form is not as important as the information on the form.** If you can describe yourself properly, the actual form you use is just a way to satisfy the agency's requirements. You will find that more effort goes into preparing for the application and describing how well you meet the needs of the job than in actually completing the forms!

The various application forms have spaces for a variety of information about job applicants. Unfortunately, the accompanying instructions do not always give applicants enough help in completing the forms or the resume. Many of the questions and concerns people have about the application process are answered in the following pages.

As a <u>standard</u> form, the SF 171 tries to deal with all kinds of applicants.

The second chapter examines myths and misconceptions some people have about the process of applying for a federal job and working for the federal government. A short quiz tests you on both of these topics. The balance of the chapter debunks some of the common myths about each topic.

The third chapter provides background to the federal government's hiring methods. The application process can best be understood when you understand its purpose in the federal government and the government's hiring process. A subtle, but major factor in the federal hiring process is that the focus is not on hiring people (be they the "most skilled," "disadvantaged," veteran, or whatever) but rather **the focus is on filling positions**. As many former military personnel know, battles cannot be won unless you know your "enemy." Not everyone who applies for a federal job is "at war" with the federal government, of course, but this analogy does help prepare you for the form while Chapter Three describes the position management process.

In Lewis Carrol's story *Alice in Wonderland*, at one point, she is walking through a forest and comes to a fork in the trail and sees Cheshire Cat sitting on a branch..

> "... Would you tell me, please, which way I ought to go from here?"
> "That depends a good deal on where you want to get to," said the Cat.
> "I don't much care where—" said Alice.
> "Then it doesn't matter which way you go," said the Cat.
> "-so long as I get somewhere," Alice added as an explanation.

Unless you know how your application will be evaluated, in other words what kinds of information will be used by personnel specialists to rate your application, it is hard to know what to put in your application and what to leave out. How can you prepare your most effective replies? The main problem with the shift away from the SF 171 to resumes and less comprehensive forms is the lack of guidance given to applicants on what to include. Some people ramble on for several paragraphs without providing enough information to evaluate their qualifications. Others use jargon that is misunderstood or not credited. What in your background is relevant for the job you seek? How do you ensure that what you write will be understood by people who read and evaluate your application? Regardless of the form you use, you need a way to effectively show that you have the education, work experience, or knowledge, skills and abilities sought by the hiring agency.

> ## *You need a goal, a target job and grade, and knowledge about the goal's requirements, to prepare the right SF 171.*

The fourth chapter covers both position qualifications and position classification, the heart of the federal government's position management process. The federal Office of Personnel Management has created and published, for most federal job series, fairly detailed descriptions of the kinds of information a personnel specialist should seek when evaluating and rating a job applicant or when creating or modifying a position. The logical conclusion is that if you are applying, for example, for a grade seven secretarial position which has an emphasis on office automation, your application can score more points if you first determine what kinds of education and experience the rating officer will be seeking in your application. If the standards apply to you, then you need to clearly, almost forcefully, include these in your application. Where do you find these standards, how do you get them, how do you read them, and finally, and perhaps most importantly, how do you incorporate them into your application? You do not want to lose a chance at a good rating because you explain your work history in a way that is unclear to a personnel specialist. If they don't understand what you have written, they will assume you are either bluffing (and do not know how to properly explain the work you did) or assume that what you did is not relevant to the qualification standards. Chapter Four should help you use the *Qualification Standards Handbook*, as well as the *Position Classification Standards* to your advantage.

Chapter Five discusses various sections of the SF 171. The attempt here is to review the kinds of information sought from the section by both personnel specialists and hiring supervisors. Also, if you have enough information for the SF 171, you have more than enough for the alternative formats an application may use. Here, when discussing work experience, education, and selected other factors, three different perspectives will be provided as illustrations of the particular section topic. The first perspective will be of actual job announcements. These are the federal government's "HELP WANTED" signs. They describe in some detail what work is required, what the position offers (pay *and* career wise), and also gives hints about the kinds of information you need to put on your SF 171.

The second perspective focuses on completing parts of the SF 171 and describes and shows examples of the kinds of information you need to provide in the SF 171. The appropriate federal standards will be examined for several example jobs, and they will be used to complete the SF 171 sections on work experience and education. The purpose here is to illustrate how important it is to clearly describe **relevant** work. Finally, several different hypothetical people will illustrate good (and bad) answers to questions in particular sections of the SF 171, thus providing a third perspective on completing each part of the SF 171.

The right SF 171 writer has three goals:

- *Set a target (job series and grade)*
- *Gather information about the target*
- *Follow an action plan to reach the target.*

Chapter Five makes reference to a computer program called *The Quick and Easy Federal Application Kit*. An application must be typed or completed using a computer program such as this to look professional. You do **not** need this or any other program (or a computer) to benefit from this book or to complete the SF 171. This program "tackles" the various application tools in the same way this book does and we have to acknowledge the similarities in approaches, especially since they are so logical, or the sponsors of the computer program might call a foul on us. Also, if you do have a computer, your job search can be simplified with a program such as this.

Typically, there are other materials required to support the SF 171 when one applies for a federal government job. Commonly, there are forms to indicate your racial heritage, veteran status, as well as evaluations of one sort or another by your current (or past) supervisor. Many of the higher-graded white collar jobs (that is, jobs normally done in offices [wearing shirts with white collars, no less!]) also ask for descriptions of your knowledge, skills and other abilities peculiar to the work required by the job. These are referred to as KSAs or sometimes "kay-sos" (No, it doesn't seem to be spelled as it is pronounced; given the variety of information they seek and the many formats used by different agencies, they probably should more properly be called knowledge, abilities and other skills—KAOS). The last chapter examines many of these supplemental materials which often accompany an application for a federal job. Example jobs will be used to illustrate the kinds of supplemental material required in an application packet. Examples of both good and bad hypothetical application packets will be presented and discussed to illustrate the role of such material in an application packet. The samples will also illustrate how the same application would look when submitted as a resume, as an OF 612, or as an SF 171. New copies of *The Quick and Easy Federal Application Kit* allow you to enter the basic information, then customize an application using any of the three major application tools (resume, OF 612 or SF 171).

Chapter Six describes both the OF 612 or "Optional Application for Federal Employment" and *briefly* discusses how a resume can be built to successfully describe your qualifications for a federal job. Examples will be shown of how to translate a current SF 171 into these other formats.

The last chapter provides an "action plan" to guide you through the federal job application process. A step-by-step plan is described and a check list is provided to help you track your applications. The action plan implements the ideas described here for writing the right federal job application.

Upon completion of this material, you should understand what role a job application plays in the federal hiring process, how you can get the greatest impact from your application packet, and how to use it and the accompanying materials to sell yourself to a federal employer. Of course, no **guarantees** are given here; we cannot anticipate all problems that may arise with one person's application for a particular job. However, the advice contained here comes from people currently working for the federal government, including some of its personnel specialists. If an agency follows normal federal practices in filling a position, then the advice here should prepare you to sell yourself in the most positive way for that position.

The appendices provide a number of resources to assist you in preparing your application. The serious job applicant will have to contact several government agencies or private firms to acquire job announcements, supplemental materials and forms, X-118 Qualification Standards, and extra copies of the SF 171 or OF 612 (if the forms are being prepared on a typewriter). The first appendix has a list of the terms used in the federal hiring process. Later appendices include descriptions of the kinds of positions available with the federal government, pay rates, where to go for information, several standard forms you may need, and examples of job announcements and completed application packages. Finally, there is a copy of the action plan, in a checklist format, for doing a job search and application forms. The action plan identifies each step to be pursued in the process of completing an application packet for a particular job announcement.

Good luck!

2

MYTHS AND REALITIES

TEST YOUR JOB APPLICATION SMARTS

The following section tests your knowledge of the federal application process and how to get a federal job. A series of statements are presented. Circle one of the five numbers following each question to indicate whether you: 1) Strongly Agree; 2) Agree; 3) Have no opinion; 4) Disagree or 5) Strongly Disagree with the statement.

1. You need a college degree to qualify for most federal jobs.

   1   2   3   4   5

2. Federal jobs are "white collar" or office jobs.

   1   2   3   4   5

3. A professional-quality *resume* can be used to apply for any federal job.

    1   2   3   4   5

4. The SF 171 is no longer used in federal job applications.

    1   2   3   4   5

5. Anyone can fill out an SF 171, no special knowledge is required.

    1   2   3   4   5

6. An SF 171 made ten years ago is still valid today.

    1   2   3   4   5

7. An exam has to be taken to get any federal job.

    1   2   3   4   5

8. There are no federal jobs for people with a liberal or a fine arts college degree.

    1   2   3   4   5

9. A background in the military will not help someone get a federal job.

    1   2   3   4   5

Now go back through the list and add the number circled with each statement. If the total score is less than 36 then some of your knowledge of the federal government or the job application process is based on commonly-held misconceptions or myths. The next section briefly addresses each of these myths; later chapters will deal with each in more detail.

FEDERAL JOB APPLICATIONS: MYTHS AND REALITIES

MYTH 1:   **You have to have a college degree, or at least some college credits, before "they" will even look at your job application.**

REALITY: Depends on the job. A rocket scientist probably should have cracked a college book or two sometime during his or her life. However, the federal government recognizes alternatives to college education, including the General Education Development (GED) equivalency certificate, technical and vocational schools, and in some cases, just work experience. That is, many of the positions will allow you to substitute relevant work experience for college education. The trick is to know what education or experience is relevant to the job you want.

You don't need a college degree for many federal jobs and some federal jobs are not done in offices.

MYTH 2: **I don't want to work in an office pushing paper, so I'll never apply for a federal job.**

REALITY: Although a majority of the federal jobs ARE "white collar" or office jobs, there are also many federal jobs that are not office-bound. Jobs ranging from park rangers to forestry technicians, archaeologists through firefighters to animal health technicians can be found in the General Schedule. Also, roughly twenty percent of the federal jobs fall into something known as the Wage Grade schedule, a group of trade, craft and labor occupations commonly called "blue collar" jobs. These jobs include machine tool operating, stevedoring, plumbing, and carpentry jobs, as well as repairing various types of equipment (air conditioners, aircraft, vending machines, and bowling alley equipment, to name a few), working on ships and river boats, or in kitchens or laundries.

MYTH 3: **I'm trying to get a job as an electrician; I don't need to learn about the federal job application process.**

REALITY: You do if it is a federal job, Sparky! All federal jobs, both white collar and blue collar, require basically the same information from applicants for the job. This book can help you prepare and present the information in an effective format, whether using a resume, the SF 171 or the OF 612.

MYTH 4: **The SF 171 is no longer used in federal job applications.**

REALITY: Although the Office of Personnel Management has discontinued the requirement to use the SF 171, many agencies will probably be using the form until, or even after 1996. Over twenty-four million copies of the form were printed by the federal government in the last three and a half years! No single standard has arisen to replace the SF 171, so for the immediate future, an applicant may be able to pick either the resume, the SF 171, or the OF 612 and use it for most applications. This is especially beneficial for people currently in federal service who need to prepare current application packets in anticipation of RIFs or other changes in employment (see below).

As long as the application looks professional, it need not be prepared by a professional service.

MYTH 5: **You need to pay a professional to make a good application package.**

REALITY: Not if you follow the suggestions in this book! If you go to a professional resume service, they will ask you for the same information that you would need to put into an application package if you did it yourself. Of course, they *should* at least know what questions to ask you. Note that you will probably only get one version of your application packet (good for just one job vacancy application); if you want to apply to several jobs, most professional agencies will ask you to pay for each version of your application packet. If you have a typewriter and follow the suggestions in this book, most of the work only has to be done one time; to apply for other jobs, just a few blocks need to be changed.

MYTH 6: **Anyone can fill in the application for a federal job; there's no special trick involved.**

REALITY: Yes, of course, dealing with the federal government is very easy, simple, and uncomplicated. Sarcasm aside, there actually is a trick to the federal job application process. Your information will be evaluated by personnel specialists who will determine if you have the minimum qualifications for the job you are seeking. The determination will be made on the basis of what you put into your application packet. Now, these are **personnel** specialists, not specialists in the kind of work related to the job you are seeking. They won't necessarily know the ins and outs of tax examiner work. What they will do is compare what you write with government- or agency-wide standards; if what you write *clearly* indicates you meet the standards, then your application won't end up in the *rejected* file. So the trick is to explain yourself in terms the personnel specialists can understand. Make their work easier!

MYTH 7: **If my application packet has lots of jargon and five syllable words, it will be so impressive, "they" will have to give me a job.**

REALITY: Many occupations, both white and blue collar, develop their own special languages—have their own meanings for words (or jargon). What a job applicant needs to remember is that the first federal employee to evaluate an application packet will probably not understand the specialized jargon that was used. A personnel specialist who may not know all the cute little buzz words will, instead, compare what the application says with what the position requires. If the application does not have the same phrasing and key words as do the qualification requirements, then the application will not be rated highly and may not get sent to the hiring official.

MYTH 8: **I filled out an SF 171 twelve years ago when I got my current federal job; I don't need to make any more SF 171s.**

REALITY: Even if you found your perfect federal job back during the halcyon days of the Gerald Ford administration, have only four years to go until you retire to your worm ranch in

Florida, and have no desire to get a promotion to a GS-7, you may not be prepared for a reorganization or a reduction-in-force (RIF) in your agency. Your sixteen year old SF 171, describes your education and work experience **before** you assumed your current job. If your agency reorganizes and you lose your position in the agency, your "most recent" SF 171 may be the one you prepared sixteen years ago! If you want to change agencies, for example, you will need to either prepare a new SF 171 or, at the very least, prepare an SF 172. Your various specialized training classes, the rich variety of work experiences you have had with the federal government, even the names of people who can give you glowing job references, are probably not in your old SF 171.

Current federal employees need to update their SF 171s in their personnel jackets, to reflect changes in work done, training completed, and to update references.

Every federal employee needs to periodically update his or her SF 171 as more education is completed or new work experiences are gained. At the very least, if you work for the federal government now, you need to add to the SF 171 that got you your current job a description of what you do *in* that job.

MYTH 9:   **I have to take exams to get a federal job.**

REALITY: Actually, very few federal jobs require exams. The wage grade jobs usually do not require exams. Above grade nine, most if not all federal jobs require relevant work experience (and maybe some college courses or degrees) instead of exams. There are many different kinds of jobs with the federal government; depending on the job series and the requirements to do the work, you may not have to take an exam.

MYTH 10: **I have a college degree, but it is in history/archaeology/ literature; there won't be a federal job given my background.**

REALITY: Scan through the Appendices B and D that list General Schedule and Wage Grade job series and families. There are more different kinds of work with the federal government than most people imagine. Also, for some federal jobs, the education requirements are often expressed as having a certain number of college semester hours (or equivalent) in RELATED disciplines. For example, the Operations Research job series (GS-1515) requires twenty-four college semester hours in courses such as math, operations research, statistics, logic, or subject matter courses which require substantial competence in math or statistics. A number of these courses are normally taken just meeting the general education requirements at most colleges and universities; a few more classes could qualify some people for a professional job such as this. Alternatively, there are a number of job series that seek people with just a "liberal arts" background. After some digging, you can probably find a federal job for almost any college major.

MYTH 11: **I retire from the military soon; I'd like a federal job but I don't think my military experiences will be of any use in getting me a job.**

REALITY: People who have served in the military may actually have one of the best backgrounds for federal jobs. First, examine the job series in the General Schedule and Wage Grade pay plans (Appendices B and D); almost every Military Occupational Specialty (MOS) has a federal civilian job series counterpart and many military skills can translate to civilian jobs. Recent alumni of the U.S. military should request DD Form 2586, "Verification of Military Experience and Training" from their transition office. This form itemizes the skills and training the vet received during his or her military service. The trick is to examine both the general qualification standards for a particular position, as well as the agency-specific standards and required knowledge, skills and abilities. A retired enlisted infantryman, for example, may find that he[1] has had experiences required for a program analyst position at Coyote Junction, Texas, as stated in the job announcement. For the combat support and combat service support arms, virtually every MOS has a counterpart in either the GS or WG pay plans. And finally, when SF 171s are evaluated, veterans, especially disabled veterans, receive preferential treatment, not only when applying for work, but during those dreaded Reduction-in-Force (RIF) exercises (when an agency is eliminating positions).

---

[1] As of the spring of 1995, no women were in the Infantry Branch of the U.S. Army.

3

WORKING FOR THE FEDERAL GOVERNMENT

The process of applying for a federal job is currently undergoing its greatest change in almost thirty years. For most of the last generation, the SF 171 has been the core of all application packets submitted by job seekers. Now, and probably for the next year or more, the SF 171 is no longer the sole core. People may use other formats to describe themselves when searching for a federal job. This chapter reviews the federal employment scene and the role of the application packet in that scene. The next chapter reviews the kinds of information and the ways to organize the information to write an effective job application packet.

POSITION MANAGEMENT

The federal government, in an effort to treat employees and job applicants impartially, or at least without the pattern or practice of discrimination, manages positions, not people. That is, in a typical office, for example, a number of **positions** will be authorized or created and tasked to do the work of the office. Personnel specialists, working with the Agency, will first identify, for the new position(s):

- What supervision will the position(s) receive;
- What supervision will the position(s) exercise; and

15

- What tasks will the position(s) perform.

After identifying what the position(s) will do, personnel specialists will then determine which occupational groups are required to do the work, and will determine the appropriate pay grade for that work, based on federal standards (more on this in Chapter Four). People will then be recruited and hired based on the extent to which they match, in educational background and work experience, the knowledge, skills and other abilities required by the position.

> *When filling a federal job, applicants are evaluated on how well they meet the position's minimum requirements; winners meet or exceed position requirements.*

OCCUPATIONAL GROUPS

There are three major occupational groups of federal positions: the General Schedule (usually, white collar career positions), the Wage Grade (usually, trade, craft and labor positions), and the Excepted Service (such as political appointments).

GENERAL SCHEDULE JOBS

Federal General Schedule (or GS) jobs comprise over eighty percent of the federal work force. Most of the discussion here applies to GS jobs. Where necessary, though, Wage Grade (WG) positions will also be discussed. Jobs in the GS are further grouped into twenty-one occupational groups (see Figure 3.1). Appendix B has a description of each occupational group, including a listing of most of the positions within each group.

White collar federal employees fall into three major pay systems: the General Schedule (GS), the Foreign Service (some Department of State employees), and a third pay system for some employees of the Department of Veterans Affairs.

As will be described in the next chapter, the more difficult the work or responsibility of a position, the higher the pay grade (hereafter, just grade will be used). The federal government has attempted to be competitive in pay with other employers and, in many cases, has been successful (see Appendix C for more information on federal pay plans). Federal employees in some "high cost of living" metropolitan areas, for example, now receive supplemental or "locality" pay. Hard to fill positions (such as secretarial positions) have, in the past, also received income supplements as inducements to remain in their positions. The Federal Pay Comparability Act, signed by President Bush in 1990, will cause federal white collar salaries to slowly change from the values on the one General Schedule (shown in Appendix C) to as many as twenty-nine different schedules for white collar employees! As of January, 1994, pay increases for the 1.5 million federal white collar employees in General Schedule jobs are supposed to be based on wages for comparable private sector jobs **in their localities**! By 2004 (assuming Congress and the President support the Act's provisions), the salaries of employees in General Schedule grades 1 through 15 should be comparable to those of private sector employees, judged on a case-by-case

Figure 3.1
Federal Occupational Groups

Occupational Group No.	Occupational Group Title	Occupational Group No.	Occupational Group Title
GS-000	Miscellaneous	GS-1000	Public Information and Arts
GS-100	Social Science, Psychology and Welfare	GS-1100	Business and Industry
		GS-1200	Copyright, Patent and Trademark
GS-200	Personnel Management and Industrial Relations	GS-1300	Physical Sciences
GS-300	Administrative, Clerical and Office Services	GS-1400	Library and Archives
		GS-1500	Mathematics and Statistics
GS-400	Biological Sciences	GS-1600	Equipment, Facilities and Service
GS-500	Accounting and Budget	GS-1700	Education
GS-600	Medical, Hospital, Dental and Public Health	GS-1800	Investigation
		GS-1900	Quality Assurance, Inspection and Grading
GS-700	Veterinary Medical Science		
GS-800	Engineering and Architecture	GS-2000	Supply
		GS-2100	Transportation
GS-900	Legal and Kindred		

basis in twenty-six metropolitan areas with large concentrations of federal employees. However, a few employees, such as some secretaries, will not receive this locality pay; other supplements may already apply. Since January, 1994, federal GS workers have been given pay raises to close the gap between their pay and the pay of comparable private sector employees.

The GS consists of eighteen grades for white collar workers. Further, grades one through fifteen are divided into ten steps (based on time-in-grade); grade sixteen has nine steps, seventeen has five steps, and eighteen has but one step. Usually, one can anticipate moving up a step every fifty-two weeks (for steps one through three), one hundred and four weeks (steps four through six), or one hundred and fifty-six weeks (steps seven through nine). Reaching step ten in a pay grade is the last step for that grade; a person would have to move to a new position (with a higher pay grade) to advance beyond step ten for a grade. Exceptional workers may also be given "quality step increases".

> ### *The General Schedule is one of many federal pay plans and pay adjustment schedules for federal employees.*

Appendix C shows the proposed 1995 GS pay plan for grades one through fifteen. Appendix C also shows pay schedules for other special "white collar" occupations, including the Foreign Service and Department of Veterans Affairs.

WAGE GRADE JOBS

Trade, craft and labor occupations are grouped under the Wage Grade (WG) system. Compensation in these occupations are set through local wage surveys (which help find the prevailing local wage rates). A job announcement for one of these positions will list available grades and pay rates per hour. Appendix D lists WG Occupational Groups.

Figure 3.2
Wage Grade Occupational Families

Job Code	Occupational Family	Job Code	Occupational Family
2500	Wire Communications Equipment Installation & Maintenance	4600	Wood Work
2600	Electronic Equipment Inst. & Maintenance	4700	General Maintenance & Operations Work
2800	Electrical Inst. & Maintenance	4800	General Equipment Maintenance
3100	Fabric & Leather Work	5000	Plant and Animal Work
3300	Instrument Work	5200	Miscellaneous Occupations
3400	Machine Tool Work	5300	Industrial Equipment Maintenance
3500	General Services and Support Work	5400	Industrial Equipment Operating
3600	Structural & Finishing Work	5700	Transportation/Mobile Equipment Operation
3700	Metal Processing	5800	Transportation/Mobile Equipment Maintenance
3800	Metal Work		
3900	Motion Picture, Radio, TV and Sound Equipment Work	6500	Ammunition, Explosives, and Toxic Materials Work
4000	Lens & Crystal Work	6600	Armament Work
4100	Painting and Paper Hanging	6900	Warehousing and Stock Handling
4200	Plumbing and Pipefitting	7000	Packing and Processing
4300	Pliable Materials Work	7300	Laundry, Dry Cleaning and Pressing
4400	Printing	7400	Food Preparation and Serving

EXECUTIVE SCHEDULE AND SES

Executive Schedule pay system was established by Congress for senior Executive Branch political appointees. There are five levels of ES positions, each with its own pay. The SES or Senior Executive Service consists of senior policy, supervisory or managerial positions in the Executive Branch which are not held by people on the Executive Schedule. SES employees typically are long-service career civil servants. The six pay levels within the SES, as well as the five ES levels, are linked with the GS; as Congress raises the GS pay plan, so too can pay for these other two pay plans be raised.

EXAMPLE OF POSITION MANAGEMENT

Figure 2.3 shows the positions in a hypothetical finance office.

This hypothetical office has eleven positions or "slots" which can be used as authorizations to hire or retain people. The office is authorized two people to work as grade 7 Accountants (the expression under the word "Accountant" describes the position as General Schedule, job series number 0510, pay grade 7). If there were,

Figure 3.3
Hypothetical Finance Office

```
              Supervisory Financial Manager
                     GS-0505-12

   Accountant        Secretary-Typing      Voucher
   GS-0510-11          GS-0318-05          Examiner
                                           GS-0540-05

   Accountant
   GS-0510-09

   Accountant
   GS-0510-07
```

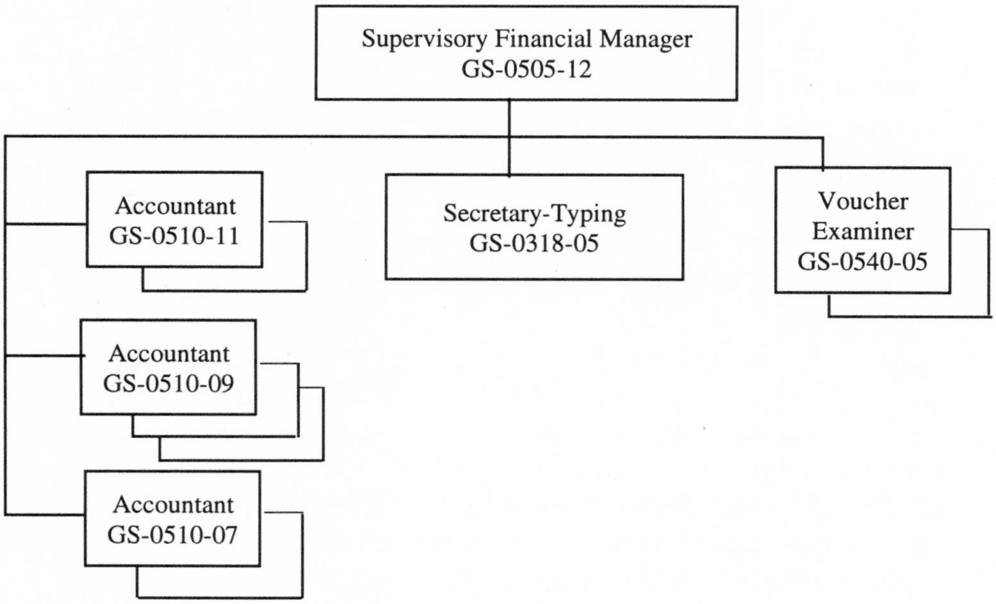

for any reason, a third grade 7 Accountant in the office, that person would be in an unauthorized position and would constitute an "overhire." The third person does not have a "slot" to occupy in the office. When offices are rapidly expanding (or just being established), some supervisors may use the overhire practice to hire someone in advance of, and in anticipation that the agency personnel office will establish such a position in the near future.

There are two grade 7, three grade 9 and two grade 11 Accountant positions in this office, plus a grade 12 supervisory position. These could constitute a "career ladder" for the people in the grade 7, 9 and 11 positions; the people in this ladder may anticipate that time in grade at the grade 7, 9 and 11 positions would prepare them for promotion to positions "higher" on the career ladder when one becomes vacant. Theoretically, the work experiences they have in these positions would fulfill the kinds of work experience required of applicants for higher level positions within the office. That is, they would be assigned various tasks and responsibilities which are required by people applying for the higher graded positions. Under normal circumstances, the secretary and the two voucher examiners would not be in the career line of the Accountant positions and would not get the assignments or responsibilities to prepare them for promotion in the Accountant series.

Further, when recruiting for a new grade 11 Accountant, the job announcement might refer to the position as a GS-0510-07/09/11 or just as a grade 11 position. In the former case, by advertising the position at three grade levels, a person could be hired at grade 7 or 9 and, within a year, if performance has been satisfactory, the person would be promoted two grades (7 to 9 or 9 to 11). From the supervisory perspective, this creates a larger applicant pool than one limited to people only qualified for grade 11. Also, when recruiting someone from outside the agency, a supervisor may actually prefer to recruit at a lower grade level. Before the new employee does the more difficult work associated with the higher grade position, a year would be spent in the lower graded position "learning the ropes" of the way the agency operates.

WHERE ARE THE JOBS?

Figure 3.4 shows, in general terms, the organization of the federal government. After the Constitution was ratified in the 1780s, the prevailing sentiment was that Congress (the Senate and House of Representatives) would make national laws, the Supreme Court (and later, lesser federal courts) would interpret (through their findings) the Constitution, and the Executive Branch, led by the President, would execute the laws of the land.

Two hundred years later, this neat and simple separation of powers has, to some extent, fallen by the wayside. Congress has created its own bureaucracy (including the Congressional Budget Office, General Accounting Office, and the Senate and House staffs). Various officials in the Executive Branch make rules and policies

Figure 3.4
The Federal Government

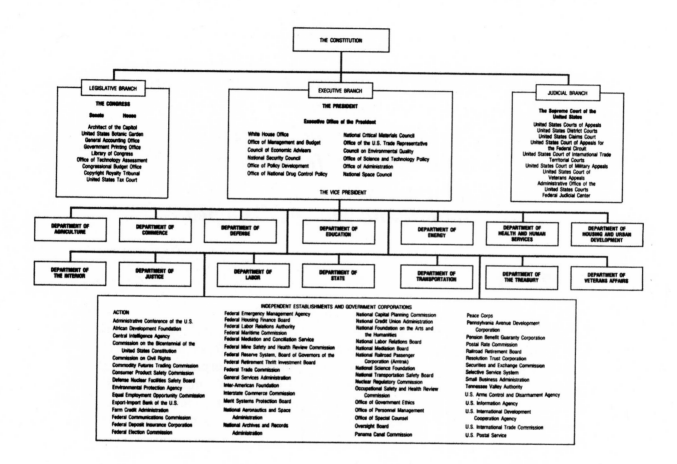

which, to the average citizen, are indistinguishable from Congress' laws. Other officials, such as Administrative Law Judges, act like judicial system judges in interpreting the Constitution, U.S. laws, and treaties. Finally, in addition to adjudication, the federal courts have established their own small bureaucracies to ensure compliance with judicial findings. The bottom line is that there are jobs in all three branches of government.

The 1991 Statistical Abstract reports federal civilian employment for 1989 (see Figure 3.5); when compared to 1992 data, the changes in agency sizes during the years of President Bush reflect the end of the Cold War.

As the data shows in Figure 3.5, not only are there federal jobs outside the Executive Branch, there are also a number of jobs outside the United States. Within the United States, most of the federal jobs are located outside the metropolitan

Washington, D.C. area. Depending on the position and the employing agency, federal jobs can be found anywhere from a one-person office in a small rural community to a large Federal Regional Center containing hundreds of workers from a number of different agencies.

> *A key point to remember when working for an agency undergoing a RIF is that the agency personnel office will, in most instances, refer to the records of the employees to determine who bumps, and who gets bumped.*

TURNOVER

Federal hiring and firing patterns vary slightly from year to year but can vary widely across agencies from year to year. For example, in 1989, while roughly 635,500 people were hired into federal jobs, only 605,700 people left federal jobs. Changes in program, lack of funds, decrease in work, reorganization, insufficient personnel, or the need to place a returning employee with re-employment rights may require a federal agency to conduct a reduction-in-force (RIF). This means the agency would lay off, furlough for more than thirty days, reassign or demote some employees (5 CFR Part 351).

Currently, some parts of the federal government, notably the Department of Defense, are reducing their workforces in response to shrinking budgets and changes in agency mission. Federal activities have three ways to reduce their workforces:

- by attrition (when people leave a position, the position is either not filled or is abolished);

- by "early out" or other similar voluntary separations ("early out" allows employees to retire earlier than their eligibility would allow); and

- by Reductions-in-Force (RIFs), in which positions are abolished (whether occupied by someone or not).

Figure 3.5
Federal Civilian Employment

AGENCY	TOTAL		PCT CHANGE 1989 - 1992	U.S. ONLY		PCT CHANGE 1989- 1992
	1989	1992		1989	1992	
Total, all agencies*	3,123,731	3,086,317	-1.2	2,977,621	2,965,634	-0.4
Legislative Branch, total *	37,690	38,509	2.2	37,637	38,446	2.1
Congress *	19,504	20,084	3.0	19,504	20,084	3.0
Senate	7,401	7,620	3.0	7,401	7,620	3.0
House Summary	12,090	12,446	2.9	12,090	12,446	2.9
Judicial Branch *	21,915	27,987	27.7	21,663	27,683	27.8
Supreme Court	327	353	8.0	327	353	8.0
U.S. Courts	21,588	27,551	27.6	21,336	27,247	27.7
Executive Branch, total *	3,064,126	3,018,821	-1.5	2,918,321	2,899,505	-0.6
Executive Office of the Pres. *	1,577	1,866	18.3	1,879	1,859	-1.1
Office of Management & Budget	527	586	11.2	527	586	11.2
Executive Departments	2,065,038	2,038,674	-1.3	1,939,431	1,939,260	-0.0
State	25,327	25,734	1.6	9,152	9,519	4.0
Treasury	152,548	161,951	6.2	151,517	160,805	6.1
Defense	1,075,437	982,773	-8.6	975,047	909,792	-6.7
Justice	79,667	96,927	21.7	78,217	95,173	21.7
Interior	77,545	85,260	9.9	77,175	84,847	9.9
Agriculture	122,062	128,324	5.1	120,567	126,754	5.1
Commerce	45,091	38,086	-15.5	44,366	37,197	-16.2
Labor	18,125	17,889	-1.3	18,085	17,848	-1.3
Health and Human Services	122,259	131,191	7.3	121,550	130,468	7.3
Housing and Urban Development	13,544	13,701	1.2	13,416	13,578	1.2
Transportation	65,615	70,558	7.5	65,104	70,004	7.5
Energy	17,130	20,962	22.4	17,123	20,956	22.4
Education	4,696	5,113	8.9	4,692	5,108	8.9
Veterans Affairs	245,922	260,205	5.8	243,420	257,211	5.7
Independent Agencies *	997,511	978,281	-1.9	977,323	958,386	-1.9
Environmental Protection Agency	15,590	18,196	16.7	15,572	18,173	16.7
Equal Employment Opportunity Committee	2,743	2,899	5.7	2,743	2,899	5.7
Federal Deposit Insurance Corp.	9,031	22,467	148.8	9,017	22,457	149.1
Federal Emergency Management Agency	3,048	5,632	84.8	3,038	5,465	79.9
General Services Administration	20,063	20,770	3.5	19,981	20,671	3.5
National Aeronautics & Space Adminstration	24,165	25,425	5.2	24,156	25,418	5.2
Nuclear Regulatory Commission	3,288	3,528	7.3	3,288	3,528	7.3
Office of Personnel Management	6,859	6,941	1.2	6,829	6,916	1.3
Small Business Administration	4,653	5,897	26.7	4,572	5,769	26.2
Tennessee Valley Authority	26,676	19,493	-26.9	26,676	19,493	-26.9
U.S. Information Agency	8,723	6,342	-27.3	4,370	4,340	-0.7

NOTES: 1989 figures are from the *1991 Statistical Abstract of the United States,* Table 529. 1992 was provided by the Office of Personnel Management from their *Monthly Report of Federal Civilian Employment (SF-113A).*

* Includes other branches not shown separately.

A RIF is often very traumatic, especially if the person has few opportunities for work outside the federal government. When an agency conducts a RIF, one or more positions are abolished. If someone is in one of those positions, the person is often given "bumping rights" or "retreat rights."

"Bumping rights" means they can move into positions occupied by people with a lower "competitive standing" in the same occupational group, bumping those employees out of their position. The "bumped" employee now gets to bump someone with yet a lower competitive standing at the same or a lower grade. If a person is "bumped" into a lower grade, the person would retain his or her pay from the position occupied before the RIF "bumping" began. Four factors are used to establish an employee's competitive area during a RIF:

- type of appointment (career, probationary or indefinite or temporary);
- veteran's preference (especially disabled vets);
- total length of civilian and creditable military service; and
- performance ratings on the job

Highly successful or exceptional evaluation ratings during the past three rating periods can add years to a person's competitive standing.

The process of setting competitive standing for an individual is very complex. Basically, though, employees in an agency undergoing a RIF are put into one of six broad retention categories (see Figure 3.6). Within each of the six categories, there are further breakdowns by job series and then by total length of creditable service.

Figure 3.6
RIF Retention Categories

	Career Employees	Non-Career Employees
30% Disabled Vets	I A	I B
Other Veterans	II A	II B
Non-Veterans	III A	III B

"Retreat rights," unlike bump rights, refer to a movement by an employee **back** to a previously held position, or to one essentially with duties identical to one previously held, when the position is held by someone with lower retention rights. If in the past one of the grade 12 people worked in another job series, such as computer scientist, GS-1550, retreat rights would enable that person to go back to a position with identical duties in the GS-1550 series; he or she is "retreating" to a previously-held position. (Note that technically, a retreat can be a "bump" under certain cases.)

Surprisingly enough, an activity undergoing a RIF might also be recruiting! Hard to fill positions, such as secretaries, clerk-typists, and some entry-level positions, might be advertised as open while more technical or specialized positions in the same agency are eliminated.

A job held many years earlier, and described briefly on an SF 171, could very well mean the difference between securing a position within the agency or being out of work! Personnel specialists reviewing your records will determine whether you have had experiences that qualify you for any of the various occupational groups (and determine for which grades you are eligible) based on position descriptions in your records. If you performed work *not* described on the position descriptions (and this occurs under the category of "other duties as required"), current federal employees need to get this into their records. The best way to do that is to file an SF 172, "Amendment of Application for Federal Employment" (see Appendix K), clearly stating that the amendment describes "other duties" done in the position.

Current federal employees need to review and perhaps update their personnel jackets, using SF 172 to describe workloads not covered by position descriptions, and provide recent addresses and phone numbers, in preparation for transfers, RIFs, or other changes in standing.

ORGANIZATIONS IN THE HIRING PROCESS

There are a number of organizations with responsibilities in the Federal hiring process. They can all affect, in one way or another, your success in completing an application for a federal job.

Office of Personnel Management (OPM)

The Office of Personnel Management is a separate agency in the Executive Branch and is responsible for establishing government-wide standards for hiring, firing, promotions, equal employment opportunities, and a host of other personnel functions. In the past, OPM played a crucial role in the hiring process as the initial point of contact for someone seeking a federal job.

Until the mid-1980s, OPM tested job applicants, evaluated SF 171s, rated applicants, and maintained registers of qualified applicants for federal jobs. If an agency needed candidates for a vacant position, OPM would supply a list of people to interview for the position. If someone wanted a federal job, the first *big* step was to contact OPM for job announcements, blank SF 171s, take any required tests, submit finished SF 171s, get rated and put on a register or list of qualified applicants.

This excessively-centralized process was changed to allow agencies more responsibility in the hiring process. Today, OPM plays an "honest broker" role in the hiring process. OPM establishes government-wide guidelines and procedures to be used by agency personnel offices to manage aspects of the personnel process. These general guidelines and procedures help standardize the ways jobs are defined, how people are recruited, what criteria are used to evaluate job applicants, and what an agency must do to ensure that equal employment opportunities are provided. One example of such a guideline is that which determines which criteria should be used to rank an applicant. OPM creates, among other things, the standards used to evaluate applicants for GS (X-118 Qualification Standards) and Wage Grade (X-118C Qualification Standards) positions. As will be shown in the next chapter, these standards help a personnel specialist review job applicants' backgrounds and rate their suitability for a vacancy.

OPM is responsible for several other products which may be of interest to someone seeking a federal job:

- *Civilian Personnel Law Manual:* This covers the legal entitlements of federal employment, and has summaries of the statutes and regulations which establish employees' rights in the areas of compensation, leave, travel and relocation;

- *Handbook of Occupational Groups and Series:* This helps the separate agencies classify positions, determine what grade is appropriate for the kind of work and responsibility in the position;

- *Handbook X-118 or Qualification Standards Handbook:* This describes the criteria to be used by agency personnel specialists to rate a job applicant's background and experience; standard "work performed" lists for each grade of each GS job (grades 1 through 15) are in this handbook;

- *Handbook X-118C or Job Qualification System for Trades and Labor Occupations:* This is the WG counterpart to Handbook X-118.

- *Career America Connection (912-757-3000):* This is a phone answering service available 24 hours a day, seven days a week, that provides information about current employment and career opportunities, special programs for students, veterans, and people with disabilities, the Presidential Management Intern Program, and salaries and benefits.

- *Federal Job Opportunities Bulletin Board (912-757-3100):* This and four regional electronic bulletin boards provide information about open examinations and job vacancy announcements worldwide. Anyone with a computer equipped with a modem can contact one of these information sources (see Appendix E for more information).

- *Federal Occupational and Career Information System (FOCIS):* This is a computer program which describes work in the federal service, helps users determine positions for which they might be eligible (including job series and grade), and identifies where (geographically and by agency) such positions exist. Copies are available at federal job centers (see below) and in some state employment offices and larger city libraries.

The Office of Personnel Management consists of the Central Office or Office Headquarters, the Washington Area Service Center (WASC), five Regional Offices, and the Federal Employment Information Centers. The Central Office in Washington, D.C. takes the lead in establishing federal policies for federal personnel management. This means they make policy on recruitment, examinations, leader development, training, administration of pay plans, job classification, personnel investigations, and employee evaluation procedures. They also administer employee retirement and insurance programs and advise agencies in labor relations and affirmative action.

The WASC and the five Regional Offices ensure that OPM programs and policies are followed in their areas (the WASC covers the metropolitan Washington, D.C. area, Atlantic overseas, and some worldwide activities). Daily administration within each region is conducted by one of the six or more Area Offices subordinate to the Regional Office. Area Offices handle the distribution of job information within an Area, and manage recruitment and examining in their Areas.

A Federal Employment Information Center is usually contained in each Area Office. FEICs help people seeking federal employment. A job seeker may visit a FEIC and obtain job announcements, application forms, advice on how to apply for work, and how to be tested for federal jobs. (Please note, however, that some FEICs are "self service" and do not provide advice to someone seeking a federal job, and many are shutting down or consolidating with other offices.) Appendix E lists OPM Regional and Area Offices, FEICs, and the WASC.

Federal Agencies

Agency personnel offices, using policy and procedure guidance from OPM, play key roles in the personnel process. Agencies establish positions by securing funding for a position, determining the appropriate pay plan, job series and grade for the position, recruiting applicants for the position, evaluating and ranking applicants, and "in-processing" newly hired people (assisting new employees in selecting insurance and retirement plans, apprising them of their rights, preparing personnel records' files

> *OPM has delegated to many federal agencies responsibility for establishing positions, advertising vacancies, recruiting, and hiring new employees.*

and so on). Agencies also manage their own RIFs. While smaller federal agencies may only have one personnel office, larger activities such as the Department of Defense, have established personnel offices throughout the United States and overseas. The Department of Defense also has created, at large or centrally-located installations, "One Stop Job Shops" which, much like the FEICs, help people get federal jobs (primarily in the Department of Defense). A One Stop Job Shop also often includes personnel trained to assist an applicant in getting a federal job. Also, One Stop Job Shops list Defense Department positions not listed elsewhere, especially those positions funded by *non-appropriated* funds (NAF). Post/Base Exchanges, libraries, morale/welfare/recreation positions and other activities at military installations may have one or more positions which are funded by money raised primarily at the installation through Officers' and Noncommissioned Officers' Clubs, golf courses, and other morale, welfare or recreational activities at the installation (that is, the position is not paid from Congressional appropriations but from locally generated income, hence the term *non-appropriated*).

Federal agencies play another role in the SF 171 process. While the OPM establishes, in the *X-118* and *X-118C Handbooks*, guidelines for evaluating job applicants, federal agencies may create additional guidelines. The *X-118 Handbook*, for example, establishes in general terms the education and work experience someone needs to become a system accountant. The agency may establish additional requirements unique to the kinds of work a system accountant does for the agency (for example, requiring experience with a particular computer system). General Schedule positions for which single agency standards have been published are marked with an asterisk in Appendix B.

State Employment Offices

Employment offices in many states play a vital role in helping people find and apply for federal jobs. State employment offices typically will have a listing of federal job openings within the state. Some state employment offices also have copies of *X-118 Handbooks* available for people to examine when preparing applications. Finally, employment offices in some states offer training seminars to help people prepare for interviews, or otherwise market themselves for jobs. These confidence-building exercises can be particularly useful for people who plan on federal jobs but have not had military experience or prior federal employment.

Public Libraries

A final resource organization for the process of applying for federal jobs is the local library. Public libraries in or near metropolitan areas and university or college libraries will often have copies of the *X-118 Handbooks* available. Many also subscribe to *Federal Career Opportunities* or *Federal Jobs Digest,* two publications which list federal vacancies around the world. While not all federal jobs are listed in these publications, they do provide a host of employment opportunities for people seeking federal jobs. A large library will typically have other assets which can provide the kinds of background information needed to successfully complete an application packet. They may, for instance, have a copy of the FOCIS computer program to help people determine which career in federal service is right for them.

Summary

Several important points were presented here about the federal job process. First, the focus of federal employment is on **positions**; a position is like an open box within an office or activity. The box is defined in terms of the tasks required by people in the position, which position supervises the position, and which positions it supervises, in turn. These characteristics of the position help personnel specialists assign a job series and grade (such as Budget Analyst, GS-560-09) to the position.

Secondly, there is a wide variety of positions available in the federal government, ranging from Wage Grade Laborer positions through Senior Executive Service positions. Further, there are opportunities throughout the country and even overseas, and across all three branches of government. Despite the great variety of work available in the federal government, a standard form (the SF 171) was created to evaluate applicants for federal jobs.

The SF 171 is not just a tool for people who want to make their first application for a federal job; even people who have been federal employees for many years need to regularly update their SF 171 in preparation for promotions, transfers, and reductions-in-force. Given the importance the SF 171 plays for both federal job applicants and employees, the fact that it is still being accepted by federal agencies in application packets, and the fact that much of the information needed to complete an SF 171 is required in any application packet, people have an advantage when they know how to most effectively complete an SF 171. The next two chapters address this crucial issue and show the relationship of the SF 171 to the new OF 612 and federal guidelines for resumes.

4

POSITION STANDARDS

The preceding chapter showed how an application packet is used in federal personnel actions. The application packet is one part of a method for the personnel specialist, who is engaged in evaluating job applicants or administering a RIF or any of several other tasks, to evaluate people. The other part of the method for evaluating people is the qualification standards associated with any federal position. At the most basic level, the person's education and work experience have meaning to a personnel specialist only when compared with "objective" standard qualifications assigned to a position.

Personnel specialists are not, nor, perhaps, should they be required to understand the work of, for example, a biochemist. That is, requiring a personnel specialist to know enough about biochemistry to assign different biochemistry knowledges and skills to different federal grade levels is unreasonable. The personnel specialist should know the work of his or her own position; specialists in biochemistry and other career groups can provide personnel specialists criteria for evaluating candidates for biochemistry positions.

The criteria used to evaluate candidates for government-wide careers have been standardized and serve as objective yardsticks for measuring a job applicant's background. Some government agencies go one step further, refining and clarifying the standards they wish to use in addition to the government-wide standards. When a person's application packet is evaluated by personnel specialists, then, the evaluation is made with reference to OPM (and, if any exist, agency) qualification standards.

The way white and blue collar job applicants are evaluated is of considerable importance to someone applying for a federal job. In fact, two very different approaches are used and this difference **must** be addressed when applying for a federal job. Basically (and this simplification is used to highlight the differences), *white collar applications must show how much education and work experience one has had in preparation for the vacant position.* If general or specialized experience at "the next lower grade" is required, how much time was spent doing the tasks of that lower grade? *Blue collar applicants must show how much ability or potential they have for the vacant position.* The length of time spent on prior jobs is not as critical for blue collar jobs as for white collar. This chapter discusses in some detail the treatment of white, and then blue collar applications, identifying the kinds of information needed for strong application packets.

An announcement for a white collar, grade eleven position might include as a standard a specific number of college hours in social science, history or English. Any applicants without those college hours do not meet that particular standard. Similarly, if an agency's standard is expressed as "at least one year's experience working with *LOTUS 1-2-3*, *VisiCalc*, or Borland's *Quattro Pro*" (those are popular spreadsheet software trade names), then even though an applicant says she has five years experience with **spreadsheet** software, to a personnel specialist unfamiliar with computer software, the applicant lacks the appropriate experience. Even though the hiring official at the agency level does understand that *VisiCalc* is a spreadsheet software program, the applicant's packet might not get sent to the hiring official simply because the information (as interpreted by the personnel specialist) did not justify rating the applicant as qualified for the position!

Obviously, some effort has to be taken to successfully prepare an application packet. The applicant knows the facts of his or her work history, but how those facts are explained makes all the difference in preparing the right application packet. The SF 171 (or OF 612 or resume) is one (admittedly a major) part of an application package which will be reviewed (and possibly rejected), not on the quality of the typing done to prepare the package or how rich and exciting one's life has been, but **how well does the information provided correspond to position qualification standards!**

This chapter will describe a plan of action to prepare an application packet to meet the standards used to evaluate applicants. Most applications for work with the federal government will require a number of forms. Although the following section refers to the SF 171, the kinds of information provided will also be useful if one is submitting an OF 612 or even a resume. A successful application packet will be that which:

- identifies the criteria used to evaluate applicants; and

- establishes in a clear, concise manner that the applicant has the prior work experience or education needed.

The first part of this chapter will examine standards for white collar positions with the federal government. The next section will examine standards for trade or labor occupations with the federal government.

X-118 QUALIFICATION STANDARDS

Background

The Classification Act of 1949 established a classification standards program for General Schedule (GS) positions (codified in Chapter 51 of title 5, United States Code). The statute:

- sets forth the principle of equal pay for equal work;
- defines each grade in the GS;
- directs OPM, after consulting with federal agencies, to prepare standards for agencies to use in placing positions within their proper classes and grades; and
- requires that OPM shall:

  - define the various types of positions in terms of duties, responsibilities and qualification standards;
  - establish official class titles; and
  - set forth the grades in which the classes of positions have been placed.

A number of federal publications discuss the process of position management but the most important one, in this context, and which also has the greatest coverage, is the *X-118 Qualification Standards Handbook.* This handbook has instructions and standards used to determine applicants' qualifications for General Schedule (both GS and managerial GM) positions at grades GS-1 through GS-15. In fact, the handbook identifies the **minimum requirements** that **MUST** be met

"by all appointees to positions in the competitive service and to positions in the excepted service that are filled under Schedule B authorities, but do not apply to positions filled under Schedule A and C authorities."[1]

For most federal positions, a combination of education and work experience can

---

[1] *X-118 Qualification Standards Handbook,* U.S. Office of Personnel Management, TS-230, p. A-4, March, 1990.

be used to meet the minimum requirements specified in the handbook. Be advised, however, that for some positions there are minimum educational requirements which must be met, regardless of previous work experience (for example, appropriate medical degrees for dentists, optometrists, medical doctors and so on).

> ## *The Vacancy Announcement will indicate whether specific college courses or degrees are mandatory requirements of the position.*

The relationship between general experience, education, and specialized experience can be illustrated (see Figure 4.1) as a sliding scale. The basic rule of thumb is that for lower grades in a job series, general experience and "lower" levels of education can satisfy the minimum requirements for a job. For higher grades, generalized experience often drops out of the equation and is replaced by specialized experience. Also, education can often be less useful as a substitute for specialized experience at the higher grades in some job series.

Quite simply, the rationale here is that in many federal positions, specialized experience virtually requires that an applicant has been a "journeyman," learning the skills necessary to do the work of the higher graded position. A private company normally would not hire someone to be the lead mechanic just on classwork alone. Similarly, for some GS jobs, education alone is not sufficient. One has to learn certain skills on the job to qualify for the higher grades. This is **especially** true for the GS grades 13 through 15, the GM (manager or supervisor) grades, and the SES (Senior Executive Service) grades.

Responsibilities

Figure 4.1
Education/Experience Mix

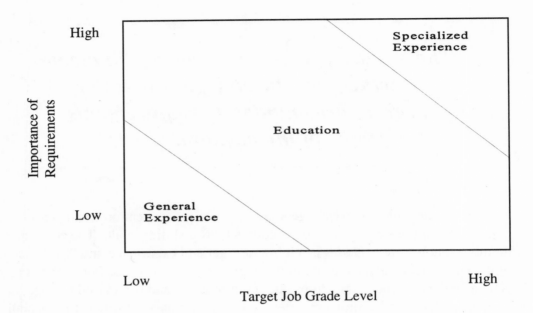

The Office of Personnel Management has responsibility for the development of minimum qualification standards and policies, and for their distribution. Federal agencies can participate in this tasking, but OPM is ultimately responsible for the product. OPM is also responsible for approving single-agency standards for particular positions (in instances where a federal agency establishes unique qualification standards for positions, beyond those in the handbook). This means that the *X-118 Qualification Standards Handbook* (hereafter referred to as QSH) is the starting point for anyone who wants to learn the minimum requirements for a federal job.

The higher the grade of your target job, the more important specialized experience becomes.

Executive branch agencies of the federal government must apply OPM's standards during personnel actions (hiring, RIFs and so on). Agencies may develop additional factors, as needed, to do personnel actions (such as knowledge of a particular programming language). Agency personnel officers are given some leeway in applying the standards to Veterans Readjustment Appointment applicants.[2] Also, agencies can modify qualification requirements for *inservice* placement actions. Inservice means a personnel action affecting someone already employed by the federal government (or with "reemployment" rights to a position with the federal government); as, for example, when an agency limits applications to people already working for the agency or when a RIF is under way.

What Are the Standards?

The standards in the QSH are the minimum education and experience requirements for federal positions. When used with agency selection factors, the personnel system works to cull applicants who, on paper, cannot do work assigned to the position. An applicant for a federal position must, at least on paper, demonstrate that his or her background does meet the minimum requirements.

The standards may be viewed as a series of hurdles an applicant faces in the race for a federal position. There may be up to three hurdles in the lane for a particular position: general standards, OPM standards for the particular job series, and agency-created standards or selection factors.

General standards exist for four broadly-defined groups of positions, covering most of the GS or GM job series:

- Clerical and Administrative Support Positions;
- Technical, Medical and Program Support Positions;
- Administrative, Management and Specialist Positions;
- Professional Positions[3]

In addition to the general standards for groups of positions, individual job series will usually have their own set of standards, and in some instances, agencies will have developed their own standards for some series. Requests for any applicable agency-created standards may be sent to:

U.S. Office of Personnel Management
Office of Staffing Policy and Operations
Career Entry Group
1900 E Street, N.W.
Washington, DC 20415
(202) 606-0960

---

[2] See Chapter 307 of the *Federal Personnel Manual*.

[3] There are also qualification standards for student-trainee positions in the competitive service and for Schedule B student trainee positions.

A typical federal job, such as the Secretary (Office Automation), GS-318-5/6 position shown in Appendix G, would have qualification standards from the Clerical and Administrative Support positions (see Appendix H) and possibly standards generated by the agency, Department of Commerce.

Quite possibly, there is a large number of people who have not worked for the federal government (and probably some who have), and who miss the key phrase

"one year of specialized experience at the next lower grade level in the General Schedule or equivalent experience outside the General Schedule."

The whole section of the application, listing qualification standards, tells applicants that their applications will be reviewed using the X-118 standards. Thus, an applicant cannot know how to determine what experience outside the federal service is "equivalent" until he or she knows how the reviewer defines equivalence! And how does the reviewer define experience outside the federal service as equivalent? By referring to the standards in the QSH and any applicable agency standards!

The best definition of "specialized experience" is in the Position Standards *for the next lower grade.*

The standards in Appendix H show that at grade GS-5, the minimum requirement (for positions other than Clerk-Steno) is four years above high school **OR** at least one year of specialized experience equivalent to GS-4 (which we will view later). Thirty college semester hours equals one year of this experience. For grade GS-6 or higher positions in clerical and administrative positions, education is not applicable as a minimum requirement. This means post-high school education would not substitute for specialized experience.

The way the federal government personnel specialist combines education and experience is simple. The minimum requirement for a GS-4 Secretary position is one year of general experience or two years of education beyond high school. If the applicant has eight months of work experience for which credit is given (8 months is 67 percent of the required experience of one year [8 divided by 12 months = 0.67]) and twenty college semester hours (20 hours is 33 percent of the required education [one year of college = 30 hours; two years = 60 hours; so 20 divided by 60 = 0.33]), thus the applicant has a combined experience and education background which meets one hundred percent of the requirement (0.67 plus 0.33 = 1.00).

Relevant Experience

The GS-5 secretary position refers to experience equivalent to GS-4. This means a successful applicant will have spent at least one year doing work comparable with the work done by a GS-4 secretary. Job announcements seem to be written as if the expected applicants will all be people who already work for the federal government in the "next lower grade." The crucial point here is that when an application is sent in response to the position announcement, people who did not **work** as GS-0318-04 secretaries for the required 52 weeks have to show the personnel specialist reviewing their application that they have done **comparable work**. Someone who just reports "I typed letters and memos" will not persuade a personnel specialist that GS-4 level work was done.

The first question this raises is "How do I find out what **experiences** are comparable to the 'next lower' grades?" If the person applying for the GS-5 secretary job does not have a year's experience as a GS-4 secretary, then he or she must show that work was done that was comparable to what is found in a GS-0318-04 position. There are three possible sources for such information:

- Qualification standards in the QSH;
- Single agency standards; or
- Position classification standards.

There are no specific, grade by grade experience standards in the QSH for some positions; often there are no single agency standards for a position. There are **general** requirements for clerical and administrative support positions, for example (see Appendix G) but nothing else. In such cases, then, personnel specialists would usually refer to **position classification standards** for the vacant position.

Now, this may be a new idea for many people, perhaps even those who already work for the federal government. There is an important distinction:

- The job announcements describe what work the position will require, what grades are available, and the minimum requirements (education and experience);
- The QSH (plus, if they exist for the position, any single agency) standards describe the minimum education, work experience, and other requirements;
- Position classification standards[4] describe in detail the kinds of tasks done in federal jobs, grade level by grade level.

---

[4] Separate booklets are published by OPM for various General Schedule job series; TS-34, for example is the *Position Classification Standard for Secretary Series GS-318*.

Assume for the moment that someone is applying for a GS-9 position which has minimum educational and work experience requirements. Also assume the applicant has never worked for the federal government. First, the applicant scans the announcement and finds that the **only** minimum requirement is "one year of specialized experience equivalent to the next lower level." Since this is a one-grade interval technical position (see Appendix G), the applicant has to determine whether previous work she has done is comparable to work done by a GS-8 in the same series.

The applicant scans the QSH and finds that at grades six and above in this position, only specialized experience (plus possibly special training classes) fulfills the minimum requirement for this position. The best way for this applicant to determine whether she has the required experience is to review the *Position Classification Standards* (hereafter referred to as PCS) for the job series. Then, when describing previous work experiences, the applicant needs to be sure to list all work which is comparable to work done by a GS-8. Assuming the applicant has spent at least 52 weeks doing tasks comparable to a GS-8, and assuming the applicant **clearly** reports this, then the applicant makes it much easier for a personnel specialist to translate this non-federal work experience into federal job requirements.

Personnel specialists use the PCS when creating or modifying federal jobs. Typically, a supervisor trying to create or change the grade of a position would work with a personnel specialist from the supervisor's agency. The supervisor would list the kinds of tasks to be done, the amount of supervision received, and so forth. The personnel specialist would then use this information, plus the PCS, to rate the job (both grade and job series).

This means that if an applicant for a federal position above grade six has not worked in "the next lower grade," the PCS should be reviewed to learn what tasks establish the needed "relevant experience."

X-118C QUALIFICATION STANDARDS

Background

There are separate qualification standards for blue collar or wage grade personnel. The Office of Personnel Management has a group of roughly forty different WG jobs, between grades one and fifteen, which are called key ranking jobs. These non-supervisory jobs

"reflect the relative worth of different key lines of work and levels within lines of work, and control the alinement (sic) of the grade levels in all non-supervisory job grading standards."[5]

---

[5] *Job Grading System,* U. S. Office of Personnel Management, TS-44, Section II, p. 5, September 1981.

Figure 4.2
WG Key Ranking Jobs[6]

Grade	Title		Grade	Title
1	Laundry Worker		8	Machine Tool Operator
1	Janitor (Light)		9	Water Plant Operator
2	Janitor (Heavy)		9	Painter
2	Food Service Worker		9	Carpenter
2	Laborer (Light)		9	Plumber
3	Laborer (Heavy)		10	Motor Grader Operator
4	Sales Store Worker		10	Automotive Mechanic
5	Forklift Operator		10	Aircraft Mechanic
5	Warehouseman		10	Welder
5	Helper (Trades)		10	Pipefitter
5	Truck Driver (Light)		10	Sheet Metal Worker
6	Truck Driver (Medium)		10	Electrician
6	Packer		10	Machinist
6	Stockroom Attendant		11	Electronics Equipment Mechanic
6	Sewing Machine Operator		12	Radar Mechanic (Ground)
7	Bindery Worker		13	Tool, Die and Gage Maker
7	Office Appliance Repairer		14	Die Sinker
7	Truck Driver (Heavy)		14	Modelmaker
8	Truck Driver (Trailer)		15	Instrument Maker
8	Cook			

When establishing or changing a job, the key ranking jobs help identify "peg points" or points of reference for comparison with existing jobs and standards. The new or modified position is compared with what is done in the key ranking jobs to help determine the grade for the new or modified job. Most standards are specific to one job family, such as Tool and Die Maker. There are, however, general standards for "common jobs" such as Helper, Inspector, Supervisor, and Leader.[7]

WG Job Grading

Blue collar federal jobs are graded, based on the work done, on how the job relates to other jobs, and by comparisons with grade definitions in an appropriate job grading standard. Individual aspects of a job (skills needed, responsibility, and so on) are not considered **individually**, but as part of the overall job. Thus, the fact that some WG employees need licenses or certificates is not as important as the nature of

---

[6] *Job Grading System,* U.S. Office of Personnel Management, TS-44, Section II, pp. 5-6, September, 1981.

[7] See, for example, the *Job Grading Standards for ... Leaders,* TS-39, *Inspectors,* TS-47, or *Supervisors,* TS-49.

the job, overall. Nevertheless, job grading standards provide a way to distinguish the requirements of different grade levels in terms of the knowledge, skill, responsibility, physical effort and conditions of work for a particular job. Thus, the X-118C standards, for WG jobs, can help job applicants determine whether their previous work experience outside the federal government qualifies them for a particular grade level. Again, as with the X-118 standards for white collar workers, sometimes the job grading standards for a particular job or occupation family need to be consulted to get more detailed information about a particular position. Like the *Position Qualification Standards* (for white collar jobs), *Job Grading Standards* may be obtained from the references in the last chapter of this book.

STATUS

Finally, mention must be made about "Status" and KSAOs. Many federal job announcements require applicants to have "status" with the federal government. This means people who apply for the vacancy must already have some kind of relationship with the government. The military services, for example, may have any one of several status requirements. The Army, for example, might advertise a job and require: DA (Department of the Army); DoD (Department of Defense); all federal employees within a geographic area; all federal employees; or anyone. Other federal organizations may make similar requirements.

When a position announcement has a status requirement, anyone who does not meet the requirement (that is, have the required status) will not be rated for the opening, regardless of any other qualifications. This practice limits the pool from which an activity could select applicants. Sometimes this practice is used to ensure that applicants are familiar with the way the activity works. By restricting the applicant pool, though, the hiring activity is probably reducing its chances to get the best possible applicant. The secretary and the social science analyst jobs listed in Appendix F show two different kinds of status requirements. The secretary job is open for anyone currently employed by the federal government (or someone with reemployment rights), plus people eligible for a special appointment. Someone interested in this job who is not currently a federal employee should call the Point of Contact (POC) listed at the end of the announcement for information about special appointments. The social science analyst position is more restrictive; only current "career" employees of the agency IN METRO D.C. may apply. The sole exception is someone who either works outside the area, or for another activity, but who is serviced by the personnel office that services the hiring agency. Not too complicated!

KSAOs are also used as qualification standards for many federal jobs. By requiring job applicants to meet the "standard" minimum education and experience requirements for a position, some potential applicants are screened out of a job. "Status" screens out more people. Requiring applicants to demonstrate that they have specific other knowledges, skills and abilities is a third way to screen applicants.

From the perspective of the hiring activity, using KSAOs means that additional standards may be established for an application without rewriting the job description. One KSAO, for example, may require that GS-0343-09 Management Analysts be familiar with Department of Agriculture programs and policies for farm price supports. The agency has taken steps to ensure that applicants for the position have some knowledge of the work assigned to the position; at the same time, people who have not worked with such programs are effectively blocked from being rated for the vacancy.

When looking at federal job announcements, be sure you qualify in terms of "status." Don't waste time applying for jobs for which you are ineligible.

Generally, the use of such KSAOs is more prevalent at senior levels or at supervisory or managerial levels. If a particular job series is particularly hard to fill (for whatever reason), KSAOs are less likely to be required. The important point to keep in mind, regardless of the presence of KSAOs, is that the minimum requirements (education and work experience) will still apply.

SUMMARY

The use of standards to define what work is assigned to a job means that the **minimum** requirements to enter a position, as well as the **minimum** work assigned to a position, will be the same for that position throughout the federal government. A GS-343-09 Management Analyst position with the U.S. Navy in Naples, Italy, will have the same minimum entry requirements and the same minimum set of tasks to perform as will a GS-0343-09 Management Analyst position with the Department of Agriculture in Dallas, Texas. However, many agencies build upon these minimum requirements by imposing KSAOs on certain jobs.

Anyone who is not currently employed by the federal government AND applying for a position in the same job series but at the same or a higher grade will have to show that the minimum job requirements have been met. The easiest way to do that is to have the right amount of education or have had work experiences which, according to qualification or classification standards, are comparable to those in the "next lower grade." Someone who has not worked for the federal government but is applying for a job should seriously attempt to view the qualification standards and the position classification standards for those jobs.

5

THE APPLICATION PACKET

The typical application for a federal job will require more than just an SF 171 or resume or OF 612. Depending on the vacant position, a host of additional forms and information will be needed to apply for just one vacancy. Since not everyone gets the first federal job for which they apply, one can reasonably expect to make **several** fairly thick packets to apply for several jobs.

This chapter reviews the typical pieces of an application packet, giving guidance on how to complete the various items with the minimum of blood, toil, sweat and tears. Every effort should be made to type all parts of the packet (except your signature); this document will be used to "sell" you to an unseen potential employer. This can amount to quite a bit of typing unless a computer is used. However, some typing shortcuts described here can help keep the workload to a minimum.

Before beginning this effort, gather information to prepare three "background" documents. The first is a list of all jobs (including part-time and volunteer work) for roughly the past ten years. The second list will consist of all education and training you have had since high school. If you did not complete high school, this list is not necessary. Finally, prepare a third list which consists of all awards or honors you have received (include community or service awards as well as those relating to previous jobs).

43

*The application packet may
be the first chance a prospective
employer has to look at you; sloppy
work, typographical errors, or poor
organization reflect badly on you.*

BASIC INFORMATION REQUIREMENTS

The core of any application packet for a federal job will require certain pieces of information from the applicant, whether put into an SF 171, and OF 612 or a resume. Also, for current federal employees, the most important way to update your personnel files is to update your SF 171. Regardless of the form you select for your application, you should plan to start with **two** copies of the form, a file or "master" copy and the "mail-in" copy which becomes your application packet. If an application packet will be prepared using one of the computer programs, such as *Quick and Easy,* the same principles and practices will apply, usually without regard to the main form you decide to use. For the balance of this chapter, the SF 171 will be used as the main example, but we will also show how this information is fit into a resume or OF 612.

The heart of any application packet will have to contain the following information:

- **Job Information:** the announcement number, title and grade(s) for which you are applying;

- **Personal Information:** full name, mailing address (with ZIP Code), and day and evening phone numbers; SSN; country of citizenship; veteran's preference; reinstatement eligibility; and highest federal grade held;

- **Education:** high school name, city and state, date of diploma or GED; all college and university courses and degrees; and (if requested in the announcement, a college transcript);

- **Work Experience:** for both paid *and non-paid* work, provide the following information: job title (series and grade for federal jobs); duties and accomplishments; employer's name and address; supervisor's name and phone number; starting and ending dates; hours per week; salary; and whether your current supervisor can be contacted about your performance on your current job;

■ **Other Information:** job-related training courses (title, year, and time spent in class); job-related certificates and licenses (currently held); job-related skills (such as computer skills, foreign languages, abilities with tools or machinery, typing speed, and so forth); job-related honors, awards and special accomplishments (such as memberships in professional or honorific organizations, leadership or public speaking experiences, bonuses, and so forth).

As you will see here and in the examples in the back of the book, the SF 171 and the OF 612 gather at least this basic set of information. If a resume is to be used as the heart of an application packet, it must contain **at least** this information! (The newer versions of *Quick and Easy* allow you to enter the above information into one type of form, such as the OF 612, and will then prepare and print the OF 612, an SF 171 or even a resume with all the information you entered.)

The master copy of your SF 171 will be used as a template or starting point for the mail-in copy and for other, future mail-in copies should you apply for other, similar positions over the next few months. You may need more than one master if you plan to apply for jobs from very different groups (for example, different masters might be made for budget analyst [GS-560] and appraiser [GS-1171] vacancies to emphasize different work experiences).

When you prepare a master, you **must** have in mind both a minimum grade and at least one occupational group or job family (or at least one job series). This is your **target job**, such as a GS-318-05 Secretary (that is, the target job is a job vacancy for grade XX and job series YYY). As shown in the last chapter, federal standards are keyed to existing federal position types. Further, the standards are broken into broad families (such as "Administrative, Management, and Specialist" positions in the General Schedule or the "Inspectors" in the Wage Grade). As shown in Appendix G, there are specific minimum standards for positions in the set of "Administrative, Management and Specialist" positions. If you plan to apply for vacancies in this group, you will need to meet the minimum education and experience requirements for a desired grade level. If education alone will not qualify you for a position, then you may need to examine the qualification standards or even the position classification standards for the target job. You have to meet **and communicate you have met** these minimum standards to be considered for the target.

*The more you know about the target
job, the easier it is to complete an
application. What tasks are done on the
job, what kind of experiences are
useful for applicants, and what are
the minimum educational requirements?*

You need to complete most of an SF 171 so that, by work experience and education, you clearly demonstrate that you qualify for the position. For a different vacancy, different standards may apply, hence the need to make different "masters." Each would be written for a specific target job. When you are ready to make a mail-in copy of a master, you complete the rest of the blocks, sign and date it, and submit the mail-in packet.

The mail-in copies are reproduced copies of masters to which you will have added most of the detailed information about yourself.[1] By leaving several sections empty, the master can be reproduced and then the blank blocks on the mail-in copy can be completed. The SF 171 is a "reproducible" form which, to the federal government, means you do not need to submit their green and white copies. A **good quality** reproduction (or a computer created copy) is acceptable. Bear in mind that the application packet says something about you and how you work; a sloppy packet suggests a sloppy worker.

PAGE 1

Block 1: Leave this blank on the master copy. On the mail-in copy, type the position title and the announcement number, such as (from Appendix F) "Laborer, WG-3502-02, Number 3/93." This applies to blocks 1 - 3 on OF 612.

Blocks 2 - 9: Complete all these blocks. If you do not want to be contacted at work by a hiring official, block 9 may be left vacant. Block 7 is especially useful for people

---

[1] Note that if you are using a computer program to make the SF 171, making copies is much easier than with a typewriter. If you do not have a computer, either use a typewriter or carefully print your master copy, then if typewritten, have a professional typist "fill in the blanks" for you or rent a typewriter and do it yourself.

who have other names on their transcripts, for example. Blocks 4 - 7 on OF 612 apply here.

Block 10: Indicate previous federal employment by type of appointment (example, career-conditional) and the dates of your **highest** (not necessarily your last) grade. This information is reported in the experience blocks of a resume and OF 612, and also in block 16 in OF 612.

Block 11: Leave this blank on the master copy of the SF 171 (this is optional on a resume and not required on OF 612). On a mail-in copy, give a specific month and year when you are available for the position. If you are available now, indicate a date at least two weeks after the closing date of the position, or three weeks after you mail the packet if the position has "open and continuous" instead of a closing date. This allows time for your application to be processed and does not indicate how desperate you are for work (if you say "NOW," regardless of the circumstances, some employers will consider you desperate).

If a block does not apply to you, mark it "N/A" and move to the next block.

Block 12: Usually a minimum grade level should be specified here on an SF 171 (it is not required on OF 612 but if several vacancies are open at different grades, the lowest grade you will accept should be included in block 2 of OF 612 and a resume should indicate the lowest grade which you will accept), especially if the position is open at several levels (for example, a position advertised as open at grades 7/9/11 means someone could be hired at any of the three grades). Wage grade employees **should** indicate a minimum salary since pay levels are set through competitive bargaining and reflect local conditions; grade level *per se* is not an accurate indicator.

Blocks 13 - 16: Complete these as truthfully as possible. What conditions of work will you accept if offered to you? Where are you willing to work? Are you available for travel—that means being away from home and family for several days a month. The announced position may require work patterns which you cannot meet; better to excuse yourself now than risk a bad work situation and probably unsatisfactory evaluations. Neither a resume nor OF 612 will ask you about the conditions under which you will work.

Blocks 17 - 22: Complete all appropriate blocks. If you are eligible for a five or ten point Veteran Preference, complete form SF 15 (see Appendix K for a copy) and provide any requested proof. Also be sure to check with a Federal Job Information Center (Appendix E) for information about the Veteran's Readjustment Act. Block 15 on OF 612 is used to identify claims for veterans preference. On a resume, you have to include a section on military experience which describes your branch and length of service, type and date of discharge and attach your DD Form 214 or other proof of service. In Appendix L, there is a copy of SF 15, Application for 10-Point Veteran Preference and detailed information about the rights of veterans and relatives of veterans.

PAGE 2

Block 23: Leave this block (and block 9 on OF 612) blank on the master. Mark "Yes" only if you want potential employers talking to your current supervisor. If you mark "No," your current supervisor will only be contacted if you are likely to be offered the target job.

Block 24: Skip this block (block 8 on OF 612) for the moment. Block 24 is discussed at some length later in this chapter, given the importance of the information in this block.

PAGE 3

Blocks 25 - 27: These three blocks (blocks 10 and 11 on OF 612) help establish in general terms how much education you have had. Complete all three blocks on the master copy that apply to you.

Blocks 28 - 31: Some people have educational histories that require WAY more space than the three rows in block 28 (block 12 of OF 612). If your educational background will run beyond three rows, you should try to prepare a supplemental sheet (see Appendix K). You can show your educational background in a more organized and thorough way if it is all done on a supplemental sheet than by trying to put part in the SF 171 and part on a supplemental sheet.[2]

Blocks 28 through 30 (block 12 on OF 612) are for college education, block 31 (block 13 on OF 612) is for other types of education or training (vocational school, military or government training seminars, and so forth). People who have spent a few years with the federal government are likely to need more than the two available answer areas for this, simply to record all the training government officials receive. Note that if you do work for the federal government and do not recall all your training classes, your personnel activity may have a complete listing in your personnel records; a few minutes there will help you compile information for an

---

[2] See the example provided in Example 5.2 on page 55.

impressive listing of courses. Also include here **self-study** projects, such as "spent approximately 36 hours studying tutorials for C computer language" (and describe the tutorials). If you are preparing a resume, of course you will want to include a section which identifies all the training classes you had which relate to the job for which you are applying.

Block 32 (Block 13 on OF 612): What separates the qualified candidates from the newly hired employees? Having the minimum requirements to do a job are enough if there are not many applicants for a vacant position. If there are more than a few applicants, the recruitment specialist in the personnel office is supposed to identify those who are minimally qualified for the job, then rate them. Special skills, accomplishments and awards go a long way toward helping separate the pool of applicants. Someone who has special skills or has been given awards or honors is someone who does more than is just minimally required. This person is an achiever. When these skills, awards and honors relate to the target job, you float toward the top of the applicants.

At the start of the chapter, you should have prepared a listing of these special skills, accomplishments and awards. If you need to do so, put this information on a continuation sheet (see Appendix K). If working with a resume, be sure to include a section that provides this information. This is a way to identify special accomplishments you have attained in your paid and non-paid work history. You should try to group information in this block by type and date (starting with the most recent and going back in time). The "types" here are skills, accomplishments and awards.

Use this block to list such special skills as:

- various types of computer skills;
- ability to work with heavy equipment or special machines (copiers, printing presses, x-ray equipment, etc.); and
- special diagnostic or repair skills (repair small engines, perform CPR, analyze electrical circuits, etc).

What you list should either be job relevant OR list skills which demonstrate initiative (for example, someone with clerical experience who knows how to work with publishing equipment, anyone taking a first aid class).

Also use this block to list accomplishments. Accomplishments cover a wide variety of sins including:

- being a member of professional, community or fraternal organizations (be sure to list offices held);
- **any** publications you have done (books, articles, even a short three-page "Office Procedures" publication should be listed);
- **any** public speaking experiences you have had;

- special one-time service on a board, team, or committee (such as a team investigating an EEO complaint, a hiring panel, or organized a church picnic, etc.);
- hobbies that pertain to the target job (rebuilt a classic motorcycle [for any target job involving small engines or automotive work], wrote a "share-ware" computer game [for any target job in which computers would be used] and so forth).

Finally, this is where you can list any honors or awards you have received. List the date of the honor and briefly describe why you received the honor. College scholarships, scholastic honors, military commendations and awards, honors from civic, community or fraternal organizations (for example, a certificate of appreciation from the local school district for running a successful PTA book drive) should all be listed here. The objective in this section is to provide a list of instances when someone recognized your performance. You want to call attention to every such instance when what you did shows you to be an asset for an organization. A golfing trophy normally does not apply here, unless your target job requires a sports background. Any award for effort that demonstrates planning, organizing, leading people, evaluating people, managing resources, working independently, or resolving conflict, for example, demonstrates that you have performed a generic skill in an above-average way.

Blocks 33 - 35: The information required in these blocks is obvious. For blocks 33 and 35, don't claim skills which you do not have, or which are not relevant to the target job. In block 34, list only those certificates or licenses which pertain to the target job. A driving license is not relevant for office jobs, for example. Block 13 on OF 612 is the place to list typing speed, licenses and certificates, and foreign languages. Although the SF 171 has these three blocks, do not consider it necessary to complete these blocks if the information is not relevant to the job you seek. Someone will not be excluded from consideration for a welding job, for example, because typing speed or foreign language skills were not indicated.

Block 36: List the names of three friends who can talk about your qualifications for the target job. If possible, list the name of at least one person who already works where the target job is located. Then the hiring official could ask someone nearby to discuss your strengths and weaknesses (and in this case, be sure to list the person's business address). Alternatively, list the names of people who have worked with you and can talk about your work on the job. Be advised that although these references might not be contacted at all, they may be contacted and also may be asked whether they have information about certain skills you said you had. Also consider giving the name of someone who knows you outside work, such as someone from your church or in an outside organization (neighborhood association, Moose lodge or whatever). This person would talk not so much about what you do at work but what kind of person you are. Neither OF 612 nor the guidelines for resumes request, or have spaces for the names of references.

PAGE 4

Blocks 37 - 44: Self-explanatory. These blocks on the SF 171 basically ask for information that often is not relevant during the recruitment process. Block 14 on OF 612 asks for your citizenship status, but your criminal record, if any, is not required. If you would have to mark any of blocks 38 through 44 with a "Yes," you should consider using an OF 612 or resume as the core document for your application packet. However, if the position requires any kind of clearance or handling of sensitive information, a record of convictions, repeated firings, or debt problems may affect your employment. Lying on any of these blocks **can** get you fired or even subject you to criminal prosecution. There is no way to avoid any bars to employment that these blocks may create. A "Yes" in blocks 38 through 40 and 42 or 43 will not necessarily bar employment opportunities, depending on the target job. As will be shown in the next chapter, if you answer these questions truthfully, you may be able to get feedback from the recruitment specialist about their effect on future applications.

Block 45: This is one block for which you do not want to have to use a continuation sheet. Provide the requested information. Artful wording under the explanation block ("left the job because I was unhappy and not working at my level of skill") may soften the blow for block 38. For blocks 39 through 43, provide the least amount of information that you can: the violation and when it occurred. Again, neither OF 612 or a resume would have you provide reasons on why you left a job or your history of debt or convictions.

Blocks 46 - 47: Answer both questions truthfully. If more than three relatives work for the federal government or the U.S. military, use a continuation sheet instead of Block 47. The information in these blocks will normally not cost you a chance at the target job. These blocks are also not necessary unless you use an SF 171 as the core of your application packet.

Blocks 48 - 49 (Block 18 on OF 612): Do not complete these blocks on the master copy of the SF 171. These blocks will be completed only on mail-in copies just before you submit your application packet.

BLOCK 24 (BLOCK 8 On OF 612)

Most of the boxes here are obvious. Include enough information so that someone can call or write a current or previous employer to verify the information in each block. Basically, describe each **job** you have had, **including unpaid positions** starting with your current job(s) and working back through time, *if the work applies* to the target job. For example, serving as a youth group leader/advisor, regardless of anything else, may earn you credit for dealing with the public. Organizing projects and other activities could also work to your advantage. When in doubt, lay it out (and let the recruitment specialists sort it out).

Begin this block by listing your most recent job or activity, then work backward through previous jobs and unpaid work for at least the past ten years. Before putting the information into the block, though, type it on a separate, clean sheet of paper. First, this will allow you to organize your information. Also, this will help determine if your information will fit into the block. If the result looks too compressed or sloppy, plan to type "See Attachment ..." under the description of work. A separate page can be prepared, containing all the necessary information and a full, thorough description of your work.

Additional work descriptions can be submitted on SF 171-A or OF 612 Work Experience Continuation Page (copies are provided in Appendix K). As with Block 24 on the SF 171, if the description of work done in a job mentioned on an SF 171 does not fit the space available, use another sheet to continue your description. The large square boxes beside each Block 24 section on form SF 171-A are for letters; your most recent jobs would be described on SF 171 in parts A and B of Block 24. When you begin to describe other previous jobs on SF 171-A or on the Work Experience Continuation Page, identify each job with a different letter (the first would be job C, the next would be job D, and so on). When you finish, this block will consist of one or more lettered sections, A for your current job, B for the next most current, C (on SF 171-A) for the next most current, and so forth. If you have to refer to particular jobs elsewhere in your application packet (for example, when completing the KSAOs), you would refer to a particular job or activity as Block 24-x (or Block 8-x), where x is the block's letter.

For the dates employed, remember that you should be establishing how much general and specialized experience you have had "at the next lower grade level" (and this is especially critical if you did not have a federal job at the next lower grade level). Recruitment specialists will be calculating how many months you worked on different tasks to determine whether you meet the minimum requirements. Note that 120 hours constitutes one month and 40 hours constitute 0.25 month—one quarter of a month. If you worked two hours a month for two years in volunteer work, explain at the start of the Description of Work that you "worked" one quarter of a month in the job over a two year period.

DESCRIPTION OF WORK

This is one of the most crucial, and most difficult to complete portions of the application packet. Information here has to be carefully organized to sell your strengths and demonstrate that you have the ability to do the target job. While you want to sell yourself as qualified for the target job, you also must not fabricate experiences and work; a recruitment specialist or the potential hiring official may call to clarify something said about one of your jobs and a misstatement about your experiences could cost you the target job.

Before putting information into this block, make a list of all jobs you had over the last six to ten years. The start and end dates should show continuous employment throughout the period. If there are periods when you were unemployed, your reason for leaving a job should be "position eliminated, employer cutback, etc." Now add to the list all the part time "jobs" (paid and unpaid) which you had: positions in church, the neighborhood, clubs, children and youth activities all count. Each of these activities often includes tasks, such as communicating with the public, organizing events, planning, supervising teams, and others which should be listed.

The right application writer will review position and qualification standards for a job before describing work experience. If you are not now in the "next lower position," the standards are the best description of what experiences qualify you for the target job.

Ideally, the qualification or even the position classification standards for your target job will be used to help describe your experience. If they are not available, vacancy announcements will normally give at least some indication of both the minimum requirements of the position, as well as the work assigned to the position. Figure 5.1 shows the duties and minimum qualifications for the GS-318-5 announcement from Appendix F. This typical announcement does not indicate what constitutes "specialized" experience. As noted in the last chapter, every effort must be made to get the qualification standards or the position classification standards if you lack the necessary "time in grade" at the next lower level (GS-4) in federal service. That is the best way to compete against people who have specialized experience. Position classification standards for GS-318-5 jobs are shown in Appendix H.

If you plan to use a resume as the core of your application packet, for each job you list, you should provide sections that: 1) describe the job in general terms, 2) list your duties in the same way as if you were completing an SF 171 or OF 612, 3) list any accomplishments you earned in the job; and 4) list the highest (or current) pay and hours worked in each job.

Example 5.1
Position Requirements

DUTIES: This position is located at Eastern District Headquarters; it is primarily that of Secretary performing duties which are auxiliary to the work of the Systems Operations Division. As required, incumbent performs a variety of secretarial, clerical and typing duties for the administrative, professional and technical personnel of the Division.

QUALIFICATIONS REQUIRED: 52 weeks of specialized experience equivalent to the next lower grade level. Specialized experience is experience which is directly related to the position to be filled and which has equipped the candidate with the particular knowledge, skills and abilities to successfully perform the duties of that position. In addition to meeting the above experience requirement, the applicant must be a qualified typist.

BASIS FOR EVALUATING CANDIDATES: Candidates who meet the minimum qualifications requirements will be evaluated on type and quality of job-related experience, education, training, awards, and performance appraisals and on the basis of the following factors:

Appendix G lists the standard education and experience requirements for most GS positions (nothing comparable exists for other types of federal positions). For clerical workers, including GS-318-5 positions, the minimum requirement is four **years** of education beyond high school OR one year of "specialized" experience equivalent to a GS-4 (this is also noted in the job announcement excerpt in Example 5.1). As stated in Chapter Four, only standards specifically for the GS-318 series would explain the duties of a GS-4 or a GS-5 for the series. If the standards are unavailable and education cannot be substituted, then each experience block needs to describe all the clerical work done, both in paid jobs (full or part-time) and volunteer work.

Rather than say "I typed memos and reports for the office," be more specific about what THAT task required. For example, a stronger statement would say:

"Using an electric typewriter, I was responsible for setting up memorandum formats and typing memos from handwritten drafts prepared by any of eight professionals. I had to translate the drafts into a standard memo format, check spelling and typographical errors (and correct any if found), and type the memo. After typing the memo, I had to proofread the memo, correcting any errors, before submitting a final copy for signature. I was required to work with minimal direction from either my direct supervisor or from the professionals in the office.

"I also prepared four types of reports . . ."

By accurately describing the specific tasks you did (such as "typing memos from handwritten drafts"), you help recruitment specialists determine whether your experience fulfills the requirements. Recruitment specialists will often look for such things as the kinds of contact you had with your supervisor, co-workers, the public, and, for some positions, contact with people above your supervisor. Other important skills include computer skills

". . . entered receipts into Lotus spreadsheets, entered data into a FoxPro database to create a mailing list . . ."

amount of travel required

". . . traveled to clients throughout a three state . . ."

how much supervision did you require

". . . after getting assignments from my boss, I had to make weekly reports of progress . . ."

how much supervision did you exercise

". . . supervised six junior accountants. I made their work assignments and evaluated their work performance. I trained eleven junior accountants over a three year period . . ."

and describe any especially noteworthy achievements you made in a job

". . . designed a telephone solicitation form which reduced average time spent with customers from five minutes to three minutes, saving the company approximately $70 per hour of solicitation."

You should also consider indicating the percentage of time spent on each major task. You could, for example, indicate in the margin to the right of your experience statement, that you spent "65%" of your time doing a specific task.[3]

---

[3] On the one hand, this helps you get proper credit for what you did and illustrates the kind of work environment from which you came. On the other hand, recruiters may calculate the percentages times the length of employment and conclude you do not have enough time on a particular task. If you can provide work breakdowns by percentages, you indicate that you are organized and methodical in your work and record-keeping.

Avoid using such words as "assisted" or "participated" or "helped." These words do not tell what you did; be specific. Instead of "helped" you might say

". . . cleaned the work site at the beginning and end of the shift. Determined what tools were needed based on orders from the master machinist. Got the right tools and jigs from the tool crib, checking and sharpening the tools as needed . . ."

You may have to write and rewrite the descriptions of work several times before you get the information you need. One easy way to check your work is to prepare your statements of work experience, then give the statements and a copy of the standards to another person. Ask that other person to mark off each standard that you met, as described in your work experience statement. This will help verify that you have expressed your work history in a way that another person can understand and evaluate in light of the standards. Your goal, again, is to describe tasks you performed, and describe them in ways that would be clear to someone who does not understand what you do. Use short, simple sentences if possible. If you use any jargon, use only the jargon from either the qualification or the position classification standards.

> *After preparing your statements of work history, have someone else compare what you wrote with the position standards for the job you seek, to see if they can check off all the standards for the next lower job, based on your work history, qualifying you for the target job.*

When you finish, each description of work should read as a list of the tasks you did in the job or activity, show the amount of supervision you received or exercised over others, and describe any notable achievements you performed. Use short sentences, relatively free of jargon or "buzz words." The length of your description is unimportant if you accomplish all these guidelines. Again, though, remember that when your packet gets to a hiring official, that is your first chance to make an impression. Would *you* rather hire someone who rambles on page after page or who describes work clearly and briefly?

SF 171-A/OF 612 WORK EXPERIENCE CONTINUATION

This form is a continuation sheet for the work experience block. You want to list and describe, in reverse order, all previous full and part-time jobs you held. Also list any unpaid jobs and volunteer work in which you performed tasks which are related to work done in your target job.

Complete *only* the blocks for your, name, Social Security Number, and the "Additional Work Experience Blocks" (below the dark line) for your master SF 171 or OF 612. After you reproduce the master for a mail-in copy, **complete** the continuation form by typing the information in blocks 3 and 4. Block 3 should have the information from block 1 of the SF 171, describing the position you seek, and block 4 *must* have a date that is *after* the opening date of the target job.

SUPPLEMENTAL INFORMATION SHEET

Appendix K has a continuation sheet for supplemental information. Before you prepare your master you should make photocopies of this sheet. Use this form to report information which was too lengthy to fit into the appropriate SF 171 Block. Complete only block 2 on this form for your master copy. When you make reproductions of the master to mail-in, you will complete blocks 1, 3 and 4. Below the four blocks at the top of the page, begin providing your supplemental information. Each block which had too much information to fit on the SF 171 should be completed here, in order of its appearance on the SF 171. (See the example in Example 5.2)

Example 5.2
Supplemental Information

SUPPLEMENTAL INFORMATION:

1. Name (Last, First, Middle Initial)	2. SSN 332-55-9999
3. Job Title/Announcement Number	4. Date

BLOCK 28:

School	At:	From	To	Sem. Hrs.	Degree	Grad.
1) Greeley Univ.	Kingston, Jamaica	1/73	6/77	119	B.S.	6/77
2) Rachkam Tech. Univ.	Rutland, VT 01011	9/72	12/72	8		
3) Miskatonic Univ.	Arkham, MA 19666	9/69	5/70	30		
4) Harrad College	Cambridge, MA 19669	9/67	5/69	38		

BLOCK 29:

Major	Sem. Hrs.
1) Biology	45
2) Astrophysics	3
3) Cultural Anthropology	3
4) Anatomy	12

KSAOs

Many federal job announcements will have a section which asks for additional knowledge, skills and other abilities (variously called KSAs, KSAOs, Qualification Requirements, *et al.*). Example 5.3 shows "Minimum Qualification Requirements" from the WG-3502-02 vacancy listed in Appendix G. These KSAOs are qualification requirements in addition to those found in the *X-118* or *X-118C* or the classification standards. Typically, these will include special experiences one must have which are related to work done in the job.

Example 5.3
KSAOs For a Laborer Job

QUALIFICATION REQUIREMENTS: Candidates will be rated on the following elements which **must** be addressed in the application:

- Ability to do the work of the position without more than normal supervision.

- Ability to follow simple oral and written instructions.

- Ability to lift or carry objects weighing 80-85 pounds.

- Ability to use and maintain tools and equipment such as hand and power saws, drill motors, simple hand tools, etc.

- Ability to work safely.

Activities trying to hire new people will often advertise a requirement to be able to perform certain other tasks in addition to the tasks listed in the *Position Classification Handbook.* These additional tasks result from the work assigned to the person in the task. Also, there are some "catch all" job series that agencies use, such as GS-301, that do not have detailed task listings in the *Standards.* Rather, candidates for the job will be evaluated solely on the extent to which their work history meets the requirements of the KSAOs. The laborer in this position, for example, may have to work alone for several hours each day, without supervision from a WL or WS leader. Thus the hiring official is interested in someone with a track record of working independently.

When completing KSAOs, use the Supplemental Information Sheet provided in Appendix K and indicate that the sheet contains information (in the example here) about "Additional Qualification Requirements." Now, for each of the jobs or tasks that you listed, describe and reference things you did which fulfill the qualification requirements. Using the Laborer example, an applicant described a previous job in Block 24-D. *Even though* he described the work quite well in that block, he copies the following information from Block 24-D:

"Ability to work . . . with normal supervision: as a night janitor, I had to clean all rooms on three floors . . . I normally only saw the supervisor once an hour. At the end of shift, the supervisor would come by and inspect my work. My supervisor was around less than two hours a shift."

Treat these additional requirements or KSAOs just like the qualification or classification standards. These are *required* tasks. You need to demonstrate in your SF 171 that you did work comparable to these required tasks (if that is the case). The same guidance given in the Description of Work section applies here. Also, although a different announcement may have different KSAOs, when you prepare these (on Supplemental Information Sheets), do not include the position announcement number or the preparation date. Start building a file of KSAO sheets. Some KSAOs (like ". . . working alone . . ." or "ability to follow . . . instructions" or "ability to communicate orally and in writing") will appear on other vacancy announcements. Rather than retype these, save them as masters and reuse them as necessary.

6

THE APPLICATION ACTION PLAN AND CAREER RESOURCES

The right federal job application writer needs three things:

- A target (job series AND grade)
- Information about the target
- An action plan to reach the target

This last chapter reviews an action plan for pursuing a federal job. Information from preceding chapters is organized into a sequence of steps which should be taken to prepare, submit, and track an application packet. A checklist version of the plan is provided in Appendix J. This chapter gives brief explanations of each part of the checklist and also describes the log sheet (in Appendix K) for managing your federal job search.

1. LIST YOUR ASSETS

A. Identify, in general terms, your:

1. Educational background: Locate or get copies of all diplomas, certificates, and college transcripts. For some positions, you may need

60

to have copies of course contents (from college catalogs) to justify educational experiences which are not readily apparent from the course titles on transcripts. You may need to prepare lists of relevant college or post-high school courses, on-the-job training, and short term training.

2. **Previous paid and unpaid work/efforts:** make two lists covering the past ten years. One list will have your paid work, starting with the most recent job and working back through time. You will need start and end dates, highest pay, job series and grade if a federal job, and a point of contact, phone, and address. The second list shows all outside activities, volunteer work, and unpaid jobs in which you demonstrated skills appropriate to your target job. Recently discharged veterans may be eligible to get DD Form 2586, "Verification of Military Experience and Training," which lists their job skills and experiences acquired while on active duty which may apply to civilian jobs (including federal jobs).[1]

B. **Identify, in general terms, where you want to work:** Consider where you want to work (what cities or states appeal to you). Check Appendix E and find the Federal Job Information Center (FJIC) serving the area where you want to work. This is the first place to contact for job announcements, examination announcements, and information about your application package.

C. **What federal organizations appeal to you?** Do you have any interest in working for specific federal agencies? Are you interested in work for Congress or the Courts, or independent agencies and commissions? The cost of obtaining job announcements can be significantly reduced if you limit the number of organizations which interest you. Also, perhaps the mission of certain federal organizations appeals to you more than the missions of other organizations.

---

[1] Call 800-258-8638 or write to PRC, Inc., Attn: VMET, G-3.03, 12001 Sunrise Valley Drive, Reston, VA, 22091. Discharged/released veterans who separated after 1 October 1990, Reservists who have served 180 consecutive days of active duty since that date, and active duty military members within 180 of their projected and approved separation may be eligible.

2. IDENTIFY JOBS AND GRADES FOR WHICH YOU ARE ELIGIBLE:

A. **Use FOCIS:** Check Federal Job Information Centers, state employment offices, and local libraries for a copy of this computer program. This can be used by anyone to quickly find jobs which might interest you or help you narrow the list of jobs to which you might apply.

B. **Get advice from OPM or state employment counselors:** If FOCIS is unavailable or if more help is needed, counselors at FJICs, some federal personnel offices within departments, and state employment counselors can help you narrow the list of jobs for which you might apply.

C. **Scan appendices in this book (job series and, for GS jobs, the general qualification standards):** Appendix B has a comprehensive list of General Schedule (GS) jobs. Appendix D has a list of Wage Grade jobs. If a GS job series sounds attractive, Appendix G lists general education and experience requirements for most GS jobs.

3. FOCUS ON THE REQUIREMENTS FOR TARGET JOBS: After you have identified one or more target jobs, agencies and parts of the country where you would like to work, contact FJICs in the appropriate area (or, if you have a computer and modem, contact the Federal Jobs Hotline) for further information.

A. **Identify any required exams:**

1. **Call nearest OPM for test dates and sites:** Ask whether any exams are required for the target job; get the name and any information available about any exams. College placement offices and large post offices will also have examination announcements.

2. **Check libraries for hints, sample questions, or copies of old exams:** Some libraries have information about federal exams; ask them about exams for your target job.

B. **Review X-118/X118C standards and agency-made standards:**

1. **Determine whether your assets qualify you for the target job:** Check Appendix G for the qualification standards for major groups of GS jobs. If more information is needed, check position classification standards. At this time, be sure to check the job's "Status" requirement. Do you meet this requirement? (For example, if the "Status" is "Federal employees," are you currently a federal employee?)

2. Does the target series/grade appeal to you (does it seem to offer what you want in terms of work and pay)?

3. Are you almost qualified for other series or grades? Check similar jobs in the same job family (or other families that interest you) and check other grades in the interesting jobs. Do the standards indicate whether you are qualified? Can you qualify by taking one or a few post-high school course(s)?

4. GET CURRENT JOB ANNOUNCEMENTS FROM:

A. **OPM's FEICs or the *Career America Connection*** listed in Appendix E.

B. **Agency personnel offices** should be checked if you want to work for a specific agency. The FJIC can provide you with the address for the nearest personnel office for the desired agency. If interested in working for the Department of Defense, check the nearest military base to determine whether there is a "One Stop Job Shop" at the base or post.

C. **State employment offices** usually carry recent federal announcements within the state.

D. ***Federal Career Opportunities/Federal Jobs Digest*** list recently announced vacancies, as well as open and continuous hire positions. Also check the ***Federal Times,*** a weekly newspaper.

E. **Federal Job Opportunities Bulletin Boards** usually carry recent federal announcements grouped by geographic region and job family.

5. BEGIN PREPARING THE APPLICATION PACKET

A. **Get *X-118* or *X-118C Qualification Standards* for the target job**: Use the job series number and grade and contact an FEIC, state employment office or local library for the qualification standards. Note that qualification standards for GS job families are in Appendix G.

B. **If more information is needed, get *Position Classification Standards* for the target job** from a FEIC or state employment office.

C. **Examine announcement: Are additional forms needed?** Note all the other forms listed on the announcement. Some key forms are in Appendix K. Current federal employees in need of a recent SF 50 should contact their servicing personnel office.

D. **If not already prepared, make a "master" SF 171/OF 612 for the target series and grade** see the discussion in the previous chapter about what blocks to leave blank on a "master."

E. **Call for more information about the vacancy:** There will be a phone number and point of contact (POC) on the announcement; record this number and name on the Log Sheet (Appendix K) and contact the POC for more information about the position (is it still open, does "closing date" on the announcement mean the date the application packet has to be in their hands or is the closing date the last acceptable postmark date on the packet; what is the schedule for filling the position; can you call the hiring official for more information about the job).

6. PREPARE A "MAIL-IN" PACKET

A. **Make a clear copy of the master SF 171 or OF 612 and complete any unfilled blocks, including block 1 and your signature and date:** Follow the instructions in Chapter Five.

B. **Prepare the supplemental forms (race and sex surveys, SF 15, KSA sheets, etc.)**

C. **Make a photo copy of the completed packet:** If not using a computer to make your application packet, after making a master, make at least one good, clear photocopy of the master. This copy will be completed and mailed in your application packet. **You also need to make a copy of the mail-in packet.** If your packet is lost, you will need to rush another copy to the POC. At the very least, copy those pages in the mail-in copy that have blanks which you completed (example, the first, second and last pages, have blocks that are blank on the master but are completed on the mail-in copy).

D. **Mail the application packet and complete a log record:** using the Log Sheet in Appendix K. Make every effort to mail the packet at least a week before the closing date. Some offices require the packets **postmarked by the closing date**; some require the packets **in their hands by the closing date**. Use special delivery services (one-day, two-day, etc.) and try to allow at least two days of slack (that is, plan to get your packet to the personnel office at least two days before the vacancy closes).

7. FOLLOW-THROUGH

A. **Call the POC a few days later and ask:**

1. **Whether the packet arrived:** Try to call *before* the closing date of the announcement; you should have planned to get the packet to the personnel office at least two days before the closing date (see 5.E., above). If they do not have your packet, you may still have time to ship another copy before the deadline.

2. **Has anything changed regarding that vacancy:** Was the closing date extended? Was the position closed? Log any changes into your Log Sheet.

3. **What timetable will be followed in rating the applications and sending ratings to hiring officials:** When does the POC expect to have the packets ranked and when will the packets be sent to the hiring official? Note this schedule in the Log Sheet. Also ask for a good time to call back for the status of your application.[2]

B. **Based on the timetable given by the POC, call later to find out if you were rated:**

1. **If you were not rated, ask why not:** The purpose of this question is not to chastise the recruiting official but to find out why your application was not ranked and forwarded to the hiring official. This is a learning experience; your application is being critiqued by a pro; use his or her recommendations to make your next submission even better. On your Log Sheet, note the date of your call and the name of the person with whom you talked.

2. **If your application was misread, ask to appeal the rating:** If you believe that your packet was misread by the recruiting official, ask to discuss why you believe a mistake was made and ask whether something can be done to put you back in the running. Again, you do *not* want to be angry with the recruiting official; he or she may have had to process dozens of applications and may have made an honest mistake that can be corrected to your satisfaction. If not, you can still

---

[2] Recruiters sometimes have scores of applications to process and each call interrupts their work. You need to call only at the key steps in the review process to track your application and the recruitment specialists can tell you the best time to make such calls.

use this as a learning experience to apply when you submit future application packets.

3. **Again ask for timetable and other information about this vacancy:** If you can resubmit a corrected packet for this vacancy, ask the recruiting official for a deadline **and meet those deadlines!** Note the deadlines on your Log Sheet.

C. **If rated, call back every two weeks and ask:**

1. **Has the application gone to the hiring activity**

2. **Has anything changed regarding the vacancy:** Record the date of each call, the name of the person who talked to you, and the information you got from the call. Normally, a personnel official will not call you about changes in the status of a vacancy. If your packet was not rated and sent to a hiring official, you probably will not be notified until someone was hired, so you need to regularly check the status of your application and log the information in your Log Sheet.

D. **If not selected, call the POC and ask why:** Try to find out what would have made your application stronger.

E. **Update the log records:** Close your Log Sheet by describing why your application was not successful and make any necessary changes in your master application.

RESOURCES

The following resources include valuable information for assisting you with your federal job search. Most of these resources are available directly from the publisher or through Impact Publications. For your convenience, please refer to the "Career Resource" section at the end of this book which includes those resources available directly through Impact Publications.

JOB HOTLINES

Career America Connection: (912) 757-3000, lists federal jobs and has forms and announcements. Requires a touch tone phone.

GOVERNMENT PUBLICATIONS

All federal government publications may be purchased from US Government

Book Stores (usually found in cities with FEICs) or from:

> The Superintendent of Documents
> U.S. Government Printing Office
> Washington, D.C. 20402-9325
> (202) 783-3238

FEDERAL JOB STANDARDS

Federal job standards such as qualification or classification standards, may be obtained from:

> U.S. Office of Personnel Management
> Office of Staffing Policy and Operations
> Career Entry Group
> 1900 E Street, N.W.
> Washington, D.C. 20415
> (202) 606-0960

JOB LISTINGS/SUBSCRIPTION SERVICES

Federal Career Opportunities: P.O. Box 1059, Vienna, VA 22183, (703) 281-0200

Federal Jobs Digest: 325 Pennsylvania Ave., SE, Washington, D.C., 20003, (800) 543-3000 are published biweekly.

Federal Times: 6885 Commercial Drive, Springfield, VA, 22159, a weekly newspaper.

BOOKS AND CATALOGS

Damp, Dennis V., ***The Book of U.S. Government Jobs***, 1995, D-Amp Publications.

Government Directory of Addresses and Telephone Numbers, 1993, Omnigraphics.

Hammer, Hy, ***The Civil Service Handbook***, Arco/Prentice-Hall.

Hammer, Hy, ***Complete Guide to U.S. Civil Service Jobs***, Arco/Prentice-Hall.

Hammer, Hy, ***General Test Practice for 101 U.S. Jobs***, Arco/Prentice-Hall.

"Jobs and Careers for the 1990's:" a free catalog of over 2,700 resources to help someone seeking *any* kind of employment, from Impact Publications, 9104-N Manassas Drive, Manassas Park, VA 22111, (703) 361-7300 (fax 703-335-9486).

Krannich, Ronald L. and Caryl Rae, *Directory of Federal Jobs and Employers*, 1996, Impact Publications, see address above.

Krannich, Ronald L. and Caryl Rae, *The Complete Guide to Public Employment*, 1995, Impact Publications, see address above.

Krannich, Ronald L. and Caryl Rae, *Find a Federal Job Fast! How to Cut the Red Tape and Get Hired*, 1995, Impact Publications, see address above.

Kraus, Krandall, *How to Get a Federal Job*, 1989, Facts on File.

Lauber, Daniel, *The Government Job Finder*, 1996, Planning/Communications.

Troutman, Kathy, *The Federal Resume Guidebook*, 1996, Resume Place Press.

U.S. Office of Personnel Management, *X-118 Qualification Standards Handbook*, TS-230, March 1990, order from The Superintendent of Documents (above).

U.S. Office of Personnel Management, *Handbook X-118C, Job Qualification System for Trades and Labor Occupations*, order from The Superintendent of Documents (above).

U.S. Office of Personnel Management, *Position Classification Standards for the _____ Series GS-_*, TS-(various numbers), various dates, order from The Superintendent of Documents (above) the standards for the target job with which you are most interested.

Waelde, David, *How to Get a Federal Job*, 1989, FEDHELP Publications.

Warner, John W., *Federal Jobs in Law Enforcement*, 1992, Arco/Prentice-Hall.

Wood, Patricia B., *The 171 Reference Book*, 1991, Workbooks, Inc.

Wood, Patricia B., *Promote Yourself*, 1991, Workbooks, Inc.

COMPUTER SOFTWARE PROGRAMS

FOCIS—Federal Occupational and Career Information System, U.S. Office of Personnel Management.

Quick and Easy Federal Job Kits, DataTech. (Contact Impact Publications for both DOS and Windows versions.) Available in four versions—individuals (1 user), family (2 users), office (8 users), and professional (unlimited users).

COMPUTER BULLETIN BOARDS

Federal Job Opportunities Bulletin Boards, provided by the U.S. Office of Personnel Management, require a computer and a modem to access job announcements. See Appendix E for a list of the boards and connection parameters.

Appendix A

EXPLANATION OF TERMS

The Office of Personnel Management's *X-118 Qualification Standards Handbook* and their *X-118C Job Qualification System for Trades and Labor Occupations* use a number of terms which have very specific meanings to federal personnel specialists. This appendix lists the key terms, taken from the handbooks.[1]

Accredited Education is education above the high school level completed in a U.S. college, university, or other educational institution which has been accredited by one of the accrediting agencies or associations recognized by the Secretary, U.S. Department of Education.

Administrative Series are occupational series which typically follow a two-grade interval pattern and involve the application of a substantial body of knowledge of

---

[1] *X-118 Qualification Standards Handbook,* U.S. Office of Personnel Management, Washington, D.C., TS-230, March 1990, pages A-5 through A-7, inclusive; *X-118C Job Qualification System for Trades and Labor Occupations,* U.S. Office of Personnel Management, Washington, D.C., *passim.*

principles, concepts, and practices applicable to one or more fields of administration or management.

Career-Conditional Appointment: A probationary appointment of one year; if work is satisfactory, then for the next two years, some aspects of civil service protection are withheld, allowing the agency to dismiss the employee; after the third year as a career-conditional appointee, a satisfactory employee is eligible for transition to the competitive service.

Certification is the ranking of all qualified applicants for a vacant position.

Clerical Series are occupational series which follow a one-grade interval pattern and involve structured work in support of office, business, or fiscal operations.

Competitive Appointment is an appointment to a position in the competitive service following open competitive examination or under direct-hire authority. The competitive examination, which is open to all applicants, may consist of a written test, an evaluation of an applicant's education and experience, and/or an evaluation of other attributes necessary for successful performance in the position to be filled.

Competitive Service includes all positions in which appointments are subject to the provisions of chapter 33 of title 5, United States Code. Positions in the executive branch of the federal government are in the competitive service unless they are specifically excluded from it. Positions in the legislative and judicial branches are outside the competitive service unless they are specifically included in it.

Concurrent Experience is experience gained in more than one position, during the same period of time, with either the same employer or with a different employer.

Delegation occurs when job application examinations are done by a federal agency instead of the Office of Personnel Management; full delegation means the agency announces vacancies, recruits applicants and then rates or ranks the applications against the position's qualification standards.

Education above the High School Level is successfully completed progressive study at an accredited business or technical school, junior college, college, or university where the institution normally requires a high school diploma or equivalent for admission.

Fill-in Employment is employment held by persons during the time period after leaving their regular occupation in anticipation of, but before entering, military service.

Foreign Education is education acquired outside the United States, the District of Columbia, the Commonwealth of Puerto Rico, a Trust Territory of the Pacific Islands, or any territory or possession of the U.S.

Full-Time Equivalent (FTE): To federal personnel specialists, a position requiring approximately 40 hours per week of work is one full-time equivalent position. A position requiring 20 hours per week of work is one-half of a FTE position.

Generic Standards are standards prescribed for groups of occupational series which have a common pattern of education and/or experience.

Graduate Education is successfully completed education in a graduate program for which a bachelor's or higher degree is normally required for admission. To be creditable, such education must show evidence of progress through a set curriculum, i.e., it is part of a program leading to a master's or higher degree, and thus does not include post-baccalaureate education consisting of undergraduate and/or continuing education courses which would not lead to an advanced degree.

High School Graduation or Equivalent means the applicant has received a high school diploma, General Education Development (GED) equivalency certificate, or proficiency certificate from a state or territorial-level Board or Department of Education.

Individual Occupational Requirements are requirements (experience, education, etc.) for individual occupational series and are used in conjunction with a generic standard.

In Service Placement for the purposes of the *X-118 Qualification Standards Handbook* includes promotion, reassignment, change to a lower grade, transfer, reinstatement, reemployment, and restoration, based on an individual's current or former competitive service employment. In service placement also includes noncompetitive conversion of excepted appointees whose federal excepted positions are brought into the competitive service under 5 CFR 316.702 and Department of Defense/Non-appropriated Fund (DOD/NAF) employees whose positions are brought into the competitive service. It does not include noncompetitive appointment of non-federal employees whose public or private enterprise positions are brought into the competitive service under 5 CFR 316.701.

Job Family refers to a collection of Wage Grade occupations and job families, based on the nature of the work they do. A job family is a broad grouping of occupations which are related in one or more ways such as: similarity of functions performed, transferability of knowledge and skills from one occupation to another, or similarity of materials or equipment worked on.

Knowledge, Skills and Abilities (KSAs): Knowledge is a body of information applied directly to the performance of a function. Skill is an observable competence to perform a learned psychomotor act. Ability is competence to perform an observable behavior or a behavior that results in an observable product.

Merit Pay is an incentive pay system for GM-13 through GM-15 supervisory personnel; pay increases are based on performance.

Modification of an OPM qualification standard means substitution by an agency or OPM of qualification requirements that differ from those in the published standards. While applicants who qualify under a modified standard may not meet all of the specific requirements described in the published standard, their overall backgrounds show clear evidence of their potential success in the position to be filled. A modified standard may apply to any number of positions within an organization.

Noncompetitive means a promotion, demotion, reassignment, transfer, reinstatement, or appointment in the competitive service that is not made by selection from an open competitive exam or under direct-hire authority.

Normal Line of Promotion is the pattern of upward movement from one grade to another for a position or group of positions in an organization.

Occupation is a subgroup of a Wage Grade job family which includes all jobs at the various skill levels in a particular kind of work. Jobs within an occupation are similar to each other with regard to subject matter and basic knowledge and skill requirements.

Overhire refers to a job which does not have an authorized *position*; a person who is an "overhire" has benefits and rights similar to someone in an authorized position but is also most likely to be the first one to be RIFed when the agency cuts its expenses.

Pay category indicates the type of job and the specific schedule from which the job is paid:

- SES—Senior Executive Service
- GM—General Schedule positions with management responsibilities
- GS—General Schedule positions
- WS—Wage Grade supervisory positions
- WL—Leader jobs in the Wage Grade pay category
- WG—Wage Grade positions, non-supervisory

Position means the officially assigned duties and responsibilities which make up the work performed by an employee.

Professional series are occupational series which follow a two-grade interval pattern and are identified as "professional" in the series definition. They involve work which is characteristically acquired through education or training equivalent to a bachelor's or higher degree with major study in a specialized field.

Quality Ranking Factors are knowledge, skills and abilities which could be expected to enhance significantly performance in a position, but are not essential for satisfactory performance. Applicants who meet the quality ranking factors may be ranked above those who do not, but no one may be rated ineligible solely for failure to meet a quality ranking factor.

Related Education is education above the high school level which has equipped the applicant with the knowledge, skills, and abilities to perform successfully the duties of the position being filled. Education may relate to the duties of a specific position or to the occupation, but must be appropriate for the position being filled.

Research positions are positions in professional series which primarily involve scientific inquiry or investigation, or research-type exploratory development of a creative or scientific nature, where the knowledge required to perform the work successfully is acquired typically and primarily through graduate study. The work is such that the academic preparation will equip the applicant to perform fully the professional work of the position after a short orientation period.

Selective factors are knowledge, skills, abilities, or special qualifications that are in addition to or more specific than the minimum requirements in the qualification standard, but which are determined to be essential to perform the duties and responsibilities of a particular position. Applicants who do not meet a selective factor are ineligible for consideration.

Series or **Occupational Series** means positions similar as to specialized work and qualification requirements. Series are designated by a title and number such as the Accounting Series, GS-510; the Secretary Series, GS-318; the Microbiology Series, GS-403.

Single-Agency Standards are qualification standards, approved by OPM, which are established for positions in a particular agency when the agency's jobs differ substantially from those covered by an OPM standard or for which no government-wide standard is applicable. Single-agency standards supersede the OPM standard for the position they cover.

Specialized experience is experience which has equipped the applicant with the particular knowledge, skills, and abilities to perform successfully the duties of the position and is typically in or related to the work of the position to be filled.

Status candidates are job applicants who already work for the federal government. This may be further limited, for example, to "DA Status Candidates." These people already work for the Department of the Army. Applications from people without the mentioned status will not be considered for the vacancy.

Technical series are occupational series which follow a one-grade interval pattern and are associated with and supportive of a professional or administrative **field.**

Veterans Readjustment Appointment is a special appointment for eligible Vietnam era veterans which allows appointment without tests or competition with non-Vietnam veterans, to positions up to GS-11 or WG-11; after two years in such a position, a veteran may be given a competitive appointment; contact a FJIC for further information.

Waiver of an OPM qualification standard involves setting aside requirements in a published standard to place an employee in a particular position usually to avoid some kind of hardship to the employee, such as in cases of reduction-in- force or administrative error on the part of the agency. Extra training and/or skills development may be needed to help the employee adjust to the new position. Waivers are granted by OPM or an agency, as appropriate, on a case-by-case basis, and do not directly affect other positions in the organization.

Work-Study Programs are government or non-government programs that provide supervised work experience related to a student's course of study, which are a part of or a supplement to education. Federal student-trainee programs are examples of such programs.

Appendix B

GENERAL SCHEDULE OCCUPATIONS

Some of the information in this appendix was taken from FOCIS, the Federal Occupational and Career Information System, a computer program prepared by the U.S. Office of Personnel Management and designed to help people select careers in the federal service. A copy of FOCIS may be obtained from the National Technical Information Service. Call (703) 487-4650 for price and ordering information. FOCIS also is available through Impact Publications (see order form at the end of this book). Other information here comes from the *X-118 Qualification Standards Handbook*. An asterisk (*) means that single-agency standards were published for the position in question. If applying for such a position, be sure to ask whether the agency's standards are available.

GS-000 Miscellaneous Occupations

What do correctional officers, park rangers, firefighters, chaplains and guards have in common? Each of these jobs is unrelated to any other Occupational Group and is, therefore, placed in the Miscellaneous Group.

This group includes all classes of positions which have responsibilities to

76

administer, supervise or perform work not included in any other occupational group either because the duties are unique, complex or come partially under a variety of other groups. The occupations in this group include:

Bond Sales Promotion
  Representatives (GS-011)
Chaplains (GS-060)
Community Planners (GS-020)
Correctional Institution
  Administrators (GS-006)
Correctional Officers (GS-007)*
Environmental Protection
  Assistants (GS-029)
Environmental Protection
  Specialists (GS-028)
Fingerprint Identifiers
  (GS-072)*
Firefighters and Fire
  Inspectors (GS-081)
Foreign Law Specialist
  (GS-095)*

General Student Trainee
  (GS-099)
Nuclear Materials Courier
  (GS-084)*
Outdoor Recreation Planners
  (GS-023)
Park Rangers and Park Managers
  (GS-025)
Police Officers (GS-083)
Safety and Occupational
  Health Specialists (GS-018)
Safety Technicians (GS-019)
Security Guards (GS-085)
Security Specialists (GS-080)
Sports Specialists (GS-030)
U.S. Marshals (GS-082)*

GS-100: Social Science, Psychology and Welfare

Social sciences and social services deal with cultures and people. Social sciences deal with psychology, economics, history, sociology and anthropology. Social services deal with social work, recreational activities and the administration of public welfare and insurance programs.

The positions in this group carry responsibilities for advising, administering, supervising or performing research or other professional and scientific work, or subordinate technical work or related clerical work. The occupations in this group include:

Anthropologists (GS-190)
Archaeologists (GS-193)
Civil Rights Analyst (GS-160)
Economists (GS-110)
Foreign Agricultural Affairs
  Specialists (GS-135)
Food Assistance Program
  Specialists (GS-120)*
Foreign Affairs Specialists
  (GS-130)
Geographers (GS-150)

Historians (GS-170)
Intelligence Aides and Clerks
  (GS-134)
Intelligence Specialists (GS-132)
International Cooperation (GS-136)*
Manpower Development Specialists
  (GS-142)
Psychologists (GS-180)
Psychology Aides and Technicians
  (GS-181)
Recreation Specialists (GS-188)

Social Insurance Administrators
(GS-105)*
Social Science Aides and
Technicians (GS-102)
Social Scientists (GS-101)
Social Science Student
Trainee (GS-199)

Social Service Aides and
Assistants (GS-186)
Social Service Representatives
(GS-187)
Social Workers (GS-185)
Unemployment Insurance
Specialists (GS-106)*

GS-200: Personnel Management and Industrial Relations

The Federal Government operates on people power. This resource, called personnel, fluctuates. Each agency has a personnel office staffed with personnel specialists who hire, fire, train employees, administer a variety of personnel programs and overall, perform work involving the various aspects of human resources management and industrial relations. The occupations in this group include:

Apprenticeship and Training
Representatives (GS-243)*
Contractor Industrial Relations
Specialists (GS-246)
Employee Development Specialists
(GS-235)
Employee Relations Specialists
(GS-230)
Equal Employment Opportunity
Specialists (GS-260)
Labor Management Relations
Examiners (GS-244)*
Labor Relations Specialists
(GS-233)
Mediators (GS-241)*
Military Personnel Clerks and
Technicians (GS-204)

Military Personnel Management
Specialists (GS-205)
Personnel Clerks and Assistants
(GS-203)
Personnel Management Specialists
(GS-201)
Personnel Management Student
Trainee (GS-299)
Personnel Staffing Specialists
(GS-212)
Position Classification
Specialists (GS-221)
Salary and Wage Administrators
(GS-223)
Wage and Hour Compliance
Specialists (GS-249)*

GS-300: Administrative, Clerical, and Office Services

This group includes all classes of positions which have responsibilities for administering, supervising or performing work involving management analysis; stenography, typing and secretarial work; mail and file tasks; the operation of computers, office machines and communications equipment; the technical phases of photographic and art processes; and, overall, performing general clerical and administrative work. The occupations in this group include:

Administrative Officers (GS-341)
Administration and Office Support
  Student Trainee (GS-399)
Clerk-Stenographers and Reporters
  (GS-312)
Clerk-Typists (GS-322)
Closed Microphone Reporters
  (GS-319)
Coding Clerks (GS-357)
Communications Clerks (GS-394)
Communications Managers (GS-391)
Communications Relay Operators
  (GS-390)
Communications Specialists (GS-393)
Computer Clerks and Assistants
  (GS-335)
Computer Operators (GS-332)
Computer Specialists (GS-334)
Correspondence Clerks (GS-309)

Data Transcribers (GS-356)
Equal Opportunity Compliance
  Specialists (GS-360)
Equipment Operators (GS-350)
General Communications Specialists
  (GS-392)
Logistics Management Specialists
  (GS-346)
Mail and File Clerks (GS-305)
Management Analysts (GS-343)
Management Clerks and Assistants
  (GS-344)
Miscellaneous Clerks and
  Assistants (GS-303)
Program Analysts (GS-345)
Secretaries (GS-318)
Support Services Administrators
  (GS-342)

A shortage exists in the Federal government of qualified secretaries, clerks, typists and stenographers.

GS-400: Biological Sciences

Biologists and related scientists use their knowledge to detect and to control pests and diseases and to develop new strains and promote growth of useful organisms. In this group, the positions carry responsibilities for advising, administering, supervising or performing research or other professional and scientific work or subordinate technical work in any of the science fields concerned with living organisms; the soil and its properties and distribution; and the management, conservation and use of these resources. The occupations in this group include:

Agricultural Management
  Specialists (GS-475)*
Agricultural Extension
  Agent (GS-406)
Agronomists (GS-471)
Animal Scientists (GS-487)
Biological Science Student
  Trainee (GS-499)
Biological Technicians (GS-404)
Botanists (GS-430)
Ecologists (GS-408)

Entomologists (GS-414)
Fish and Wildlife Administrators
  (GS-480)
Fish and Wildlife Refuge Managers
  (GS-485)
Fishery Biologists (GS-482)*
Foresters (GS-460)
Forestry Technicians (GS-462)
General Biological Scientists
  (GS-401)
Geneticists (GS-440)

Home Economists (GS-493)
Horticulturists (GS-437)
Irrigation System Operators
  (GS-459)*
Microbiologists (GS-403)
Pharmacologists (GS-405)
Physiologists (GS-413)
Plant Pathologists (GS-434)
Plant Physiologists (GS-435)
Plant Protection and Quarantine
  Officers (GS-436)*

Plant Protection Technicians
  (GS-421)*
Range Conservationists (GS-454)
Range Technicians (GS-455)
Soil Conservationists (GS-457)
Soil Conservation Technicians
  (GS-458)
Soil Scientists (GS-470)
Wildlife Biologists (GS-486)
Wildlife Refuge Manager (GS-485)*
Zoologists (GS-410)

GS-500: Accounting and Budget

Money and accountability go hand-in-hand. Taxpayers and program managers require efficient use and management of Federal dollars; so the Federal Government employs financial experts in virtually all of its agencies. The people in these positions advise, administer, supervise or perform professional, technical or related clerical work of an accounting, budget administration or financial management nature. The occupations in this group include:

Accountants (GS-510)
Accounting Technicians (GS-525)
Auditors (GS-511)
Budget Analysts (GS-560)
Cash Processors (GS-530)
Financial Administrators (GS-501)
Financial Institution Examiners
  (GS-570)
Financial Managers (GS-505)
Financial Management Student
  Trainee (GS-599)

Insurance Accounts Specialists
  (GS-593)
Internal Revenue Agents (GS-512)*
Military Pay Specialists (GS-545)
Payroll Clerks and Technicians
  (GS-544)
Tax Examiners (GS-592)*
Tax Technicians (GS-526)*
Voucher Examiners (GS-540)

GS-600: Medical, Hospital, Dental and Public Health

The Nation's health is overseen, maintained and improved upon by the many doctors, dentists, therapists, allied health specialists, nurses, health administrators and health-care support staff employed by the Federal Government. The people in these positions advise, administer, supervise or perform research or other professional and scientific work, subordinate technical work or related clerical work in one of the many branches of medicine, surgery, dentistry and related patient-care fields. The occupations in this group include:

Autopsy Assistants (GS-625)
Consumer Safety Officers (GS-696)*
Corrective Therapists (GS-635)
Dental Assistants (GS-681)
Dental Hygienists (GS-682)
Dental Laboratory Aides and Technicians (GS-683)
Dentists (GS-680)
Diagnostic Radiologic Technologists (GS-647)
Dietitians and Nutritionists (GS-630)
Doctors (GS-602)
Educational Therapists (GS-639)
Environmental Health Technicians (GS-698)
General Health Scientists (GS-601)
Health Aides and Technicians (GS-640)
Health System Administrators (GS-670)
Health System Specialists (GS-671)
Hospital Housekeepers (GS-673)
Industrial Hygienists (GS-690)
Manual Arts Therapists (GS-637)
Medical Clerks (GS-679)
Medical and Health Student Trainee (GS-699)
Medical Machine Technicians (GS-649)
Medical Records Librarians (GS-669)

Medical Records Technicians (GS-675)
Medical Supply Aides and Technicians (GS-622)
Medical Technologists (GS-644)
Medical Technical Assistant (GS-650)*
Nuclear Medicine Technicians (GS-642)
Nurses (GS-610)
Nursing Assistants (GS-621)
Occupational Therapists (GS-631)
Optometrists (GS-662)
Orthotists/Prosthetists (GS-667)
Pathology Technicians (GS-646)
Pharmacists (GS-660)
Pharmacy Technicians (GS-661)
Physical Therapists (GS-633)
Physicians Assistants (GS-603)
Podiatrists (GS-668)
Practical Nurses (GS-620)
Prosthetic Representatives (GS-672)
Public Health Advisors and Analysts (GS-685)*
Recreation and Creative Arts Therapists (GS-638)
Rehabilitation Therapy Assistants (GS-636)
Respiratory Therapists (GS-651)
Restoration Technicians (GS-664)*
Speech Pathologists and Audiologists (GS-665)
Therapeutic Radiologic Technologists (GS-648)

There are many opportunities in the public sector for doctors and dentists, audiologists, dietitians, medical records administrators, orthotists/prosthetists, pharmacists, speech pathologists, physical therapists and nurses across the U.S.

GS-700: Veterinary Medical Science

Livestock diseases, meat and poultry processing operations, laboratory research, and animal health and welfare are areas of concern to the Federal Government. The positions in this group carry responsibilities for advising and consulting, administering, managing, supervising or performing research or other professional and scientific work in the various branches of veterinary medical science. The occupations in this group include:

Animal Health Technicians (GS-704)
Veterinarians (GS-701)
Veterinary Student Trainee (GS-799)

GS-800: Engineering and Architecture

Engineers and architects perform professional and scientific work in the design and construction of projects such as buildings, systems, equipment, materials and methods. They also review applications, designs, and plans for structures and systems.

The positions in this group require a knowledge of the science or the art, or both, in order to transform and make useful materials, natural resources and power. The occupations in this group include:

Aerospace Engineers (GS-861)
Agricultural Engineers (GS-890)
Architects (GS-808)
Biomedical Engineers (GS-858)
Ceramic Engineers (GS-892)
Chemical Engineers (GS-893)
Civil Engineers (GS-810)
Computer Engineers (GS-854)
Construction Analysts (GS-828)
Construction Control (GS-809)
Drafting Engineers (GS-818)
Electrical Engineers (GS-850)
Electronics Engineers (GS-855)
Electronics Technicians (GS-856)
Engineering and Architecture
  Student Trainee (GS-899)
Engineering Technicians (GS-802)
Engineers (GS-801)
Environmental Engineers (GS-819)

Fire Prevention Engineers
  (GS-804)
General Engineer (GS-801)
Industrial Engineering
  Technicians (GS-895)
Industrial Engineers (GS-896)
Industrial Engineer
  Technicians (GS-895)
Landscape Architect (GS-807)
Materials Engineers (GS-806)
Mechanical Engineers (GS-830)
Mining Engineers (GS-880)
Naval Architects (GS-871)
Nuclear Engineers (GS-840)
Petroleum Engineers (GS-881)
Safety Engineers (GS-803)
Ship Surveyors (GS-873)
Surveying Technicians (GS-817)

There are numerous opportunities for engineers in all specialties with the Federal Government across the United States.

GS-900: Legal and Kindred

Courtroom drama, lawyers, judges and examiners with their magnifying glasses are all part of the legal arena. Any agency is likely to employ attorneys either in its legal department or in its Office of the General Counsel.

This group includes all classes of positions which carry responsibilities for advising, administering, supervising or performing professional legal work in preparation for the trial and argument of cases; presiding at formal hearings; administering laws entrusted to an agency or department; providing authoritative or advisory legal opinions or decisions; preparing a variety of legal documents; and performing quasi-legal work. The occupations in this group include:

Administrative Law Judges
 (GS-935)
Attorneys (GS-905)
Civil Service Retirement Claim
 Examiners (GS-997)*
Claims Clerks (GS-998)
Clerk of Court (GS-945)
Contract Representatives (GS-962)
Estate Tax Examiners (GS-920)
General Claims Examiners (GS-990)
Hearings and Appeals Specialists
 (GS-930)
Land Law Examiners (GS-965)*
Law Clerks (GS-904)
Legal Clerks and Technicians
 (GS-986)

Legal Instruments Examiners
 (GS-963)
Legal Occupations Student
 Trainee (GS-999)
Loss and Damage Claims Examiners
 (GS-992)
Paralegal Specialists (GS-950)
Social Insurance Claims Examiners
 (GS-993)*
Unemployment Compensation Claims
 Examiners (GS-994)*
Veterans Claims Examiners
 (GS-996)*
Visa and Passport Examiners
 (GS-967)*
Worker's Compensation Claims
 Examiners (GS-991)*

GS-1000: Public Information and Arts

The world of public information, music, theater, language, museums, photography, writing and illustrating is a world away from the typical Federal job. The Federal Government maintains and operates theaters, audio-visual production facilities, museums, and public information programs. The positions in this group require writing, editing and foreign languages; the ability to evaluate and to interpret informational and cultural materials; the ability to apply technical or aesthetic principles in combination with manual skills and dexterity; and possess clerical skills. The occupations in this group include:

Arts Specialists (GS-1056)
Audio-Visual Production
 Specialists (GS-1071)

Editorial Assistants (GS-1087)
Exhibits Specialists (GS-1010)

General Arts and Information
 Specialist (GS-1001)
Illustrators (GS-1020)
Information and Arts Student
 Trainee (GS-1099)
Interior Designer (GS-1008)
Language Clerk (GS-1046)
Language Specialists (GS-1040)
Museum Curators (GS-1015)
Museum Specialists and
 Technicians (GS-1016)
Music Specialist (GS-1051)

Office Drafting Specialist (GS-1021)
Photographers (GS-1060)
Public Affairs Specialists
 (GS-1035)
Technical Writers and Editors
 (GS-1083)
Theater Specialist (GS-1054)
Visual Information Specialists
 (GS-1084)
Writers and Editors (GS-1082)

GS-1100: Business and Industry

The business world and the Federal world have many similar needs. Both deal daily with contracts, property, purchasing, production and finances. Industrial production methods and processes, industrial and commercial contracts, and the examination and appraisal of merchandise or property are some of the business and trade activities of the Government. The positions in this group carry responsibilities for advising, administering, supervising or performing work pertaining to and requiring a knowledge of business and industry rules, regulations and practices. The occupations in this group include:

Agricultural Marketing Specialists
 (GS-1146)*
Agricultural Market Reporters
 (GS-1147)*
Agricultural Program Specialists
 (GS-1145)*
Appraisers and Assessors (GS-1171)
Building Managers (GS-1176)*
Business and Industry Specialists
 (GS-1101)
Business and Industry Student
 Trainee (GS-1199)
Commissary Store Managers
 (GS-1144)
Contract Specialists (GS-1102)
Crop Insurance Administrators
 (GS-1161)*
Crop Insurance Underwriter
 (GS-1162)*
Financial Analysts (GS-1160)

Housing Managers (GS-1173)
Industrial Property Managers
 (GS-1103)
Industrial Specialists (GS-1150)
Insurance Examiner (GS-1163)
Internal Revenue Officers
 (GS-1169)*
Loan Specialists (GS-1165)
Procurement Clerks and Assistants
 (GS-1106)
Production Controllers (GS-1152)
Property Disposal Clerks and
 Technicians (GS-1107)
Property Disposal Specialists
 (GS-1104)
Public Utilities Specialists
 (GS-1130)
Purchasing Specialists (GS-1105)
Realtors (GS-1170)
Trade Specialists (GS-1140)

GS-1200: Copyright, Patent and Trademark

When does an invention become an invention? Who keeps track of all the designs, applications and details for copyright and patent approvals? The U.S. Patent Office within the Department of Commerce handles inquiries, applications and record keeping functions in this arena.

This group includes positions having the responsibilities for advising, administering, supervising, or performing professional scientific, technical and legal work related to copyright cataloguing and registration; patent classification and issuance; and trademark registration. The occupations in this group include:

Copyright and Patent Student Trainee (GS-1299)
Copyright Specialist (GS-1210)
Copyright Technician (GS-1211)
Design Patent Examiner (GS-1226)*
Patent Administrator (GS-1220)
Patent Advisor (GS-1221)

Patent Attorneys (GS-1222)*
Patent Classifier (GS-1223)*
Patent Examiners (GS-1224)*
Patent Interference Examiner (GS-1225)*
Patent Technician (GS-1202)

GS-1300: Physical Sciences

The physical world can be divided into three sections for scientific study: earth, water and space. The people employed in this group administer, supervise, advise or perform research, professional and scientific work or subordinate technical work in any of the science fields concerned with matter, energy, physical space, time, nature of physical measurement and the physical environment, and the fundamental structural particles. Occupations in this group include:

Astronomers and Space Scientists (GS-1330)
Cartographers (GS-1370)
Cartographic Technicians (GS-1371)
Chemists (GS-1320)
Food Technologists (GS-1382)
General Physical Scientists (GS-1301)
Geodesists (GS-1372)
Geologists (GS-1350)
Geophysicists (GS-1313)
Health Physicists (GS-1306)
Hydrologic Technicians (GS-1316)
Hydrologists (GS-1315)

Land Surveyors (GS-1373)
Metallurgists (GS-1321)
Meteorological Technicians (GS-1341)
Meteorologists (GS-1340)
Navigational Information Specialists (GS-1361)
Oceanographers (GS-1360)
Physical Science Student Trainee (GS-1399)
Physical Science Technicians (GS-1311)
Physicists (GS-1310)

GS-1400: Library and Archives

The library may outwardly seem a sedentary place. Behind the scenes, people busily collect, organize, preserve and retrieve information. The staff at any Federal library helps to keep the Government's records up-to-date. The people employed in this group work in the various phases of library and archival science and have responsibilities to supervise, administer, advise and perform professional and scientific work or subordinate technical work. The occupations in this group include:

Archivists (GS-1420)*
Archives Technicians (GS-1421)
Librarians (GS-1410)
Library and Archives Student
  Trainee (GS-1499)

Library Technicians (GS-1411)
Technical Information Services
  Specialists (GS-1412)

GS-1500: Mathematics and Statistics

People apply mathematical, statistical and financial principles to every facet of daily life and business. This group includes all classes of positions carrying responsibilities for advising, administering, supervising and performing research or other professional and scientific work or related clerical work using mathematical principles, methods, procedures or relationships. The occupations in this group include:

Actuaries (GS-1510)
Computer Science Specialists
  (GS-1550)
Cryptographer (GS-1540)
Cryptanalysts (GS-1541)
Mathematical Statisticians
  (GS-1529)

Mathematicians (GS-1520)
Mathematics and Statistics Student
  Trainee (GS-1599)
Operations Research Analysts
  (GS-1515)
Statisticians (GS-1530)

GS-1600: Equipment, Facilities and Service

Federally owned property may be located anywhere in the United States or around the world. A property site may include facilities, services and, often, buildings to be managed. The positions in this group require technical or managerial skills and abilities, plus a practical knowledge of trades, crafts or manual-labor operations.

The people employed in this group must carry out the responsibilities for advising, managing, or providing instructions and information to others in such functions. The occupations in this group include:

Cemetery Superintendents
  (GS-1630)*

Equipment and Facilities Student
  Trainee (GS-1699)

Equipment Specialists (GS-1670)
Facility Managers (GS-1640)
General Facilities and Equipment
  Specialists (GS-1601)

Laundry and Dry Cleaning Plant
  Managers (GS-1658)
Printing Specialists (GS-1654)
Stewards (GS-1667)

GS-1700: Education

The Federal Government continually trains new employees and supervisors and provides continuing, refresher and retraining courses to its employees. The curricula and opportunities are diverse. This group includes positions which involve administering, managing, supervising, performing or supporting education or training. The occupations in this group include:

Educational Program Specialists
(GS-1720)*
Education and Training Specialists
(GS-1701)
Education and Training Technicians
(GS-1702)
Education and Vocational Training
  Specialists (GS-1710)
Education Researcher (GS-1730)*
Education Specialist (GS-1740)

Education Student Trainee (GS-1799)
Elementary Teachers (GS-1724)
Public Health Educators (GS-1725)
School Administrators (GS-1722)
Secondary Teachers (GS-1726)
Special Ed. Teachers (GS-1728)
Training Instructors (GS-1712)
Vocational Rehabilitation
  Specialists (GS-1715)

GS-1800: Investigation

Sniffing out criminals, following clues, gathering and presenting evidence, observing people and merchandise entering the United States, investigating prospective Federal employees, and working undercover are all duties within the Investigation Group.

The Federal Government hires people for investigation, inspection and enforcement work to uphold and safeguard the laws, the people and the property of the United States. The occupations in this group include:

Agricultural Commodity Warehouse
  Examiners (GS-1850)*
Air Safety Investigators (GS-1815)*
Alcohol, Tobacco, and Firearms
  Inspectors (GS-1854)*
Aviation Safety Inspectors
  (GS-1825)*
Border Patrol Agents (GS-1896)*
Compliance Inspection and Support
  Specialists (GS-1802)

Consumer Safety Inspectors
(GS-1862)*
Criminal Investigators (GS-1811)
Customs Aides (GS-1897)
Customs Entry and Liquidation
  Specialists (GS-1894)*
Customs Inspectors (GS-1890)*
Customs Patrol Officers (GS-1884)*

Customs Warehouse Officer
 (GS-1895)*
Food Inspectors (GS-1863)*
Game Law Enforcement Agents
 (GS-1812)
General Inspection, Investigation
 and Compliance Specialists
 (GS-1801)
General Investigators (GS-1810)
Immigration Inspectors (GS-1816)*

Import Specialists (GS-1889)
Investigation Student Trainee
 (GS-1899)
Mine Safety and Health Inspectors
 (GS-1822)*
Public Health Quarantine Inspector
 (GS-1864)*
Securities Compliance Examiners
 (GS-1831)

GS-1900: Quality Assurance, Inspection and Grading

In this age of technological sophistication and excellence, government operations demand quality products. Quality products depend on quality materials, facilities and processes. The Federal Government performs inspections and commodities grading to bring products up to standard levels.

The people employed in this group advise, supervise or perform administrative or technical work related to quality assurance, inspection or commodities grading. The occupations in this group include:

Agricultural Commodity Aides
 (GS-1981)
Agricultural Commodity Graders
 (GS-1980)

Assurance Officer (GS-1910)
Quality Inspection Student Trainee
 (GS-1999)

GS-2000: Supply

It takes many different types of items to operate the Federal government. Each item is identified, selected and acquired; then it is counted, catalogued and distributed prior to being stored, inventoried or used. The positions in this group require knowledge of one or more elements of supply systems, and/or supply methods, policies or procedures.

Work performed within this group concerns the provision and control of supplies, equipment, material, property (except real estate) and other services to components of the Federal government, or industrial or other concerns under contract to the government or receiving supplies from the government. The occupations in this group include:

Distribution Facility and Storage
Management Specialists (GS-2030)
Inventory Management Specialists
 (GS-2010)
Packaging Specialists (GS-2032)

Sales Stores Clerks (GS-2091)
Supply Catalogers (GS-2050)
Supply Clerks and Technicians
 (GS-2005)

Supply Program Managers
(GS-2003)

Supply Specialists (GS-2001)
Supply Student Trainee (GS-2099)

GS-2100: Transportation

The federal government requires many transportation services and regulates a variety of transportation activities. This group includes positions having responsibilities for advising, administering, supervising or performing clerical, administrative or technical work involved in providing transportation service to the Government, regulating Government transportation activities, or managing Government-funded transportation programs including research and development projects. The occupations in this group include:

Aircraft Operators (GS-2181)
Air Navigation Specialist (GS-2183)
Aircrew Technician (GS-2185)
Air Traffic Assistants (GS-2154)
Air Traffic Controllers (GS-2152)
Cargo Schedulers (GS-2144)
Dispatchers (GS-2151)
Freight Rate Specialists (GS-2131)
Highway Safety Specialists
  (GS-2125)*
Marine Cargo Specialists (GS-2161)
Motor Carrier Safety Specialists
  (GS-2123)*
Railroad Safety Inspectors and
  Specialists (GS-2121)*

Shipment Clerks and Assistants
  (GS-2134)
Traffic Management Specialists
  (GS-2130)
Transportation Clerks and Assistants
  (GS-2102)
Transportation Industry Analysts
  (GS-2110)
Transportation Loss Damage Claims
  Examiners (GS-2135)
Transportation Operators (GS-2150)
Transportation Specialists (GS-2101)
Transportation Student Trainee
(GS-2199)
Travel Assistants (GS-2132)

Appendix C

SELECTED FEDERAL PAY SCHEDULES FOR 1995[1]

GENERAL SCHEDULE

GS Grade	Step 1	Step 2	Step 3	Step 4	Step 5	Step 6	Step 7	Step 8	Step 9	Step 10
1	$12,141	$12,546	$12,949	$13,352	$13,757	$13,994	$14,391	$14,793	$14,811	$15,183
2	13,650	13,975	14,428	14,811	14,974	15,414	15,854	16,294	16,734	17,174
3	14,895	15,392	15,889	16,386	16,883	17,380	17,877	18,574	18,871	19,368
4	16,721	17,278	17,835	18,392	18,949	19,506	20,063	20,620	21,177	21,734
5	18,707	19,331	19,955	20,579	21,203	21,827	22,451	23,075	23,699	24,323
6	20,852	21,547	22,242	22,937	23,632	24,327	25,022	25,717	26,412	27,107
7	23,171	23,943	24,715	25,487	26,259	27,031	27,803	28,575	29,347	30,119
8	25,662	26,517	27,372	28,227	29,082	29,937	30,792	31,647	32,502	33,357
9	28,345	29,290	30,235	31,180	32,125	33,070	34,015	34,960	35,905	36,850
10	31,215	32,256	33,297	34,338	35,379	36,420	37,461	38,502	39,543	40,584
11	34,295	35,438	36,581	37,724	38,867	40,010	41,153	42,296	43,439	44,582
12	41,104	42,474	43,844	45,214	46,584	47,954	49,324	50,694	52,064	53,434
13	48,878	50,507	52,136	53,765	55,394	57,023	58,652	60,281	61,910	63,539
14	57,760	59,685	61,610	63,535	65,460	67,385	69,310	71,235	73,160	75,085
15	67,941	70,206	72,471	74,736	77,001	79,266	81,531	83,796	86,061	88,326

Grades 16 through 18 are being converted to SES positions and are unlikely to be used for newly hired employees.

---

[1] The schedules reported in this appendix were established by Executive Order 12826 of December 30, 1992, "Adjustments of Certain Rates of Pay and Allowances," *Federal Register,* Vol 60, No.1, January 3, 1995, pp. 311-314.

METRO D.C. SPECIAL RATE CLERICAL PAY

Approximately 200,000 federal workers receive special pay rates that are three to thirty percent higher than normal General Schedule rates. Most of these positions are engineers, scientists, medical personnel, and roughly 40,000 GS-2 through GS-7 clerical positions in the Washington, D.C. metro area. This table is provided to illustrate the pay differentials available to special rate positions. Normally, a job announcement will indicate whether a special rate applies to the position. The table below applies only to the metro D.C. clerical positions; other tables exist for other special rate positions, such as federal law enforcement officers.

GS Grade	Step 1	Step 2	Step 3	Step 4	Step 5	Step 6	Step 7	Step 8	Step 9	Step 10
2	$16,411	$16,843	$17,275	$17,707	$18,139	$18,571	$19,003	$19,435	$19,867	$20,299
3	17,525	18,012	18,499	18,986	19,473	19,960	20,447	20,934	21,421	21,908
4	18,577	19,123	19,669	20,215	20,761	21,307	21,853	22,399	22,945	23,491
5	20,173	20,784	21,395	22,006	22,617	23,228	23,839	24,450	25,061	25,672
6	21,805	22,486	23,167	23,848	24,529	25,210	25,891	26,572	27,253	27,934
7	23,474	24,231	24,988	25,745	26,502	27,259	28,016	28,773	29,530	30,287

LAW ENFORCEMENT SCHEDULE

Grade	Step 1	Step 2	Step 3	Step 4	Step 5	Step 6	Step 7	Step 8	Step 9	Step 10
1	$12,379	$12,793	$13,203	$13,614	$14,026	$14,269	$14,673	$15,083	$15,102	$15,487
2	13,917	14,249	14,711	15,102	15,270	15,720	16,169	16,618	17,067	17,517
3	18,226	18,732	19,239	19,745	20,252	20,758	21,265	21,771	22,278	22,784
4	20,456	21,024	21,591	22,159	22,727	23,295	23,863	24,431	24,998	25,566
5	23,522	24,157	24,793	25,428	26,063	26,699	27,334	27,970	28,605	29,241
6	24,802	25,510	26,218	26,927	27,635	28,343	29,051	29,760	30,468	31,176
7	26,775	27,562	28,349	29,137	29,924	30,711	31,498	32,286	33,073	33,860
8	27,910	28,783	29,656	30,528	31,401	32,273	33,146	34,018	34,891	35,764
9	29,864	30,827	31,790	32,753	33,716	34,679	35,642	36,605	37,568	38,531
10	32,888	33,949	35,010	36,070	37,131	38,192	39,253	40,314	41,374	42,435
11	34,968	36,134	37,300	38,465	39,631	40,797	41,963	43,129	44,295	45,460
12	41,910	43,307	44,703	46,100	47,497	48,894	50,290	51,687	53,084	54,480
13	49,837	51,498	53,159	54,819	56,480	58,141	59,802	61,463	63,124	64,785
14	58,892	60,856	62,819	64,783	66,746	68,710	70,673	72,637	74,600	76,564
15	69,273	71,582	73,891	76,200	78,509	80,817	83,126	85,453	87,744	90,053

This table shows pay rates for law enforcement officials in the metro Washington,

D.C., Philadelphia, and Chicago areas. Rates are somewhat higher in the New York and San Diego metro areas.

FEDERAL SERVICE SCHEDULE

Step	Class 1	Class 2	Class 3	Class 4	Class 5	Class 6	Class 7	Class 8	Class 9
1	$67,941	$55,053	$44,609	$36,147	$29,290	$26,184	$23,408	$20,926	$18,707
2	69,979	56,705	45,947	37,231	30,169	26,970	24,110	21,554	19,268
3	72,079	58,406	47,326	38,348	31,074	27,779	24,834	22,200	19,846
4	74,241	60,158	48,745	39,499	32,006	28,612	25,579	22,866	20,442
5	76,468	61,963	50,208	40,684	32,966	29,470	26,346	23,552	21,055
6	78,762	63,822	51,714	41,904	33,955	30,354	27,136	24,259	21,687
7	81,125	65,736	53,265	43,161	34,974	31,265	27,950	24,987	22,337
8	93,660	67,708	54,863	44,456	36,023	32,203	28,789	25,736	23,007
9	86,066	69,739	56,509	45,790	37,104	33,169	29,653	26,508	23,697
10	88,326	71,832	58,205	47,164	38,217	34,164	30,452	27,304	24,408
11	88,326	73,987	59,951	48,579	39,363	35,189	31,458	28,123	25,141
12	88,326	76,206	61,749	50,036	40,544	36,245	32,402	28,966	24,895
13	88,326	78,492	63,602	51,537	41,761	37,332	33,374	29,835	26,672
14	88,326	80,847	65,510	53,083	43,013	38,452	34,375	30,731	27,472

VETERANS HEALTH ADMINISTRATION SCHEDULES, DEPARTMENT OF VETERANS AFFAIRS

Section 7306 Schedule[2]
Deputy Under Secretary for Health $115,384
Associate Deputy Under Secretary for Health .... 110,516[3]
Assistant Under Secretaries for Health 107,259

---

[2]Does not apply to the Assistant Under Secretary for Nursing Programs of the Director of Nursing Service. Pay for these positions is set by the Under Secretary for Health under 38 U.S.C. 7451.

[3]The rate of basic pay for this employee is limited to the rate for Level V of the Executive Schedule per section 7404 (d) (2) of Title 38, U.S.C.

	Minimum	Maximum
Medical Directors	$91,514	$103,718
Director of Service	79,684	98,960
Director, National Center for Preventative Health	67,941	98,960

Physician and Dentist Schedule

Director Grade	$79,684	$98,960
Executive Grade	73,579	93,774
Chief Grade	67,941	88,326
Senior Grade	57,769	75,085
Intermediate Grade	48,878	63,539
Full Grade	41,104	53,434
Associate Grade	34,295	44,582

Clinical Podiatrist and Optometrist Schedule

Chief Grade	67,941	88,326
Senior Grade	57,760	75,085
Intermediate Grad	48,878	63,539
Full Grade	41,104	53,434
Associate Grade	34,295	44,582

Physician Assistant and Expanded-Function

Dental Auxiliary Schedule[4]

EXECUTIVE SCHEDULES

Senior Executive Service:

ES-1	$92,900
ES-2	97,400
ES-3	101,800
ES-4	107,300
ES-5	111,800
ES-6	115,700

Executive Service:

Level I	$148,400
Level II	133,600
Level III	123,100
Level IV	115,700
Level V	108,200

[4] These positions are paid according to the Nurse Schedule in 38 U.S.C. 4107(b) as in effect on August 14, 1990, with subsequent adjustments included (Section 301a, Public Law 102-40).

LOCALITY PAY DIFFERENTIALS[5]

Pay Locality	Differential	Pay Locality	Differential
Atlanta MSA	4.66%	Los Angeles	7.39%
Boston	6.97	Miami	5.39
Chicago	6.92	New York	7.30
Cincinnati	5.33	Philadelphia	6.26
Cleveland	4.23	Portland, OR	4.71
Columbus	5.30	Richmond MSA	4.00
Dallas	5.65	Sacramento	5.27
Dayton MSA	5.19	St. Louis MSA	4.28
Denver	5.75	San Diego MSA	6.14
Detroit	6.59	San Francisco	8.14
Houston	8.53	Seattle	5.84
Huntsville MSA	4.39	Washington	5.48
Indianapolis MSA	4.58	Rest of US	3.74
Kansas City MSA	3.97		

---

[5] Each area below is a Consolidated Metropolitan Statistical Area unless indicated otherwise. MSA refers to a Metropolitan Statistical Area. Both are defined by the Office of Management and Budget (OMB) in *OMB Bulletin Number 94-07*, July 5, 1994.

Appendix D

WAGE GRADE POSITIONS

2500 Wire Communications Equipment Installation and Maintenance Family

2502 Telephone Mechanic
2504 Wire Communications Cable Splicing
2508 Communications Line Installing & Repairing
2511 Wire Communications Equipment Installing & Repairing

2600 Electronic Equipment Installation and Maintenance Family

2602 Electronic Measurement Equipment Mechanic
2604 Electronics Mechanic
2606 Electronic Industrial Controls Mechanic
2608 Electronic Digital Computer Mechanic
2610 Electronic Integrated Systems Mechanic

2800 Electrical Installation and Maintenance Family

2805 Electrician
2810 Electrician (High Voltage)

2854 Electrical Equipment Repair
2892 Aircraft Electrician

3100 Fabric and Leather Work Family

3103 Shoe Repairing
3105 Fabric Working
3106 Upholstering
3111 Sewing Machine Operating
3119 Broom & Brush Making

3300 Instrument Work Family

3306 Optical Instrument Repairing
3314 Instrument Making
3341 Scale Building, Installing and Repairing
3359 Instrument Mechanic
3364 Projection Equipment Repair

3400 Machine Tool Work Family

3414 Machining
3416 Toolmaking
3417 Tool Grinding
3422 Power Saw Operating
3428 Die Sinking
3431 Machine Tool Operating

3500 General Services And Support Work Family

3502 Laboring
3506 Summer Aid/Student Aid
3508 Pipeline Working
3511 Laboratory Working
3513 Coin/Currency Checking
3515 Laboratory Support Working
3543 Stevedoring
3546 Railroad Repairing
3566 Custodial Working

3600 Structural and Finishing Work Family

3602 Cement Finishing
3603 Masonry
3604 Tile Setting
3605 Plastering
3606 Roofing
3609 Floor Covering Installing
3610 Insulating
3611 Glazing
3653 Asphalt Working

3700 Metal Processing Family

3702 Flame/Arc Cutting
3703 Welding
3705 Nondestructive Testing
3707 Metalizing
3708 Metal Process Working
3711 Electroplating
3712 Heat Treating
3716 Leadburning
3720 Brazing & Soldering
3722 Cold Working
3725 Battery Repairing
3727 Buffing & Polishing
3735 Metal Phototransferring
3736 Circuit Board Making
3741 Furnace Operating
3769 Shot Peening Machine Operating

3800 Metal Work Family

3802 Metal Forger
3804 Coppersmithing
3806 Sheet Metal Mechanic
3807 Structural/Ornamental Iron Working
3808 Boilermaking
3809 Mobile Equipment Metal Mechanic

3815 Pneumatic Tool Operating
3816 Engraving
3818 Springmaking
3819 Airframe Jig Fitting
3820 Shipfitting
3830 Blacksmithing
3832 Medal Making
3833 Transfer Engraving
3858 Metal Tank & Radiator Repairing
3869 Metal Forming Machine Operating
3872 Metal Tube Making, Installing, Repairing

3900 Motion Picture, Radio, Television, and Sound Equipment Operating Work

3910 Motion Picture Projection
3911 Sound Recording Equipment Operating
3919 Television Equipment Operating
3940 Broadcasting Equipment Operating
3941 Public Address Equipment Operating

4000 Lens and Crystal Work Family

4005 Optical Element Working
4010 Prescription Eyeglass Making
4015 Quartz Crystal Working

4100 Painting and Paper Hanging Family

4102 Painting
4103 Paperhanging
4104 Sign Painting

4157 Instrument Dial Painting

4200 Plumbing and Pipefitting Family

4204 Pipefitting
4206 Plumbing
4255 Fuel Distribution System

4300 Pliable Materials Work Family

4351 Plastic Molding Equipment Operating
4352 Plastic Fabricating
4360 Rubber Products Molding
4361 Rubber Equipment Repairing
4370 Glassblowing
4371 Plaster Pattern Casting
4373 Molding
4374 Core Making

4400 Printing Family

4402 Bindery Working
4403 Hand Composing
4405 Film Assembly-Stripping
4406 Letterpress Operating
4407 Linotype Machine Operating
4413 Negative Engraving
4414 Offset Photography
4416 Platemaking
4417 Offset Press Operating
4419 Silk Screen Making and Printing
4422 Dot Etching
4425 Photoengraving
4440 Stereotype Platemaking
4441 Bookbinding
4445 Bank Note Designing
4446 Bank Note Engraving
4448 Sideographic Transferring
4449 Electrolytic Intaglio Platemaking

4450 Intaglio Die and Plate Finishing
4454 Intaglio Press Operating

4600 Wood Work Family

4602 Blocking and Bracing
4604 Wood Working
4605 Wood Crafting
4607 Carpentry
4616 Patternmaking
4618 Woodworking Machine Operating
4620 Shoe Last Repairing
4639 Timber Working
4654 Form Block Making

4700 General Maintenance and Operations Work Family

4714 Model Making
4715 Exhibits Making/Modeling
4716 Railroad Car Repairing
4717 Boat Building and Repairing
4737 General Equipment Mechanic
4741 General Equipment Operating
4742 Utility Systems Repairing Operating
4745 Research Laboratory Mechanic
4749 Maintenance Mechanic
4754 Cemetery Caretaking

4800 General Equipment Maintenance

4802 Musical Instrument
4804 Locksmithing
4805 Medical Equipment Repairing
4806 Office Appliance Repairing
4807 Chemical Equipment Repairing
4808 Custodial Equipment Servicing

4812 Saw Reconditioning
4816 Protective and Safety Equipment Fabricating
4818 Aircraft Survival and Flight Equipment Repairing
4819 Bowling Equipment Repairing
4820 Vending Machine Repairing
4839 Film Processing Equipment Repairing
4840 Tool and Equipment Repairing
4841 Window Shade Assembling, Installing and Repairing
4843 Navigation Aids Repairing
4844 Bicycle Repairing
4845 Orthopedic Appliance Repairing
4848 Mechanical Parts Repairing
4850 Bearing Reconditioner
4851 Reclamation Working
4855 Domestic Appliance Repairing

5000 Plant and Animal Work Family

5002 Farming
5003 Gardening
5026 Pest Controlling
5031 Insects Production Working
5034 Dairy Farming
5035 Livestock Ranching/ Wrangling
5042 Tree Trimming and Removing
5048 Animal Caretaking

5200 Miscellaneous Occupations

5205 Gas and Radiation Detection
5210 Rigging
5220 Shipwright
5221 Lofting
5222 Diving
5235 Test Range Tracking

5300 Industrial Equipment Maintenance Family

5306 Air Conditioning Equipment Mechanic
5309 Heating & Boiler Plant Equipment Mechanic
5310 Kitchen/Bakery Equipment Repairing
5312 Sewing Machine Repairing
5313 Elevator Mechanic
5317 Laundry and Dry Cleaning Equipment Repairing
5318 Lock and Dam Repairing
5323 Oiling and Greasing
5324 Powerhouse Equipment Repairing
5326 Drawbridge Repairing
5330 Printing Equipment Repairing
5334 Marine Machinery Mechanic
5335 Wind Tunnel Mechanic
5341 Industrial Furnace Building and Repairing
5350 Production Machinery Mechanic
5352 Industrial Equipment Mechanic
5364 Door Systems Mechanic
5365 Physiological Trainer
5378 Powered Support Systems Mechanic
5384 Gasdynamic Facility Installing & Repairing

5400 Industrial Equipment Operating Family

5402 Boiler Plant Operating
5403 Incinerator Operating
5406 Utility Systems Operating
5407 Electric Power Controlling
5408 Sewage Disposal Plant Operating

5409 Water Treatment Plant Operating
5413 Fuel Distribution System Operating
5414 Baling Machine Operating
5415 Air Conditioning Equipment Operating
5419 Stationary-Engine Operating
5423 Sandblasting
5424 Weighing Machine Operating
5426 Lock & Dam Operating
5427 Chemical Plant Operating
5430 Drawbridge Operating
5433 Gas Generating Plant Operating
5435 Carton/Bag Making Machine Operating
5438 Elevator Operating
5439 Testing Equipment Operating
5440 Packaging Machine Operating
5444 Food/Feed Processing Equipment Operating
5446 Textile Equipment Operating
5450 Conveyor Operating
5454 Solvent Still Operating
5455 Paper Pulping Machine Operating
5473 Oil Reclamation Equipment Operating
5478 Portable Equipment Operating
5479 Dredge Equipment Operating
5484 Counting Machine Operating
5485 Aircraft Weight and Balance Operating
5486 Swimming Pool Operating

5700 Transportation/Mobile Equipment Operation Family

5703 Motor Vehicle Operating
5704 Fork Lift Operating
5705 Tractor Operating
5706 Road Sweeper Operating

5716 Engineering Equipment Operating
5725 Crane Operating
5729 Drill Rig Operating
5731 Mining/Tunneling Machine Operating
5736 Braking-Switching and Conducting
5737 Locomotive Engineering
5738 Railroad Maintenance Vehicle Operating
5767 Airfield Clearing Equipment Operating
5782 Ship Operating
5784 Riverboat Operating
5786 Small Craft Operating
5788 Deckhand

5800 Transportation/Mobile Equipment Maintenance Family

5803 Heavy Mobile Equipment Mechanic
5806 Mobile Equipment Servicing
5823 Automotive Mechanic
5876 Electromotive Equipment Mechanic

6500 Ammunition, Explosives, and Toxic Materials Work Family

6502 Explosives Operating
6505 Munitions Destroying
6511 Missile/Toxic Materials Handling
6517 Explosives Test Operating

6600 Armament Work Family

6605 Artillery Repairing
6606 Artillery Testing

6610 Small Arms Repairing
6641 Ordnance Equipment Mechanic
6652 Aircraft Ordnance Systems Mechanic
6656 Special Weapons Systems Mechanic

6900 Warehousing and Stock Handling Family

6902 Lumber Handling
6903 Coal Handling
6904 Tools & Parts Handling
6907 Materials Handling
6910 Materials Expediting
6912 Materials Examining and Identifying
6914 Store Working
6941 Bulk Money Handling
6968 Aircraft Freight Handling

7000 Packing and Processing Family

7002 Packing
7004 Preservation Packaging
7006 Preservation Servicing
7009 Equipment Cleaning
7010 Parachute Packing

7300 Laundry, Dry Cleaning and Pressing Family

7304 Laundry Working
7305 Laundry Machine Operating
7306 Pressing
7307 Dry Cleaning

7400 Food Preparation and Serving Family

7402 Baking
7404 Cooking
7405 Bartending
7407 Meatcutting
7408 Food Service Working
7420 Waiter

7600 Personal Services Family

7603 Barbering
7640 Bus Attending
7641 Beautician

8200 Fluid Systems Maintenance Family

8255 Pneudraulic Systems Mechanic
8268 Aircraft Pneudraulic Systems Mechanic

8600 Engine Overhaul Family

8602 Aircraft Engine Mechanic
8610 Small Engine Mechanic
8675 Liquid Fuel Rocket Engine Mechanic

8800 Aircraft Overhaul Family

8810 Aircraft Propeller Mechanic
8840 Aircraft Mechanical Parts Repairing
8852 Aircraft Mechanic
8862 Aircraft Attending
8863 Aircraft Tire Mounting
8882 Airframe Test Operating

9000 Film Processing Family

9003 Film Assembling and Repairing
9004 Motion Picture Developing/ Printing Machine Operating
9055 Photographic Solution Mixing

Appendix E

FEDERAL EMPLOYMENT INFORMATION CENTERS

When writing for job information, be sure to include "Office of Personnel Management" in the mailing address.

ATLANTA REGION

Office of Personnel Management
75 Spring Street, SW
Atlanta, GA 30303-3109

Alabama
520 Wynn Dr., NW.
Huntsville, AL 35816-3426
(205) 837-0894

Florida
Commodore Bldg., Suite 125
3444 McCrory Pl.
Orlando, FL 32803-3701
(407) 648-6148

Georgia
Richard B. Russell Federal Building
Room 940A
75 Spring St., S.W.
Atlanta, GA 30303-3309
(404) 331-4315

Mississippi
(See Alabama listing)

North Carolina
4407 Bland Rd., Suite 202
Raleigh, NC 27609
(919) 790-2822

Federal Regions

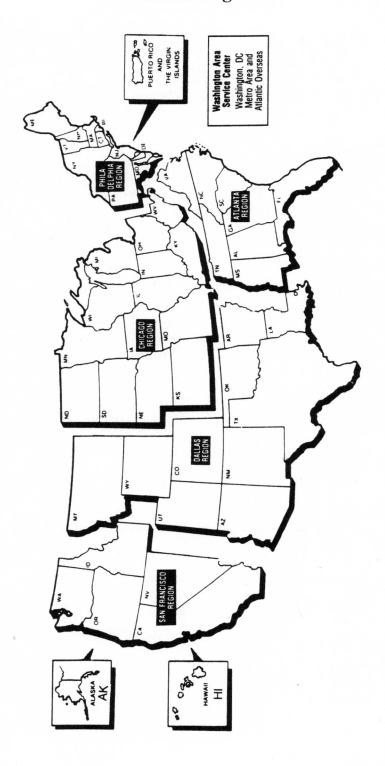

Federal Regions

South Carolina
(See North Carolina listing)

Tennessee
(See Alabama listing)

Virginia
Federal Bldg., Room 500
200 Granby Street
Norfolk, VA 23510-1886
(804) 441-3355

CHICAGO REGION

Office of Personnel Management
John C. Kluczynski Bldg.
230 South Dearborn Street
Chicago, IL 60604-1687

Illinois
230 South Dearborn St.
Room 2916
Chicago, IL 60604
(312) 353-6192

(In Madison and St. Clair Counties
[East St. Louis Area], see St. Louis,
MO listing)

Indiana
(See Detroit, Michigan)

(In Clark, Dearborn and Floyd Counties, see Ohio listing)

Iowa
(See Kansas City, MO, listing) For 24
hour job info: (816) 426-7757. In Scott
Co., see Illinois listing. In
Pottawattamie Co., see Kansas listing)

Kansas
(See Kansas City, Missouri)
24 hour job info: (816) 426-7820

Kentucky
(See Ohio listing [except Henderson
Co., see Indiana listing])

Michigan
477 Michigan Ave., Room 565
Detroit, MI 48226
(313) 226-6950

Minnesota
Federal Building, Room 501
1 Federal Drive
Ft. Snelling, MN 55111
(612) 725-3430

Missouri
Federal Building, Room 134
601 E. 12th St.
Kansas City, MO 64106
(816) 426-5702
(For counties west of and including:
Mercer, Grundy, Livingston, Carroll,
Saline, Pettis, Benton, Hickory, Dallas,
Webster, Douglas and Ozark)

St. Louis
Old Post Office Building
815 Olive St., Room 400
St. Louis, MO 63101
(314) 539-2285
(For all other Missouri counties not
listed under Kansas City)

Nebraska
(See Kansas listing.) 24 hour job info:
(816) 426-7819

North Dakota
(See Minnesota listing.)

Ohio
200 W. Second St., Room 506
Dayton, OH 45402
(513) 225-2720
(For counties north of and including
Van Wert, Auglaize, Hardin, Marion,
Crawford, Richland, Ashland, Wayne,
Start, Carroll and Columbiana, see
Michigan listing)

South Dakota
(See Minnesota listing.)

West Virginia
(See Ohio listing) 24 hour job info:
(513) 225-2866

Wisconsin
(In the counties of Grant, Iowa,
Lafayette, Dane, Green, Rock, Jefferson, Walworth, Waukesha, Racine,
Kenosha and Milwaukee, see Illinois
listing and dial 312-353-6189. For all
other Wisconsin counties, see Minnesota listing and dial 612-725-3430)

DALLAS REGION

Office of Personnel Management
1100 Commerce
Dallas, TX 75250

Arizona
Century Plaza Bldg., Rm 1415
3225 N. Central Ave.
Phoenix, AZ 85004
(602) 640-4800

Arkansas
(See San Antonio, TX listing.)

Colorado
(mail only)
P.O. Box 25167
Denver, CO 89225

(FJIC is located at 12345 W. Alameda
Pkwy, Lakewood, CO)
(303) 969-7050

For job information (24 hrs/day) in the
following states, dial:

Montana
(See Colorado listing)

Louisiana
1515 Poydras St.
Suite 608
New Orleans, LA 70112
(210) 805-2402

New Mexico
Federal Building
421 Gold Ave., S.W.
Albuquerque, NM 87102
(505) 766-5583
(In Dona Ana and Otero counties in
NM and El Paso Co. in TX, dial 505-766-1893)

Oklahoma
(See San Antonio, TX listing)

Texas
Corpus Christi: See San Antonio;
(512) 884-8113

Dallas: See San Antonio; (210) 805-2423

Harlingen: See San Antonio; (512)
412-0722

Houston: See San Antonio; (713) 759-0455

San Antonio: Room 305
8610 Broadway,
San Antonio, TX 78217
(210) 805-2406

Utah
(See Colorado listing.)

Wyoming
(See Colorado listing.)

PHILADELPHIA REGION

Office of Personnel Management
Federal Building
600 Arch Street
Philadelphia, PA 19106

Connecticut
(See Boston, MA listing)

Delaware
(See Philadelphia, PA listing.)

Maine
(See Boston, MA listing.)

Maryland
(See Philadelphia, PA listing)

Massachusetts
Thos. P. O'Neill Federal Bldg.
10 Causeway St.
Boston, MA 02222-1031
(617) 565-5900

New Hampshire
(See Boston, MA listing)

New Jersey
(For Atlantic, Burlington, Camden,
Cape May, Cumberland, Gloucester,
Mercer, Monmouth, Ocean and Salem
Counties, see Philadelphia, PA listing)

(For all other counties, see New York
City, NY listing)

New York
Jacob K. Javits Federal Bldg.
Room 120
26 Federal Plaza
New York, NY 10278
(212) 264-0422

Syracuse: James M. Hanley
 Federal Bldg.
100 S. Clinton St.
Syracuse, NY 13260
(315) 448-0480

Pennsylvania
Federal Bldg., Room 168
P.O. Box 761
Harrisburg, PA 17108
(717) 782-4494

Philadelphia: Wm. J. Green Jr.
 Federal Bldg.
600 Arch St., Rm 1416
Philadelphia, PA 19106
(215) 597-7440

Pittsburgh: Federal Building
Rm 119
1000 Liberty Avenue
Pittsburgh, PA 15222

Puerto Rico
Federal Bldg.
Room 328
150 Carlos E. Chardon St.
San Juan, PR 00918
(809) 766-5452

Rhode Island
(See Boston, MA listing)

Vermont
(See Boston, MA listing)

SAN FRANCISCO REGION

**Office of Personnel Management
211 Main Street
San Francisco, CA 94105**

Alaska
222 W. Seventh Ave., Box 22
Room 156
Anchorage, AK 99513-7572
(907) 271-5821 (From outside Alaska
call (912) 757-3000)

California
9650 Flair Drive
Suite 100A
El Monte, CA 91731
(818) 575-6510

Sacramento: 1029 J St., Room 202
Sacramento, CA 95814
(414) 744-5627

San Diego: Federal Bldg.
Room 4260
880 Front St.
San Diego, CA 92101
(818) 575-6510

San Francisco:
120 Howard St, Suite B (mail only)
PO Box 7405
San Francisco, CA 94120.
(415) 744-5627

Hawaii
(And the Pacific Area)
Federal Bldg., Rm 5316
300 Ala Moana Blvd.
Honolulu, HI 96850
(808) 541-2791 (Hawaii)
(912) 757-3000 (Outside Hawaii)

Idaho
(see Seattle, WA listing.)

Nevada
(For Clark, Lincoln, and Nye Counties,
see Los Angeles, CA) (For all other
counties see Sacramento, CA listing.)

Oregon
Federal Bldg., Rm. 376
1220 S.W. Third Ave.
Portland, OR 97204
(503) 326-3141

Washington
Federal Bldg., Rm. 110
915 Second Ave.
Seattle, WA 98174
(206) 220-6400

WASHINGTON AREA SERVICE CENTER

**Office of Personnel Management
P.O. Box 52
Washington, D.C. 20415
(202) 653-9260**

District of Columbia
(Metropolitan area)
1900 E St., NW
Room 1416
Washington, D.C. 20415
(202) 653-8468

Federal Job Telephone Device for the Deaf (TDD) Numbers:

Nationwide TDD Number .... (912) 744-2299
Washington D.C. Metropolitan Area .... (202) 606-0591
Southeastern States (AL,FL,GA,MS,NC,SC,TN,VA) ...... (919) 790-2739
Northeastern States (CT,DE,ME,MD,MA,NH,NJ,
   NY,PA,RI,VT, Puerto Rico, Virgin Islands) .... (617) 565-8913
North Central States (IL,IN,IA,KS,KY,MI,MN,MO,
   NE,ND,OH,SD,WV,WI) .... (816) 426-6022
Mountain States (CO,MT,UT,WY) .... (303) 969-2739
Southwestern States:
   Arizona .... (800) 223-3131
   New Mexico .... (505) 766-8662
   Texas (Dallas) .... (214) 767-8115
   Rest of Texas .... (210) 805-2401
   Louisiana .... (504) 589-4636
   Oklahoma/Arkansas .... (405) 231-4612

Western States:
   Alaska .... (800) 770-8973
   California .... (800) 735-2929
   Hawaii .... (808) 643-8833
   Idaho .... (208) 334-2100
   Nevada .... (800) 326-6868
   Oregon .... (800) 526-0661
   Washington .... (800) 833-6388

Federal Job Opportunities Bulletin Board:

(Requires a computer and modem set at least at 2400 baud, 8 data bits, no stop bits, no parity)

Nationwide .... (912) 757-3100
North Central States .... (313) 226-4423
Northeastern States .... (215) 580-2216
Washington, D.C. area .... (202) 606-4800
Western States .... (818) 575-6521

(The nationwide board may also be accessed through the Internet (Telnet connections only) at FJOB.MAIL.OPM.GOV or at this IP address: 198.78.46.10

Appendix F

SAMPLE JOB ANNOUNCEMENTS

Secretary GS-0318-05

VACANCY ANNOUNCEMENT
NATIONAL XXXXXX ADMINISTRATION

Announcement Number: E/NWS93-008A.CFH
Issue Date: 01/21/93
Closing Date: 02/22/93

Secretary (Office Automation)
GS-0318-05
Salary: $19,807 to $25,746[1]
No Known Promotion Potential

National XXXXX Agency
Eastern Region HQ
Bohemia, NY

COMPETITIVE SERVICE

WHO MAY APPLY: STATUS applicants and applicants eligible for appointment under special appointing authorities.

---

[1] The salary includes a Geographic Adjustment.

DUTIES: This position is located at Eastern District Headquarters; it is primarily that of Secretary performing duties which are auxiliary to the work of the Systems Operations Division. As required, incumbent performs a variety of secretarial, clerical and typing duties for the administrative, professional and technical personnel of the Division.

QUALIFICATIONS REQUIRED: 52 weeks of specialized experience equivalent to the next lower grade level. Specialized experience is experience which is directly related to the position to be filled and which has equipped the candidate with the particular knowledge, skills and abilities to successfully perform the duties of that position. In addition to meeting the above experience requirement, the applicant must be a qualified typist.

BASIS FOR EVALUATING CANDIDATES: Candidates who meet the minimum qualifications requirements will be evaluated on type and quality of job-related experience, education, training, awards, and performance appraisals and on the basis of the following factors:

- Knowledge of administrative and operational policies and practices.
- Knowledge of computer operations and desktop publishing software.
- Ability to make commitments, set priorities and apply instruction and regulations.

In order to receive appropriate credit consideration applicants should include in their SF 171 a list of courses taken and credit received (or submit a transcript of education); list all training; list all awards including the types of awards and their effective dates; list all performance ratings for the last three (3) years; list all outside job-related activities or professional association (not paid for by your employer's agency), their effective date, and a brief statement regarding the nature and extent of your participation; and should ensure that the above job-related factors are addressed in their SF 171 or in attached narrative statement.

HOW AND WHERE TO APPLY: Submit a complete SF 171 (Application for Federal Employment—Rev. 6/88) and a copy of their most recent performance appraisal (FAILURE TO SUBMIT THIS FORM MAY AFFECT CONSIDERATION UNDER THIS ANNOUNCEMENT). To: U.S. Department of XXXXXXX . . . FOR FURTHER INFORMATION CALL MS. C. XXXXX ON (804)...

This announcement is typical for higher grade jobs. Note that applicants are limited to current federal employees.

JOB OPPORTUNITY
DEPARTMENT OF YYYYYYY

Permanent Change of Station (PCS) Funds are not authorized.

POSITION: Social Science Analyst   **ANNOUNCEMENT NO.:** 33-93BB
GS-101-11/12/13 (Potential to GS-13)
(2 Vacancies)

LOCATION: YYYYYYY Manpower Data Center
Survey & Market Analysis Division
Arlington, Virginia

OPENING DATE: 01 FEB 93   **CLOSING DATE:** 17 FEB 93

AREA OF CONSIDERATION: Competitive Service Career and Career Conditional Employees of YYYYYYY in the Washington DC Metropolitan Area and Competitive Service Career and Career Conditional Employees of (the local personnel office) Serviced Activities.

DUTIES: Incumbent is responsible for managing surveys conducted under the auspices of the agency-wide personnel attitude survey program. Duties include:

(1) planning, designing, and conducting personnel surveys of military personnel to determine attitudes and opinions on specified topics such as reenlistment intent, compensation policies, promotion opportunities, voluntary education programs, and commissaries and exchanges;

(2) developing survey questions, analyzing and adapting questions used in previous surveys as well as writing new questions using standard survey measurement techniques;

(3) analyzing survey response data utilizing bivariate and multivariate statistical techniques;

(4) performing statistical analyses of survey data;

(5) developing specifications for senior technical personnel and/or preparing computer programs for storing survey data on a computerized survey data bank; and

(6) developing, maintaining, and disseminating information about the data tapes available within the survey data bank. If position is filled below the target level, duties and responsibilities will be correspondingly reduced.

QUALIFICATION REQUIREMENTS: Applicants must meet one of the following basic requirements: (a) successful completion of a 4-year course of study in an accredited college or university leading to a Bachelor's degree in behavioral or social sciences; (b) a combination of education and experience as outlined in OPM Handbook X-118; or © four years of appropriate experience which demonstrates that the applicant has acquired knowledge of one or more of the behavioral or social sciences equivalent to a major in the field. In addition, applicants must have one year of specialized experience at least equivalent to the GS-9/11/12 level, respectively, which has equipped the applicant with the particular knowledge, skills, and abilities to perform successfully the duties of the position described above and which is typically in or related to the work of the above position. Education may be substituted for experience to the extent outlined in OPM Handbook X-118. Applicants must have served at least one year at the GS-9/11/12 level, respectively, in order to meet time-in-grade requirements.

The next paragraph stresses the importance of an agency-imposed qualification, doing surveys, that is not normally part of a GS-101-XX position.

SELECTIVE PLACEMENT FACTOR: In addition to the qualification requirements outlined above, applicants must have the ability to conduct surveys in order to be minimally qualified for this position.

EVALUATION METHODS: **Maximum Point Value**

1. Quality of Experience   65
2. Performance Appraisal   20
3. Education, Training and Self Development   10
4. Awards   <u>5</u>
                                                                 100

The next section lists special requirements of the position; these are not found in X-118 qualification standards or in the classification standards.

METHOD OF RANKING: Applicants competing for promotion will be given a score on each evaluation method. The combined score on all evaluation methods will be used in ranking candidates to determine their relative standing. <u>Applicants meeting the minimum qualification requirements will be evaluated against the following criteria:</u>

1. **Ability to design and execute personnel surveys using state-of-the-art survey techniques** . . . in order to assure that surveys are representative of the population being served.

2. **Ability to analyze survey data using computer statistical packages such as SAS, SPSS, dBase III and Lotus** . . . in order to understand the findings and implications of survey results.

3. **Skill in presenting research results** . . . in order to write executive summaries and results of studies.

4. **Skill in building, managing and using research data bases** . . . in order to develop a research file and ensure that data are available for analysis.

5. **Knowledge of social science research techniques** . . . in order to plan, develop and analyze surveys.

OTHER:

1. This position may be filled through means other than the competitive promotion process. This may include reassignments or repromotion of qualified eligibles or appointment from an Office of Personnel Management Certificate of Eligibles. In such case, this announcement will be canceled and all applicants so advised.
2. Male applicants who were born . . . (registered for Selective Service)
3. This position is non-sensitive, and requires a personnel security investigation on a post-appointment basis only.
4. Applications will be accepted from VRA eligibles and 30 percent or more disabled veterans.
5. TDY (10%) is required.
6. Time in grade and qualification requirements must be met by the closing date of this announcement.
7. Management has the prerogative to select at any of the grade levels.
8. This recruitment offers promotion opportunity to target position without further competition when selectee is eligible and recommended by management. However, promotion is not guaranteed and no promise of a promotion is implied.

HOW TO APPLY: Forward a current, completed and signed SF 171, Application for Federal Employment, along with the following documents and forms to Department XXXXXXX, ATTN: DXXX-KSE, Room XYZ, Alexandria, VA. **APPLICATION MUST BE POSTMARKED BY THE CLOSING DATE INDICATED ON THE JOB OPPORTUNITY ANNOUNCEMENT.**

a. Supplemental Experience Questionnaire

b. A copy of current annual performance rating and appropriate performance standards (lists performance appraisal forms). **FAILURE TO SUBMIT A CURRENT PERFORMANCE APPRAISAL (NO MORE THAN 18 MONTHS OLD) MAY AFFECT APPLICANT'S OVERALL RATING.**
c. A list of all awards received within the past ten years, including the dates of the awards.
d. OPM Form 1386, Background Survey . . . (a standard form, optional, which reports the applicant's disability, sex, race and national origin and is provided as part of the job announcement).
e. Copy of recent SF-50, Notification of Personnel Action.
f. If qualified based on education, applicants must submit official transcripts.

The application had three pages with space to describe work experiences which pertain to the KSAOs or supplemental work experience. The original form need not be used as long as the KSAOs were described and had the applicant's name and the announcement number.

SUPPLEMENTAL EXPERIENCE QUESTIONNAIRE

POSITION: Social Science Analyst GS-101-11/12/13 (Potential to GS-13)   **JOA#** 33-93BB

NAME _____ DATE _____

INSTRUCTIONS: Prepare brief but concise responses to the following highly qualifying criteria on how your experience, education and/or training satisfies the knowledge, skills and abilities cited below. DO NOT REPEAT VERBATIM INFORMATION IN THE SF 171.

KSA# 1. Ability to design and execute personnel surveys using state-of-the-art survey techniques.

- -

Please provide the following information relating to the above experiences:
Names and telephone numbers of supervisors or other persons who can verify your statements_____
title, series, and grade of your position (if applicable)_____

From _____ To _____.

_____

KSA# 2. Ability to analyze survey data using computer statistical packages such as SAS, SPSS, DBASE III and LOTUS.

- -

Please provide the following information relating to the above experiences:
Names and telephone numbers of supervisors or other persons who can verify your statements_____
title, series, and grade of your position (if applicable) _____
From _____ To _____.

_____

KSA# 3. Skill in presenting research results.

- -

Please provide the following information relating to the above experiences:
Names and telephone numbers of supervisors or other persons who can verify your statements_____
title, series, and grade of your position (if applicable) _____
From _____ To _____.

_____

KSA# 4. Skill in building, managing and using research data bases.

- -

Please provide the following information relating to the above experiences:
Names and telephone numbers of supervisors or other persons who can verify your statements_____
title, series, and grade of your position (if applicable) _____
From _____ To _____.

_____

KSA# 5. Knowledge of social science research techniques.

- -

Please provide the following information relating to the above experiences:
Names and telephone numbers of supervisors or other persons who can verify your statements_____
title, series, and grade of your position (if applicable) _____
From _____ To _____.

_____

_____

This last example is for a Wage Grade position. Notice that ALL federal positions require quite a bit of effort to apply for a job, even a relatively low-skilled, low-paying job as a laborer.

_____

Laborer, WG-3502-02

VACANCY ANNOUNCEMENT
DEFENSE XXXXXX AGENCY

Number: 3/93

LOCATION: Headquarters, Defense XXXXXX Agency, 1234 Telegraph Road, Alexandria, VA

SALARY RANGE: $7.72 - $9.02 per hour

OPENING DATE: 2 February 1993   **CLOSING DATE:** 9 March 1993

AREA OF CONSIDERATION: All Sources

Relocation expenses will not be paid.
This is not a critical-sensitive position.

DUTIES: Position is located in the Engineering, Environmental, and Energy Division (LEEE), Assistant Directorate for Logistics and Engineering (CSLE), Command Services Directorate (DFCS). The incumbent of the position performs any one or a combination of a large variety of skilled and unskilled tasks requiring predominately physical exertion of a heavy or arduous type. Usually works alone. Lifts boxes weighing up to 80-85 pounds, heavy furniture, safes, filing cabinets, and other miscellaneous items. Much of this is done in close quarters. Periodically cleans occupied spaces of packing debris, boxes, etc., vacuums spaces, clears hallways of pallets, excess office furniture and supplies. Shovels snow and distributes salt crystals on sidewalks by hand. Assists in unloading supply/delivery vehicles, transports items within the headquarters building and stocks supply shelves. Assists in use of reproduction equipment and assembling and delivery of large production runs. Meets and escorts work crew personnel through security sensitive areas of building. Tightens screws in furniture, assembles some furniture, uses putty knife, hammer, does touch up painting, etc.

This use of additional requirements beyond those in X-118C helps recruiters select applicants with special abilities, without requiring a rewrite of Laborer standards.

QUALIFICATION REQUIREMENTS: Candidates will be rated on the following elements which <u>must</u> be addressed in the application:

- Ability to do the work of the position without more than normal supervision.
- Ability to follow simple oral and written instructions.
- Ability to lift or carry objects weighing 80-85 pounds.
- Ability to use and maintain tools and equipment such as hand and power saws, drill motors, simple hand tools, etc.
- Ability to work safely.

HOW TO APPLY: Applicants must submit a separate and current SF 171, Application . . . Indicate the VA number in Item #1.[2] Include relevant paid or volunteer public or private sector experience. Current and former Federal employees should attach a copy of SF-50 substantiating competitive service. **DO not** send position descriptions, manuscripts, personal endorsements, award justifications, training certificates, or other unsolicited material. SF 171s and supporting documents will be retained by the Civilian Personnel Office, therefore, do not submit original documents. Failure to submit appropriate application forms may affect applicants consideration in the evaluation process. Applicants are requested to submit the following:

- The attached Supervisory Appraisal or most recent performance appraisal

---

[2] In this context, VA refers to Vacancy Announcement.

(received within last 2 years) if related to the position.

- A Supplemental Statement addressing the Ranking Factors (listed under Supplemental Evaluation Criteria above). Please include the number of appropriate experience block(s) on the SF 171 with each element.
- The attached Applicant Race and National Origin Questionnaire (voluntary). Submit to: (address given).

(Other details follow)

Appendix G

POSITION QUALIFICATION STANDARDS

There are six GS families or groups of job series; each has been given a general set of qualification standards. Excerpts from the *X-118 Qualification Standards Handbook*, showing minimum requirements for five of the families, are provided here. Further information may be obtained from the *Handbook,* Part IV.

CLERICAL AND ADMINISTRATIVE SUPPORT POSITIONS

The standards listed on the next four pages are general standards for a group of similar jobs which have a single grade interval. That is, people in these jobs normally advance one grade level when they get promoted. Notice how general experience (in all the job families in this appendix) decline in importance while specialized experience increases, as grade levels increase. Also, above grade 5, education does not generally substitute for experience.

These are general standards; more specific requirements are in the *X-118 Qualification Standards Handbook.*

119

ADMINISTRATIVE, MANAGEMENT AND SPECIALIST POSITIONS

The positions in this group have two intervals between grades. Someone promoted from a grade 7 position, for example, is promoted not to grade 8 but to grade 9. As might be expected from the group name, education requirements are more stringent and after the lowest grade (5), general experience is not important. At the journeyman level (above grade 11), only specialized experience in the job series qualifies one for a position. Typically, jobs in this family will also have fairly specific KSAOs or additional qualification requirements in job announcements. Normally this makes entry from outside the federal government quite difficult for most of the jobs in the family.

MINIMUM QUALIFICATION REQUIREMENTS FOR TWO-GRADE INTERVAL ADMINISTRATIVE, MANAGEMENT, AND SPECIALIST POSITIONS

This qualification standard covers positions in the General Schedule which involve the performance of two-grade interval administrative, management, and specialist work. A list of the occupational series covered by this qualification standard is provided below. This standard may also be used for other two-grade interval positions for which the education and experience pattern is determined to be appropriate. While some of the occupational series covered by this standard include both one- and two-grade interval work, the qualification requirements described in this standard apply only to those positions which follow a two-grade interval pattern.

This standard contains common patterns of undergraduate and graduate education, general and specialized experience, and other information to be used in making qualifications determinations. Some occupations covered by this standard contain education or experience requirements which are more specific than the requirements described in the generic standard. These requirements are provided in attachments to the basic standard. Such occupations are noted below with an asterisk. For a description of the work performed in occupations covered by this standard, refer to the series definitions in the *Handbook of Occupational Groups and Series* and-or to individual positions' classification standards.

GS-011	Bond Sales Promotion*
GS-018	Safety and Occupations Health Management*
GS-023	Outdoor Recreation Planning*
GS-028	Environmental Protection Specialist
GS-030	Sports Specialist*
GS-062	Clothing Design*
GS-080	Security Administration
GS-105	Social Insurance Administration
GS-106	Unemployment Insurance*
GS-120	Food Assistance Program Specialist
GS-132	Intelligence
GS-142	Manpower Development
GS-160	Civil Rights Analysis
GS-188	Recreation Specialist*
GS-201	Personnel Management
GS-205	Military Personnel Management
GS-212	Personnel Staffing
GS-221	Position Classification
GS-222	Occupational Analysis
GS-223	Salary and Wage Administration
GS-230	Employee Relations
GS-233	Labor Relations
GS-235	Employee Development
GS-244	Labor Management Relations Examining*
GS-246	Contractor Industrial Relations
GS-260	Equal Employment Opportunity
GS-270	Federal Retirement Benefits
GS-301	Miscellaneous Administration and Program
GS-334	Computer Specialist*
GS-340	Program Management
GS-341	Administrative Officer
GS-343	Management and Program Analysis
GS-346	Logistics Management
GS-360	Equal Opportunity Compliance
GS-362	Electric Accounting Machine Project Planning
GS-391	Telecommunications*
GS-501	Financial Administration and Program
GS-505	Financial Management
GS-560	Budget Analysis
GS-570	Financial Institution Examining*
GS-669	Medical Records Administration*
GS-670	Health System Administration*
GS-671	Health System Specialist*
GS-673	Hospital Housekeeping Management*
GS-685	Public Health Program Specialist*
GS-828	Construction Analyst*
GS-920	Estate Tax Examining
GS-930	Hearings and Appeals
GS-950	Paralegal Specialist

GS-958	Pension Law Specialist*
GS-962	Contact Representative
GS-965	Land Law Examining*
GS-990	General Claims Examining
GS-991	Workers' Compensation Claims Examining
GS-993	Social Insurance Claims Examining
GS-996	Veterans Claims Examining
GS-1001	General Arts and Information
GS-1008	Interior Design*
GS-1010	Exhibits Specialist*
GS-1020	Illustrating*
GS-1035	Public Affairs
GS-1040	Language Specialist*
GS-1051	Music Specialist*
GS-1054	Theater Specialist*
GS-1056	Art Specialist*
GS-1071	Audio-Visual Production*
GS-1082	Writing and Editing
GS-1083	Technical Writing and Editing*
GS-1084	Visual Information*
GS-1101	General Business and Industry*
GS-1103	Industrial Property Management*
GS-1104	Property Disposal
GS-1130	Public Utilities Specialist
GS-1140	Trade Specialist*
GS-1144	Commissary Store Management*
GS-1150	Industrial Specialist*
GS-1160	Financial Analysis*
GS-1163	Insurance Examining*
GS-1165	Loan Specialist*
GS-1170	Realty
GS-1171	Appraising and Assessing
GS-1173	Housing Management
GS-1176	Building Management
GS-1361	Navigational Information*
GS-1397	Document Analysis*
GS-1421	Archives Specialist
GS-1630	Cemetery Administration
GS-1640	Facility Management*
GS-1654	Printing Management*
GS-1670	Equipment Specialist*
GS-1702	Education and Training Technician
GS-1712	Training Instruction*
GS-1715	Vocational Rehabilitation*
GS-1801	General Inspection, Investigation, and Compliance*
GS-1810	General Investigating
GS-1811	Criminal Investigating*
GS-1812	Game Law Enforcement

GS-1816	Immigration Inspection
GS-1831	Securities Compliance Examining*
GS-1854	Alcohol, Tobacco and Firearms Inspection*
GS-1864	Public Health Quarantine Inspection*
GS-1890	Customs Inspection*
GS-1910	Quality Assurance*
GS-2001	General Supply
GS-2003	Supply Program Management
GS-2010	Inventory Management
GS-2030	Distribution Facilities and Storage Management
GS-2032	Packaging
GS-2050	Supply Cataloging
GS-2101	Transportation Specialist*
GS-2110	Transportation Industry Analysis*
GS-2123	Motor Carrier Safety*
GS-2125	Highway Safety*
GS-2130	Traffic Management*
GS-2150	Transportation Operations*
GS-2161	Marine Cargo*

The requirements of this standard have been approved for the following occupations for use within the Veterans Health Administration of the Department of Veterans Affairs under the provisions of section 7402, title 38, U.S.C.: GS-301, Miscellaneous Administration and Program, except for GS-301, Rehabilitation Medicine Coordinator positions; GS-340, Program Management; GS-669, Medical Records Administration; GS-670, Health System Administration; GS-671, Health System Specialist; GS-672, Prosthetic Representative,; GS-673, Hospital Housekeeping Management; GS-1020, Illustrating; GS-1101, General Business and Industry; and GS-1715, Vocational Rehabilitation.

EDUCATION AND EXPERIENCE REQUIREMENTS

GS-5 and above: The following table shows the amounts of education and experience required for grades GS-5/15 for positions covered by this standard. Applicants who meet experience requirements for a higher grade also meet the experience requirements for positions at lower grades in the same occupation. Possession of an advance degree, e.g., Ph.D., without having earned the lesser degree, e.g., M.A., qualifies an applicant for both the appropriate higher and lower grades.

Grade	Education OR	Experience	
		General	Specialized
GS-5	4-year course of study above high school leading to a bachelor's degree	3 years, 1 year of which was at least equivalent to GS-4	None
GS-7	1 full academic year of graduate level education or law school or superior academic achievement	None	1 year at least equivalent to GS-5
GS-9	2 full academic years of progressively higher level graduate education or master's or equivalent graduate degree or LL.B. or J.D.	None	1 year at least equivalent to GS-7
GS-11	3 full academic years of progressively higher level graduate education or Ph.D or equivalent doctoral degree	None	1 year at least equivalent to GS-9
GS-12 & above	None	None	1 year at least equivalent next lower grade level

Equivalent combinations of education and experience are qualifying for all grade levels for which both education and experience are acceptable.

Undergraduate Education

Successful completion of a full 4-year course of study *in any field* leading to a bachelor's degree, in an accredited college or university, meets the requirements at the GS-5 level for all positions, *except* for those covered by separate attachments to this standard. Applicants for the latter positions must, in general, (1) have specific course work that meets the requirements for a major in a *particular field(s)*, or (2) have at least 24 semester hours of course work in the field(s) identified in the attachment covering the occupation. Course work in fields closely related to those specified may be accepted if it clearly provides applicants with the background of knowledge and skills necessary for successful job performance. One year of full-time undergraduate study is defined as 30 semester hours or 45 quarter hours, and is equivalent to 9 months of general experience.

The superior academic achievement provision for entry at GS-7 is applicable to all occupations covered by this standard.

Graduate Education

Education at the graduate level (including law school education) in an accredited college or university in the amounts shown in the table meets the requirements for positions at GS-7 through GS-11. Such education must demonstrate the knowledge, skills, and abilities necessary to do the work.

A year of full-time graduate education is considered to be the number of credit hours which the school attended has determined to represent 1 year of full-time study. If that information cannot be obtained from the school, 18 semester hours should be considered as satisfying the 1 year of full-time study requirement. Part-time graduate education is creditable in accordance with its relationship to a year of full-time study at the school attended.

For certain positions covered by this standard, the work may be recognized as sufficiently technical or specialized, and the working level such that graduate study alone may not provide the knowledge and skills needed to perform the work. In such cases, agencies may use selective factors to screen out applicants without actual work experience.

General Experience

Three years of progressively responsible experience which demonstrates the ability to:

1. Analyze problems to identify significant factors, gather pertinent data, and recognize solutions;

2. Plan and organize work; and

3. Communicate effectively orally and in writing.

Such experience may have been gained in administrative, professional, technical, investigative, or other responsible work. Experience in substantive and relevant secretarial, clerical, or other responsible work may be qualifying as long as it has provided evidence of the knowledge, skills, and abilities (KSA's) necessary to perform the duties of the position to be filled. Experience of a general clerical nature (typing, filing, routine procedural processing, maintaining records, or other nonspecialized tasks) is not creditable. Trades or crafts experience appropriate to the position to be filled may also be creditable for some positions. Specialized experience may be substituted for general experience.

For some occupations, applicants must have had work experience which demonstrated KSA's in addition to those identified above. Positions with more specific general experience requirements than those described here are shown in the attachment covering the occupation(s). (Also, see the information below on use of selective factors.)

Specialized Experience

Experience which has equipped the applicant with the particular knowledge, skills, and abilities to perform successfully the duties of the position and which is typically in or related to the work of the position to be filled. To be creditable, specialized experience must have been at least equivalent to the next lower grade level in the normal line of progression for the occupation in the organization.

Combining Education and Experience

Combinations of successfully completed education and experience may be used to meet total qualification requirements, and may be computed by first determining the applicant's total qualifying experience as a percentage of the experience required for the grade level; then determining the applicant's education as a percentage of the experience required for the grade level; and then adding the two percentages. The total percentages must equal at least 100 percent to qualify an applicant for that grade level. Only graduate education in excess of the amount required for the next lower grade level may be used to qualify applicants for positions at grades GS-9 and GS-11. (When crediting education which requires specific course work, prorate the number of hours of related courses required as a proportion of the total education to be used.)

The following are examples of how education and experience may be combined. They are examples only, and are not all-inclusive.

■ The position to be filled is a Loan Specialist, GS-1165-

5. An applicant has 2 years of general experience and 45 semester hours of college, which includes 9 semester hours in related course work as described in the attachment. The applicant meets 67 percent of the required experience and 38 percent of the required education. Therefore, the applicant exceeds 100 percent of the total requirement and is qualified for the position.

■ The position to be filled is a Management Analyst, GS-343-9. An applicant has 6 months of specialized experience equivalent to GS-7 and 1 year or graduate level education. The applicant meets 50 percent of the required experience but none of the required education, since he or she does not have any graduate study beyond that which is required for GS-7. Therefore, the applicant meets only 50 percent of the total requirement and is not qualified for the position. (The applicant's first year of graduate study is not qualifying for GS-9.)

■ The position to be filled is a Music Specialist, GS-1051-11. An applicant has 9 months of specialized experience equivalent to GS-9 and 2 ½ years of creditable graduate level education in music. The applicant meets 75 percent of the required experience and 50 percent of the required education, i.e., the applicant has 1/2 year of graduate study beyond that required for GS-9. Therefore, the applicant exceeds the total requirement and is qualified for the position. (The applicant's first 2 years of graduate study are not qualifying for GS-11.)

OTHER QUALIFICATION PROVISIONS

Applicants for positions in some occupations must meet certification or licensing requirements in addition to meeting the education/experience requirements described above. Applicants can qualify on the basis of licensure, certification, or registration in lieu of education or experience in some other occupations. Such provisions are noted in the attachment covering the occupation.

USE OF SELECTIVE FACTORS

Agencies may identify some positions covered by this standard that require knowledge, skills, and abilities or other qualifications, such as certification or licensure, that are in addition to or more specific than the minimum requirements described in this standard. The need for these special requirements can be met through the use of selective factors in both the competitive and inservice recruitment processes. Selective factors may be used for all of the occupations covered by this standard. They must be job related, essential for the successful performance of the position, and represent KSA's or other qualifications which could not be reasonably acquired on the job during the period of training customary for the position being filled.

WRITTEN TEST REQUIREMENTS

For information on the occupational series and positions covered by this standard which require written tests, refer to the *Test Requirements in Qualification Standards* section (Part IV) of this Handbook.

TECHNICAL, MEDICAL AND PROGRAM SUPPORT POSITIONS

MINIMUM QUALIFICATION REQUIREMENTS FOR ONE-GRADE INTERVAL TECHNICAL, MEDICAL, AND PROGRAM SUPPORT POSITIONS

This qualification standard covers positions in the General Schedule which involve the performance of one-grade interval technical, medical, and program support work. A list of the occupational series covered by this standard is provided below. This standard may also be used for other on-grade interval positions for which the education and experience patterns is determined to be appropriate.

This standard contains common patterns of creditable experience and education to be used in making qualifications determinations. Examples of qualifying experience and education for the specific occupations covered by this standard may be found in attachments to the basic standard. For a description of the work performed in these occupations, refer to the *Handbook of Occupational Groups and Series* and/or to individual position classification standards

GS-019	Safety Technician
GS-090	Guide
GS-119	Economics Assistant
GS-181	Psychology Aid and Technician
GS-186	Social Services Aid and Assistant
GS-404	Biological Technician
GS-421	Plant Protection Technician
GS-455	Range Technician
GS-458	Soil Conservation Technician
GS-459	Irrigation System Operation
GS-462	Forestry Technician
GS-621	Nursing Assistant
GS-636	Rehabilitation Therapy Assistant
GS-460	Health Aid and Technician
GS-645	Medical Technician
GS-646	Pathology Technician
GS-647	Diagnostic Radiologic Technologist
GS-648	Therapeutic Radiologic Technologist
GS-649	Medical Instrument Technician
GS-651	Respiratory Therapist
GS-661	Pharmacy Technician

GS-681	Dental Assistant
GS-648	Dental Laboratory Aid and Technician
GS-649	Environmental Health Technician
GS-704	Animal Health Technician
GS-802	Engineering Technician
GS-809	Construction Control
GS-817	Surveying Technician
GS-818	Engineering Drafting
GS-856	Electronics Technician
GS-895	Industrial Engineering Technician
GS-1021	Office Drafting
GS-1311	Physical Science Technician
GS-1316	Hydrologic Technician
GS-1341	Meteorological Technician
GS-1371	Cartographic Technician
GS-1374	Geodetic Technician
GS-1521	Mathematics Technician
GS-1541	Cryptanalysis
GS-1862	Consumer Safety Inspection
GS-1898	Admeasurement
GS-1981	Agricultural Commodity Aid
GS-2144	Cargo Scheduling

Several of the listed occupations have requirements that have been approved by the Secretary of Veterans Affairs for use the by the Veterans Health Administration under the provisions of section 7402 (formerly 4105), title 38, U.S.C. Such approval is indicated on the individual occupation requirements for those occupational series.

EXPERIENCE AND EDUCATION REQUIREMENTS

GS-1/6 and above: The following table shows the amounts of general and/or specialized experience and education that meet the requirements for each grade.

Grade/Positions	Experience		OR	Education
	General	Specialized		
GS-1	None	None		None
GS-2	3 months	None		High school graduation or equivalent
GS-3	6 months	None		1 year above high school with course(s) related to the occupation, if required
GS-4	6 months	None		2 years above high school with courses related to the occupation, if required
GS-5	None	1 year at least equivalent to GS-4		4 year course of study above high school leading to bachelor's degree with courses related to the occupation, if required
GS-6 and above	None	1 year at least equivalent to next lower grade level		See the NOTE under Education section

Equivalent combinations of education and experience are qualifying for all grade levels for which both education and experience are acceptable.

General Experience

(1) Any type of work that demonstrates the applicant's ability to perform work of the position, or (2) experience that provided a familiarity with the subject matter or processes of the broad subject area of the occupation. Specialized experience may be substituted for general experience.

Specialized Experience

Experience which has equipped the applicant with the particular knowledge, skills, and abilities (KSA's) to perform successfully the duties of the position and which is typically in or related to the work of the position to be filled. To be creditable, specialized experience must have been at least equivalent to the next lower grade level.

Education

High school graduation or the equivalent is qualifying for GS-2.

Successfully completed post-high school education is qualifying for grades GS-3 through GS-5. This education must have been obtained in an accredited business or technical school, junior college, college or university for which high school graduation or the equivalent is the normal prerequisite. One year of full-time undergraduate study is defined as 30 semester hours or 45 quarter hours in a college or university or at least 20 hours of classroom instruction per week for approximately 36 weeks in a business or technical school.

For some occupations covered by this standard, 6 semester hours of specific courses are included in the 1 year or education which meets the GS-3 requirements. The 6 semester hours allow for subjects which are common to a broad range of degree programs, e.g., subjects in the mathematical, physical, or biological sciences. This inclusion corresponds to the second part of the description of general experience, i.e., the subjects provide evidence of a familiarity with the subject matter or processes of the broad subject area of the occupation.

At grades GS-4 and above, a portion of the education is usually directly related to the work of the position to be filled. Examples of related courses are provided where applicable. However, agencies may require other courses if they are considered to be more related to the position to be filled.

NOTE: Graduate education or an internship meets the specialized experience required above GS-5 *only* in those instances where it is directly related to the work of the position. One full year of graduate education meets the requirements for GS-7. Two full years of graduate education or a master's degree meets the requirements for GS-9. A year of full-time graduate education is considered to be the number of credit hours which the school attended has determined to represent 1 year of full-time study. If that information cannot be obtained from the school, 18 semester hours should be considered as satisfying the 1 year of full-time study requirement.

Training

Completion of appropriate training such as inservice training programs, training acquired while serving in the armed forces, and government-sponsored developmental training programs will be allowed credit on a month-for-month basis, generally through the GS-5 level. Such training will meet general or specialized experience requirements depending upon its applicability.

Completion of an intensive, specialized source of study of less than 1 year may meet in full the experience requirements for GS-3. Courses of this type normally require completion of up to 40 hours per week of instruction rather than the usual 20 hours per week and are usually of *at least* 3 months duration. Such courses may have been obtained through a variety of programs such as those offered by technical schools and military training programs. To be creditable, such a course must have been designed specifically as career preparation for the work of the position being filled and must have provided the applicant with the necessary knowledge, skills, and abilities to do the work.

Combining Experience and Education

Equivalent combinations of successfully completed education and experience are qualifying for most positions. The combinations described below are those most typical for these positions, i.e., for grades GS-3 through GS-5. If education is used to meet specialized experience requirements, then such education must include courses related to the work of the position. *(When crediting education, prorate the number of hours of directly related courses required as a proportion of the total education to be used.)*

For GS-3 level positions, determine the applicant's total qualifying experience as a percentage of the 6 months' experience required for GS-3; then determine the applicant's education as a percentage of the 1 year of education which meets the requirements for GS-3. Add the two percentages. The total percentage must equal at least 100 percent to qualify an applicant for GS-3.

For GS-4 level positions, determine the applicant's total qualifying experience as a percentage of the 1 year of experience required for GS-4; then determine the applicant's education as a percentage of the 2 years of education which meets the requirements for GS-4. Add the two percentages. The total percentage must equal at least 100 percent to qualify an applicant for GS-4.

For GS-5 level positions, only education in excess of the first 60 semester hours of a course of study leading to a bachelor's degree is creditable toward meeting the specialized experience requirements. Two full academic years of study, or 60 semester hours, *beyond the second year* is equivalent to 1 year of specialized experience.

Determine the applicant's total qualifying experience as a percentage of the year of specialized experience required at the GS-5 level. Then determine the applicant's education as a percentage of the education which meets the requirements for GS-5. Add the two percentages. The total percentage must equal at least 100 percent to qualify an applicant for GS-5.

The following are examples of how education and experience may be combined. They are examples only, and are not all-inclusive.

- The position to be filled is a Pharmacy Technician, GS-3. An applicant has 2 months of experience and 20 semester hours of college. The applicant meets 33 percent of the required experience and 67 percent of the required education. The applicant meets 100 percent of the total requirements and is qualified for the position.

- The position to be filled is an Industrial Engineering Technician, GS-4. An applicant has 5 months of general experience and 36 semester hours of college. The applicant meets 42 percent of the required experience and 60 percent of the required education. The applicant exceeds 100 percent of the total requirements

and is qualified for the position. (This example assumes that education is being used to meet the specialized experience requirements and that at least 7 of the 36 semester hours are in courses directly related to the work of the position. See examples of such courses listed in the individual occupational requirements for the Industrial Engineering Technician Series, GS-895.)

- The position to be filled is a Recreation Assistant, GS-5. An applicant has 8 months of GS-4 level specialized experience and 80 semester hours of college. The applicant meets 67 percent of the required experience and 33 percent of the required education (i.e., 20 semester hours in excess of the first 60 semester hours). The applicant meets 100 percent of the total requirements and is qualified for the position. At least 8 of the 20 semester hours must be directly related to the work of the position. See examples of such courses listed in the individual occupational requirements for the Recreation Assistant Series, GS-189.

USE OF SELECTIVE FACTORS

Agencies may identify some positions covered by this standard that require knowledge, skills, and abilities or other qualifications, such as certification or licensure, that are in addition to or more specific than the minimum requirements described in this standard. The need for these special requirements can be met through the use if selective factors in both the competitive and inservice recruitment processes. Selective factors must be job-related, essential for the successful performance of the position and represent KSA's or other qualifications which could not be reasonably acquired on the job during the period of training customary for the position being filled.

OTHER QUALIFICATION PROVISIONS

Applicants for positions in some occupations must meet certification or licensure requirements in addition to meeting the education/experience requirements described above. Applicants can qualify on the basis of licensure, certification, or registration in lieu of education or experience in some other occupations. Such provisions are noted in the individual occupational requirements.

WRITTEN TEST REQUIREMENTS

For information on the occupational series and positions covered by this standard which require written tests, refer to the *Test Requirements in Qualification Standards* section (Part IV) of this Handbook.

PROFESSIONAL POSITIONS

MINIMUM QUALIFICATION REQUIREMENTS FOR TWO-GRADE INTERVAL PROFESSIONAL POSITIONS

This qualification standard covers positions in the General Schedule which involve the performance of two-grade interval professional work. The major provisions and definitions of terms pertaining to the qualification requirements of professional positions, as well as education and specialized experience requirements for most positions in grade GS-7 and above begun on page 3.

The specific requirements for entry into each occupation covered by this standard are attached as individual occupational requirements. Following is a list of the occupational series covered by this standard. For a description of the work performed in these occupations, refer to the series definitions in the *Handbook of Occupational Groups and Series* and/or to individual position classification standards.

GS-020	Community Planning
GS-101	Social Science*
GS-110	Economist
GS-130	Foreign Affairs
GS-131	International Relations
GS-140	Manpower Research and Analysis
GS-150	Geography
GS-170	History
GS-180	Psychology
GS-184	Sociology*
GS-185	Social Work
GS-190	General Anthropology
GS-193	Archeology
GS-401	General Biological Science*
GS-403	Microbiology
GS-405	Pharmacology*
GS-406	Agricultural Extension
GS-408	Ecology
GS-410	Zoology
GS-413	Physiology*
GS-414	Entomology
GS-415	Toxicology*
GS-430	Botany
GS-434	Plant Pathology
GS-435	Plant Physiology
GS-437	Horticulture*
GS-440	Genetics*
GS-454	Range Conservation
GS-457	Soil Conservation
GS-460	Forestry
GS-470	Soil Science
GS-471	Agronomy
GS-475	Agricultural Management
GS-480	General Fish and Wildlife Administration
GS-482	Fishery Biologist
GS-485	Wildlife Refuge Management
GS-486	Wildlife Biology
GS-487	Animal Science
GS-493	Home Economics
GS-510	Accounting
GS-511	Auditing
GS-512	Internal Revenue Agent
GS-601	General Health Science*
GS-630	Dietitian and Nutritionist*
GS-635	Corrective Therapist*
GS-637	Manual Arts Therapist*
GS-638	Recreation/Creative Arts Therapist*
GS-639	Educational Therapist*
GS-690	Industrial Hygienist*
GS-696	Consumer Safety

GS-800	Engineering Group, includes:
	General Engineering, GS-801
	Safety Engineering, GS-803
	Fire Protection Engineering, GS-804
	Materials Engineering, GS-806
	Civil Engineering, GS-810
	Environmental Engineering, GS-819
	Mechanical Engineering, GS-830
	Nuclear Engineering, GS-840
	Electrical Engineering, GS-850
	Computer Engineering, GS-854
	Electronics Engineering, GS-855
	Biomedical Engineering, GS-858
	Aerospace Engineering, Gs-861
	Naval Architecture, GS-871
	Mining Engineering, GS-880
	Petroleum Engineering, GS-881
	Agricultural Engineering, GS-890
	Ceramic Engineering, GS-892
	Chemical Engineering, GS-893
	Welding Engineering, GS-894
	Industrial Engineering, GS-896
GS-807	Landscape Architecture
GS-808	Architecture
GS-1015	Museum Curator
GS-1221	Patent Adviser
GS-1301	General Physical Science*
GS-1306	Health Physics*
GS-1310	Physics*
GS-1313	Geophysics
GS-1315	Hydrology
GS-1320	Chemistry*
GS-1321	Metallurgy
GS-1330	Astronomy and Space Science
GS-1340	Meteorology
GS-1350	Geology
GS-1360	Oceanography
GS-1370	Cartography
GS-1372	Geodesy
GS-1373	Land Surveying
GS-1380	Forest Products Technology
GS-1382	Food Technology
GS-1384	Textile Technology
GS-1386	Photographic Technology
GS-1420	Archivist
GS-1510	Actuary
GS-1515	Operations Research
GS-1520	Mathematics
GS-1529	Mathematical Statistician
GS-1530	Statistician

GS-1550　Computer Science
GS-1701　General Education and Training*
GS-1720　Education Program
GS-1725　Public Health Educator

GS-1730　Education Research
GS-1740　Education Services
GS-1750　Instructional Systems

Individual occupational requirements have been approved by the Secretary of Veterans Affairs for use within the Veterans Health Services and Research Administration under the provisions of Section 4105, Title 38, U.S.C.

PROFESSIONAL POSITIONS

BASIC REQUIREMENTS FOR ALL GRADES

Because of the highly specialized nature of the work classified to the occupation series covered by this standard, basic requirements vary for entry into each occupation.

All applicants for positions covered by this standard must have successfully completed the appropriate basic requirements as described in the individual occupational requirements. Applicants who meet the basic requirements are fully qualified for the entry grade specified for the occupation (generally grade GS-5). Applicants who wish to qualify for positions at higher grade levels (generally grade GS-7 and above) must also meet the requirements for such positions shown in the table on page 4, in addition to meeting the basic requirements.

The individual occupational requirements in the attachment generally provide two methods for applicants to qualify for occupations included in this standard, as outlined below:

A. Successful completion of a full 4-year course of study in an accredited college or university leading to a bachelor's or higher degree, which included a major field of study in paragraph A in the individual occupational requirements. Where specific course requirements are not indicated in paragraph A, the number of semester hours required to constitute a major field of study is the amount specified by the college or university attended. If this number cannot be obtained, 24 semester hours will be considered as equivalent to a major field of study. The nature and quality of this required course work must have been such that it would serve as a prerequisite for more advanced study in the field or subject matter area. Related course work generally refers to courses that may be accepted as part of the program major. An applicant who possesses a master's or higher degree with the appropriate major meets the basic education requirements described above.

OR

B. Appropriate combinations of education and experience, which are typically specified in paragraph B of the individual occupational requirements. The "paragraph B" method generally requires that an applicant possess a core of educational credit, as described in paragraph A above, plus additional education and/or experience.

The quality of the combination of education and experience must have seen sufficient to demonstrate that the applicant possesses the knowledge, skills, and abilities required to perform work in the occupation, and is comparable to that normally acquired through the successful completion of a full 4-year course of study with a major in the appropriate field. As in paragraph A, the number of semester hours required to constitute a major field of study is that specified by the college or university attended. If that number cannot be obtained, 24 semester hours will be considered as equivalent to a major field of study. An academic year of undergraduate study comprises 30 semester hours, or 45 quarter hours.

When combining education with experience, first determine the applicant's total qualifying education as a percentage of the education required for the grade level; then determine the applicant's experience as a percentage of the experience required for the grade level; finally, add the two percentages. The total percentage must equal at least 100 percent to qualify an applicant for that grade level. For example, an applicant for a GS-184, Sociology, position has successfully completed 60 undergraduate semester hours, including 24 semester hours in sociology, and, in addition, has 2 full-time years of appropriate sociology research, analysis, and report writing experience. This applicant would qualify for GS-5, since the 60 semester hours (the equivalent of 2 years of undergraduate education, or 50 percent of the total requirement) were supplemented by 2 additional years of appropriate professional experience, which provided the remaining 50 percent of the total required education and experience.

The individual occupational requirements for some series make no provision for substituting experience for education. Therefore, they do *not* include paragraph B provisions.

For a small number of series, applicants may possess certain kinds of experience *in lieu* of education. In such cases, applicants may meet minimum qualification requirements for those specific series through a combination of education and experience, or experience equivalent to a 4-year degree without any additional educational qualification. These situations are described in paragraph C of the individual occupational requirements.

ADDITIONAL EXPERIENCE AND EDUCATION REQUIREMENTS FOR GS-7 AND ABOVE

In addition to meeting the basic entry qualification requirements, applicants must have either specialized experience *or* directly related education in the amounts shown in the table below. Applicants who meet education requirements for a higher grade are also qualified for appropriate positions at lower grades.

Grade	Education	OR	Specialized Experience
GS-7	1 full year of graduate-level education or superior academic achievement		1 year at least equivalent to GS-5
GS-9	2 full academic years of progressively higher level graduate education or master's or equivalent graduate degree		1 year at least equivalent to GS-7
GS-11	3 full academic years of progressively higher level graduate education or Ph.D or equivalent doctoral degree		1 year at least equivalent to GS-9
GS-12 & above			1 year at least equivalent next lower grade level
Research Positions GS-11	Master's or equivalent graduate degree		1 year at least equivalent to GS-11
GS-12 research positions	Ph.D or equivalent doctoral degree		1 year at least equivalent to GS-12
GS-13 and above research positions			1 year at least equivalent to next lower grade

NOTE: Education of experience may be combined to meet the above requirements.

Specialized Experience: Experience which has equipped the applicant with the particular knowledge, skills, and abilities to perform successfully the duties of the position and which is typically in or related to the work of the position to be filled. To be creditable, specialized experience must have been at least equivalent to the next lower grade level in the normal line of progression for the occupation in the organization.

Superior Academic Achievement: The superior academic achievement provision is applicable to all occupations covered by this standard.

Graduate Education: Education in a field of study which provided the knowledge, skills, and abilities necessary to do the work.

Completion of graduate level education in the amounts shown in the table, in addition to meeting the basic requirements, is qualifying for positions at GS-7 through GS-11, and GS-12 research positions. A year of full-time graduate education is considered to be the number of credit hours which the school attended has determined represents 1 year of full-time study. If this number cannot be obtained from the school, 18 semester hours should be considered an academic year of graduate study.

Research Positions: Positions which primarily involve scientific inquiry or investigation, or research-type exploratory development of a creative or advanced scientific nature, where the knowledge required to successfully perform the work is typically and primarily acquired

through graduate study (master's or equivalent degree for GS-11, Ph.D or equivalent for GS-12). The work is such that the academic preparation will equip the applicant to fully perform the professional work of the position after a short orientation period.

1. Qualification on the basis of education—Applicants for such research positions can be considered qualified for GS-11 if they possess an appropriate master's or equivalent graduate degree, and qualified for GS-12 if they posses a Ph.D or equivalent doctoral degree.

2. Qualification on the basis of experience—Applicants who furnish positive evidence that they have performed highly creative or outstanding research that has led or can lead to major advances in a specific area of research, to a major advance in the discipline or field of science involved, or to major advances in science in general, can be rated under this provision for highly demanding research positions requiring similar abilities. Under these circumstances, applicants can be rated eligible for the next higher grade above that for which they would normally be rated, provided they have not been rated eligible at this higher grade on the basis of meeting the graduate study requirements described in paragraph 1 above. That is, applicants cannot receive an "extra" grade for education, and an additional "extra" grade for appropriate experience.

To receive this rating, the work must have been creative in the sense that it developed a basic principle, product, concept, method, approach, or technique, or provided a body of basic information that opened the way for a major advance in the discipline or field of science involved, or to advances in the discipline or field of science involved, or to advances in science in general, by providing a method of solving other problems, opening areas of research, or providing the means of exploiting the application of science in a major area.

Combination of Graduate Education and Professional Experience: Combinations of successfully completed graduate level education and specialized experience may be used to meet total experience requirements. Only graduate level education in excess of the amount required for the next lower grade level may be combined with experience. For example, an applicant with six months of appropriate experience equivalent to GS-7 (50 percent of the experience requirement for GS-9), and 27 semester hours of appropriate graduate education (50 percent of the education requirement for GS-9, in excess of that required for GS-7) would be qualified for a GS-9 position (assuming that there is no evidence that the attended college or university requires more than 18 hours as equivalent to a year of graduate study).

USE OF SELECTIVE FACTORS

Agencies may identify some positions covered by this standard that require knowledge, skills, and abilities (KSA's) or other qualifications that are in addition to the minimum requirements prescribed in the standard. The need for these special requirements can be met through the use of selective factors in both the competitive and inservice recruitment processes for positions at any grade level covered by this standard.

There are a variety of situations where agencies would be warranted in limiting consideration to applicants who possess the particular qualifications required to perform the work of such positions. For example, an agency may require specific kinds of training appropriate for filling positions concerned with scientific research and development activities, or may require specific educational courses or combinations of courses (where the individual occupational requirement permits applicants to qualify based on several combinations of educational course-work) to meet other specialized agency requirements. Also, an agency filling an international economist position may require that applicants for such a position possess certain kinds of knowledge in international economics. In this case, since applicants can qualify on the basis of education, the agency may also require certain types of educational courses. That agency may not, however,, require applicants for statistical clerk, or

other positions which do not require completion of a degree, to have a degree. Similarly, in some cases, consideration may be limited only to those applicants who possess an appropriate license, registration, or certification, if possession of such is determined to be necessary for carrying out the responsibilities of a position.

Selective factors must be job related, essential for the successful performance of the position and represent KSA's or other qualifications which could not be reasonably acquired on the job during the period of training customary for the position being filled.

ADDITIONAL QUALIFICATION REQUIREMENTS

In addition to meeting basic and additional requirements, all applicants for some positions must also meet special requirements such as certifications or licensure in a particular occupation. These situations are noted in individual occupational requirements in the attachment.

STUDENT TRAINEE POSITIONS

STUDENT TRAINING QUALIFICATION STANDARD FOR COMPETITIVE SERVICE POSITIONS

This standard describes the qualification requirements for student trainees under career-conditional or career appointments in the competitive service. Eligibility and selection requirements for prospective competitive service student trainees are described in FPM Chapter 332, Appendix G. Student trainee positions in the excepted service are covered by the Multiseries Student Trainee Qualification Standard for Schedule B Positions. This standard is not applicable to students who are temporarily employed

GS-099   General Student Trainee Series
GS-199   General Science Student Trainee Series
GS-299   Personnel Management Student Trainee Series
GS-399   Administration and Office Support Student Trainee Series
GS-499   Biological Science Student Trainee Series
GS-599   Financial Management Student Trainee Series
GS-699   Medical and Health Student Trainee Series
GS-799   Veterinary Student Trainee Series
GS-899   Engineering and Architecture Student Trainee Series
GS-999   Legal Occupations Student Trainee Series
GS-1299 Copyright and Patent Student Trainee Series
GS-1399 Physical Science Student Trainee Series

during the summer vacations and who have not been appointed to a student trainee program in the competitive service as described above.

Students may be appointed to any position which leads to qualification in a two-grade interval professional, administrative, or technical occupational series. Following is a list of the occupational series covered by this standard.

GS-1499 Library and Archives Student Trainee Series
GS-1599 Mathematics and Statistics Student Trainee Series
GS-1699 Equipment and Facilities Student Trainee Series
GS-1799 Education Student Trainee Series
GS-1899 Investigation Student Trainee Series
GS-1999 Quality Inspection Student Trainee Series
GS-2099 Supply Student Trainee Series
GS-2199 Transportation Student Trainee Series
GS-1099 Information and Arts Student Trainee Series
GS-1199 Business and Industry Student Trainee Series

This standard has been approved by the Administrator of Veterans Affairs for use within the Department of Medicine and Surgery of the Veterans Administration under the provisions of section 4105, title 38, U.S.C.

Student trainees qualify as described below.

GRADE	LEVEL OF EDUCATION
GS-2	High school diploma or equivalent
GS-3	Completion of 1 academic year post-high school
GS-4	Completion of 2 academic years of post-high school or associate's degree

The required education must lead to a bachelor's degree with specialization in or directly related to the field in which they will receive training on the job. The degree of specialization in this field must satisfy on graduation the specific educational requirements in the qualification standard for the corresponding two-grade interval positions.

PROMOTION REQUIREMENTS

Student trainees may be promoted to higher-graded trainee positions based on completion of portions of the education and student trainee work experience.

To GS-3: Completion of one full semester, or the equivalent, of post-high school study and one period of student trainee work experience.

To GS-4: (a) Completion of 1 academic year of study and two periods of student trainee work experience; or

(b) completion of 1 1/2 academic years of study and one period of student trainee work experience.

To GS-5: (a) Completion of 3 academic years of study and one period of GS-4 student trainee work experience; or (b) completion of 2 1/2 academic years of study and 6 months (at least 960 hours) of GS-4 student trainee work experience.

Upon completion of all the requirements for a bachelor's degree in an appropriate field, student trainees may be reassigned or promoted in the appropriate target series to GS-5 or GS-7, if they meet the qualification requirements of the target occupation, including minimum education requirements, if any.

EXPLANATION OF TERMS

An academic year of undergraduate education is defined as 30 semester hours, 45 quarter hours, or the equivalent in an accredited college or university.

For purposes of this standard, a period of student trainee work experience is the equivalent of 2 months (320 hours) of full-time work experience.

WRITTEN TESTS

No written test is required for these positions.

SCHEDULE B STUDENT TRAINEE POSITIONS

**MULTISERIES STUDENT TRAINEE
QUALIFICATION STANDARD FOR SCHEDULE B
POSITIONS**

This standard describes the qualification requirements for General Schedule, career-related, Schedule B student trainee positions authorized under E.O. 12015. Eligibility and selection requirements for prospective Schedule B student trainees are described in FPM Chapter 308. (Student trainee positions in the competitive service are covered by the *Student Trainee qualification Standard for Competitive Service Positions.*)

GS-099   General Student Trainee Series
GS-199   Social Science Student Trainee Series
GS-299   Personnel Management Student Trainee Series
GS-399   Administration and Office Support Student Trainee Series
GS-499   Biological Science Student Trainee Series
GS-599   Financial Management Student Trainee Series
GS-699   Medical and Health Student Trainee Series
GS-799   Veterinary Student Trainee Series
GS-899   Engineering and Architecture Student Trainee Series
GS-999   Legal Occupations Student Trainee Series
GS-1099   Information and Arts Student Trainee Series

This standard is not applicable to students who are temporarily employed during summer vacations and who have not been appointed to a career-related student trainee program as described above.

Following is a list of the occupational series covered by this standard.

GS-1199   Business and Industry Student trainee Series
GS-1299   Copyright and Patent Student Trainee Series
GS-1399   Physical Science Student Trainee Series
GS-1499   Library and Archives Student Trainee Series
GS-1599   Mathematics and Statistics Student Trainee Series
GS-1699   Equipment and Facilities Management Student Trainee Series
GS-1799   Education Student Trainee Series
GS-1899   Investigation Student Trainee Series
GS-1999   Quality Inspection Student Trainee Series
GS-2099   Supply Student Trainee Series
GS-2199   Transportation Student Trainee Series

This standard has been approved by the Secretary of Veterans Affairs for use within the Veterans health Administration under the provisions of section 7402, title 38, U.S.C.

REQUIREMENTS FOR INITIAL APPOINTMENT

Student trainees with not previous related education or experience may qualify as described below.

GRADE	LEVEL OF EDUCATION
GS-2	High school diploma or equivalent
GS-3	Completion of 1 academic year post-high school
GS-4	Completion of 2 academic years of post-high school or associate's degree
GS-5	Completion of 4 academic years of post-high school study leading to a bachelor's degree or completion of 4 academic years of pre-professional study
GS-7	Completion of 1 academic year of graduate level education, bachelor's degree with Superior Academic Achievement as provided in the "General Policies and Instructions" for *Qualification Standards Handbook,* or 5 academic years of pre-professional study
GS-9	Completion of 2 academic years of graduate level education or master's or equivalent graduate degree
GS-11	For research positions, completion of all requirements for a master's or equivalent degree

The required education must be (a) related to the field in which student trainees will receive training on the job or (b) applicable under the qualification standard for the target occupational series. Agencies may use selective factors to identify special requirements, e.g., specific courses, needed to perform the work of individual positions.

Special Provisions for Student Trainees With Previous Related Education or Experience

For both initial appointment to and concurrent with conversion from a student trainee program, the applicant's previous education and/or experience (both student trainee and non-student trainee experience) should be evaluated using the qualification standard for the target position to determine whether it is creditable.

If any portion of the education or experience meets the requirements in the qualification standard for the target position, then both initial appointment and conversion may be made at the highest grade level for which the applicant is qualified and eligible.

PROMOTION REQUIREMENTS

Student trainees may be promoted to higher-graded trainee positions based on their Federal Government student trainee work experience as follows:

To GS-2: Continued study in a high school education program and completion of one period of student trainee work experience.

To GS-3: Completion of one full semester or the equiv-

alent of post-high school study and one period of student trainee work experience.

To GS-4: (a) Completion of 1 academic year of study and two periods of student trainee work experience; or (b) completion of 1 1/2 academic years of study and one period of student trainee work experience.

To GS-5: (a) Completion of 3 academic years of study leading to a bachelor's or higher degree and one period of GS-4 student trainee work experience; or (b) completion of 2 1/2 academic years of study leading to a bachelor's or higher degree and 6 months (at least 960 hours) of GS-4 student trainee work experience.

Student trainee positions where the target occupation follows a one-grade interval pattern:

To GS-6: (a) Completion of 4 academic years of study (or all the requirements) for a bachelor's degree and completion of one period of GS-5 student trainee work experience.

Student trainee positions where the target occupation follows a two-grade interval pattern:

To GS-7: (a) Completion of 4 academic years of study (or all the requirements) for a bachelor's degree and completion of one period of GS-5 student trainee work experience, or (b) completion of 4 academic years of pre-professional study and completion of one period of GS-5 student trainee work experience.

To GS-9: (a) Completion of 1 full years of graduate level study and completion of one period of GS-7 student trainee work experience, or (b) completion of 5 academic years of pre-professional study and completion of one period of GS-7 student trainee work experience.

To GS-11: (a) Completion of 2 full years of graduate level study and completion of one period of GS-9 student trainee work experience.

EXPLANATION OF TERMS

An academic year of undergraduate education is defined as 30 semester hours, 45 quarter hours, or the equivalent in an accredited college or university, or approximately 36 weeks for at least 20 classroom hours per week in an accredited business, technical, or secretarial school. See the "General Policies and Instructions" for the *Qualification Standards Handbook* for the definition of a full year of graduate education.

Pre-professional study is study in fields that require a post-baccalaureate degree at the entry level, e.g., veterinary medicine, social worker.

For purposes of this standard, a period of student trainee work experience is the equivalent of 2 months (320 hours) of work experience.

CONVERSION

Students may be converted noncompetitively to a career or career-conditional appointment to the target position within

120 days following completion of their educational and work experience requirements. An agency may recommend noncompetitive conversion in another Federal agency provided that all parties agree that the appointment is in the best interest of the Government. Agencies may also promote students noncompetitively using this standard immediately prior to conversion.

When converting students, the following conditions must be met:

a. Students must meet the qualification standard for the position, including any minimum educational, licensing, or certification requirements; however, students who are converted at the same grade as their final student trainee grade need not meet any length of experience requirements for that grade level;

b. The position must be in the field, or in a closely related field, for which the students were trained;

c. Students must meet all the program requirements in FPM Chapter 308.

TEST REQUIREMENTS

A written test is not required for Schedule B student trainee positions at the time of initial appointment or upon conversion.

CLERICAL AND ADMINISTRATIVE SUPPORT POSITIONS

MINIMUM QUALIFICATION REQUIREMENTS FOR ONE-GRADE INTERVAL CLERICAL AND ADMINISTRATIVE SUPPORT POSITIONS

This qualification standard covers positions in the General Schedule which involve the performance of one-grade interval clerical and administrative support work. A list of the occupational series covered by this standard is provided below. This standard may also be used for other one-grade interval positions for which the education and experience pattern is determined to be appropriate. While some of the occupational series

covered by this standard include both one- and two-grade interval work, the qualification requirements described in this standard apply only to those positions which follow a one-grade interval pattern. For a description of the work in these occupations, refer to the series definitions in the *Handbook of Occupational Groups and Series* and/or to individual position classification standards.

GS-029	Environmental Protection Assistant
GS-072	Fingerprint Identification
GS-086	Security Clerical and Assistance
GS-134	Intelligence Aid and Clerk
GS-203	Personnel Clerical and Assistance
GS-204	Military Personnel Clerical and Technician
GS-302	Messenger[1]
GS-303	Miscellaneous Clerk and Assistant
GS-304	Information Receptionist
GS-305	Mail and File
GS-309	Correspondence Clerk
GS-312	Clerk-Stenographer and Reporter
GS-318	Secretary
GS-319	Closed Microphone Reporting
GS-322	Clerk-Typist
GS-326	Office Automation Clerical and Assistance
GS-332	Computer Operation
GS-335	Computer Clerk and Assistant
GS-344	Management Clerical and Assistance
GS-350	Equipment Operator
GS-351	Printing Clerical
GS-356	Data Transcriber
GS-357	Coding
GS-359	Electric Accounting Machine Operation
GS-361	Equal Opportunity Assistance
GS-382	Telephone Operating
GS-390	Telecommunications Processing
GS-392	General Telecommunications
GS-394	Communications Clerical
GS-503	Financial Clerical and Assistance
GS-525	Accounting Technician
GS-530	Cash Processing
GS-540	Voucher Examining
GS-544	Civilian Pay
GS-545	Military Pay

GS-561	Budget Clerical and Assistance
GS-592	Tax Examining
GS-593	Insurance Accounts
GS-675	Medical Records Technician
GS-679	Medical Clerk[2]
GS-962	Contact Representative
GS-963	Legal Instruments Examining
GS-986	Legal Clerical and Assistance
GS-990	General Claims Examining
GS-998	Claims Clerical
GS-1001	General Arts and Information
GS-1046	Language Clerical
GS-1087	Editorial Assistance
GS-1101	General Business and Industry
GS-1105	Purchasing
GS-1106	Procurement Clerical and Assistance
GS-1107	Property Disposal Clerical and Technician
GS-1152	Production Control
GS-1411	Library Technician[2]
GS-1421	Archives Technician
GS-1531	Statistical Assistant
GS-1702	Education and Training Technician
GS-1802	Compliance Inspection and Support
GS-1897	Customs Aid
GS-2005	Supply Clerical and Technician
GS-2091	Sales Store Clerical
GS-2102	Transportation Rate and Tariff Examining
GS-2131	Freight Rate
GS-2132	Travel
GS-2133	Passenger Rate
GS-2134	Shipment Clerical and Assistance
GS-2135	Transportation Loss and Damage Claims Examining
GS-2151	Dispatching

---

[1] Under 5 U.S.C. 3310, appointment to Messenger positions is restricted to persons entitled to veteran preference as long as such persons are available.

[2] These qualification requirements have been approved for use within the Veterans Health Administration of the Department of Veterans Affairs under the provisions of section 7402, title 38, U.S.C.

EDUCATION AND EXPERIENCE REQUIREMENTS

GS-1/6 and above: The following table shows the amounts of general and/or specialized experience and education that meet the requirements for each grade.

Grade/Positions	Experience		OR	Education
	General	Specialized		
GS-1 All positions	None	None		None
GS-2 All positions	3 months	None		High school graduation or equivalent
GS-3 Clerk-Steno				High school graduation or equivalent
All other positions	6 months	None		1 year above high school
GS-4 All positions	1 year	None		2 years above high school
GS-5 Clerk-Steno	2 years	None		4 years above high school (There is no educational substitution for Reporting Stenographer, Shorthand Reporter, or Closed Microphone Reporter positions.)
All other positions	None	1 year at least equivalent to GS-4		
GS-6 and above All positions	None	1 year at least equivalent to next lower grade level		Generally, not applicable

Equivalent combinations of education and experience are qualifying for all grade levels and positions for which both education and experience are acceptable.

General Experience—(All positions except Reporting Stenographer, Shorthand Reporter, and Closed Microphone Reporter): Progressively responsible clerical, office, or other work which indicates ability to acquire the particular knowledge, skills, and abilities (KSA's) to perform successfully the duties of that position and which is typically in or related to the position to be filled. To be creditable, specialized experience must have been at least equivalent to the next lower grade level.

Specialized Experience—(All positions except Reporting Stenographer, Shorthand Reporter, and Closed Microphone Reporter): Experience which has equipped the applicant with the particular knowledge, skills, and abilities (KSA's) to perform successfully the duties of that position and which is typically in or related to the position to be filled. To be creditable, specialized experience must have been at least equivalent to the next lower grade level.

Experience for Reporting Stenographer, Shorthand Reporter, and Closed Microphone Reporter—One year of experience at least equivalent to the next lower grade level using the skills and equipment appropriate to the position to be filled is required for all positions. Following is a description of qualifying experience for these positions.

Reporting Stenographer, GS-5: Experience as a clerk-stenographer, secretary, reporting stenographer, or in another position which included application of stenography and typing skills as a significant part of the work. Reporting Stenographer, Shorthand Reporter, and Closed Microphone Reporter, GS-6: Experience as a reporting stenographer, hearing reporter, or in another position in which the primary duty was to make and transcribe manual or machine-written shorthand records of hearings, interviews, or similar proceedings.

Shorthand Reporter and Closed Microphone Reporter, GS-7 and above: Experience as a court reporter, or hearing reporter, or in another position in which the primary duty was to make verbatim records of proceedings.

Education

High school graduation or the equivalent is creditable at the GS-2 level for the occupations listed, except Clerk-Stenographer, where it is creditable at the GS-3 entry level.

Successfully completed education above the high school level in any field for which high school graduation or the equivalent is the normal prerequisite is creditable at grades GS-3 through GS-5 for all positions except Reporting Stenographer, GS-5. This education must have been obtained in an accredited business, secretarial or technical school, junior college, college or university. One full year of full-time academic study is 30 semester hours, 45 quarter hours, or the equivalent or college or at least 20 hours or classroom instruction per week for approximately 36 weeks in a business, secretarial, or technical school.

As a general rule, education is not creditable above GS-5 for most positions covered by this standard; however, graduate education may be credited in those few instances where the graduate education is directly related to the work of the position.

Intensive Short-Term Training—Completion of an intensive, specialized course of study of less than 1 year (such as for computer operator) may meet in full the experience requirements for GS-3. Courses of this type normally require completion of up to 40 hours per week of instruction rather than the usual 20 hours per week and are usually of *at least* 3 months duration. Such courses may have been obtained through a variety of programs such as those offered by business or technical schools, and through military training programs. To be creditable, such a course must have been designed specifically as career preparation for a work of the position being filled and must have provided the applicant with the necessary knowledge, skills and abilities to do the work.

Combining Education and Experience

Equivalent combinations of successfully completed post-high school education and experience may be used to meet total experience requirements at grades GS-5 and below, except for Reporting Stenographer, GS-5.

For GS-3 and GS-4 level positions, determine the applicant's total qualifying experience as a percentage of the experience required for the grade level; then determine the applicant's education as a percentage of the education required for the grade level; then add the two percentages. The total percentage must equal at least 100 percent to qualify an applicant for the grade level.

For all GS-5 level positions (except Clerk-Stenographer, which does not require specialized experience), only education in excess of the first 60 semester hours (i.e., beyond the second year) is creditable toward meeting the specialized experience requirement. One full academic year of study (30 semester hours) *beyond the second year* is equivalent to 6 months of specialized experience.

The following are examples of how education and experience may be combined. They are examples only, and are not all inclusive:

- The position to be filled is a Payroll Clerk, GS-4. An applicant has 8 months of qualifying experience and 20 semester hours of college. The applicant meets 67 percent of the required experience and 33 percent of the required education. The applicant meets 100 percent of the total requirements and is qualified for the position.

- The position to be filled is a Clerk-Typist, GS-4. The applicant has 4 months of qualifying experience and 1 year of business school. The applicant meets 33 percent of the required experience and 50 percent of the required education. The applicant meets 83 percent of the total requirements and is not qualified for the position.

- The position to be filled is a Clerk-Stenographer, GS-5. An applicant has 1 year of qualifying experience and 90 semester hours of college. The applicant meets 50 percent of the required experience and 75 percent of the required education. The applicant exceeds 100 percent of the total requirements and is qualified for the position.

- The position to be filled is a Personnel Clerk, GS-5. The applicant has 9 months of specialized experience and 75 semester hours of college (15 semester hours beyond the second year and the equivalent of 3 months of specialized experience). The applicant meets 75 percent of the required experience and 25 percent of the required education. The applicant meets 100 percent of the requirement of 1 year of specialized experience and is qualified for the position.

USE OF SELECTIVE FACTORS

Agencies may identify some positions in an occupation, especially at the higher grade levels, that require KSA's that are in addition to or more specific than the minimum requirements described in this standard. The need for these special requirements can be met through the use of selective factors in both the competitive and inservice recruitment processes. Selective factors must be job related, essential for the successful performance of the position, and represent KSA's which could not be reasonably acquired on the job during the period of training customary for the position being filled.

WRITTEN TEST REQUIREMENTS

For information on the occupational series and positions covered by this standard which require written tests, refer to the *Test Requirements in Qualification Standards* section (Part IV) of this Handbook.

PROFICIENCY REQUIREMENTS

Clerk-Typist, Office Automation Clerk/Assistant, Clerk-Stenographer, Data Transcriber, and Positions with Parenthetical Titles of (Typing), (Office Automation), (Stenography), or (Data Transcription)

In addition to meeting experience or education requirements, applicants for these positions must show possession of the following skills, as appropriate. Applicants may meet these requirements by passing the appropriate performance test, presenting a certificate of proficiency from a school or other organization authorized to issue such certificates by the Office of Personnel Management local office, or by self-certifying their proficiency. Performance test results and certificates of proficiency are acceptable for 3 years. Agencies may verify proficiency skills of self-certified applicants by administering the appropriate performance test.

Clerk-Typist, GS-2/3, Office Automation Clerk/Assistant (any grade), (typing) (any grade), and (Office Automation) (any grade):
 40 words per minute typing speed

Data transcriber, GS-2/4, and (Data Transcription) (any grade):
 skill in operating an alphanumeric data transcribing machine,
 or 20 words per minute typing speed for GS-2 transcription duties,
 or 25 words per minute typing speed for GS-3 and GS-4 transcription duties

Clerk-Stenographer, GS-3/4:
 40 words per minute typing speed *and*
 80 words per minute dictation speed

Clerk-Stenographer, GS-5:
 40 words per minute typing speed *and*
 120 words per minute dictation speed

(Stenography) (any grade):
 40 words per minute typing speed *and either*
 80 words per minute dictation speed for GS-3 and GS-4 stenographic duties or
 120 words per minute dictation speed for GS-5 stenographic duties

NOTE: The level of proficiency for stenographic and data transcribing duties required by positions with parenthetical titles is based on the grade level of those duties and not necessarily on the overall grade of the position. For example, a position classified as Secretary (Stenography), GS-318-5, may required either 80 or 120 words per minute dictation speed depending upon the level of difficulty of the stenographic duties. Or, a position classified as a Payroll Clerk (Data Transcription), GS-544-4, may require either 20 or 25 word per minute typing speed depending upon the level of difficulty of the transcribing duties. Therefore, before filling positions of this type, first determine the grade level of the duties which require the additional skill, and then determine the skill level required.

Reporting Stenographer, Shorthand Reporter, and Closed Microphone Reporter

In addition to meeting the experience requirements, applicants for these positions must show possession of the following skills with equipment appropriate to the specific position.
 Reporting Stenographer, GS-5/6: 120 words per minute dictation speed

Shorthand Reporter and Closed Microphone Reporter, GS-6: 160 words per minute dictation speed
Shorthand Reporter and Closed Microphone Reporter, GS-7 and above: 175 words per minute dictation speed

Applicants must also be able to produce accurate typewritten transcripts of recorded proceedings.

Applicants for competitive appointment and inservice applicants for initial assignment to these three positions at all grade levels must demonstrate the specific skill and level of proficiency required by the position to be filled. Also, inservice applicants for promotion of positions which

have a higher proficiency requirement than the position previously held must demonstrate the higher level of proficiency. Applicants may demonstrate the proficiency by either passing a dictation test at the required speed or presenting a certificate of proficiency showing speed and accuracy equivalent to those used in the Office of Personnel Management performance tests for these positions. The certificate must show that the candidate demonstrated the required proficiency, i.e., dictation speed and accuracy, to a teacher or stenography, shorthand reporting, or closed microphone reporting, within the past year. Applicants for these positions may not self-certify dictation proficiency.

Appendix H

POSITION CLASSIFICATION STANDARDS

The information here is excerpted from *Position Classification Standards for GS-0318*. Only the standards for grades four and five are reproduced here. The kinds of detailed descriptions provided in this appendix are similar to what a successful application packet will have in its description of work experience. Refer to the wording here, for a fairly common position, for examples of how to describe clearly and in detail the **tasks** you have done in the past.

SERIES   GRADE   BMK ≈
GS-318   04   01

SECRETARY (TYPING)

Duties

Performs various clerical support and typing duties for the chief of a regional supply division and the staff.

— Receives and files correspondence, records, and reports. Maintains file plans and checks subordinate unit files for proper disposition. Receives and files changes to regulatory publications.

— Maintains employee record cards for personnel within the division.

— Receives incoming correspondence, screening material prior to distribution for suspense dates, establishing controls, and following up for division chief.

— Receives visitors and phone calls to the division office, ascertaining the nature of requests and directing callers to appropriate staff, or personally providing the information desired when routine or procedural matters of the office are involved.

— Types from voice recordings dictated by the division chief, the assistant division chief, and others in the organization. Types correspondence, reports, and similar material.

— Reviews correspondence prepared for the division chief. Checks for spelling, typographical errors, conformance to formats and procedural requirements.

— Requisitions office supplies, equipment, and publications, and performs similar office maintenance duties.

— Schedules appointments and makes arrangements for time, participants, and location of meetings in accordance with instructions from the supervisor.

Factor 1. Knowledge Required by the Position—Level 1-3—350 points

Knowledge Type II

— Knowledge of the organizational functions and procedures of the supply division to perform such duties as distribute and control mail, refer phone calls and visitors, and provide general, non-technical information.

— Knowledge of the office filing system and various references and handbooks commonly used by the staff in order to classify, search for, and dispose of materials.

— Knowledge of procedures required to requisition office supplies, maintenance, and printing services. This requires knowledge of the procedures applicable to the control, authorization, securing, and justification of such services.

— Knowledge of procedures required to maintain leave records of division staff and to prepare forms required for various personnel actions.

— Skills in operating a typewriter. A qualified typist is required.

— Knowledge of grammar, spelling, punctuation, and required formats.

Work Situation A

The division is of limited organizational complexity and is divided into three subordinate units. The chief directs the staff primarily through face-to-face meetings. Internal procedures and administrative controls are simple and informal.

Factor 2. Supervisory Controls—Level 2-2—125 points

The supervisor provides assignments, generally indicating what is to be done, quantity expected, deadlines, and priorities. Additional instructions are provided for new, difficult, or unusual assignments.

Employee uses initiative to independently perform recurring office work. Work is performed as it arrives, or in accordance with established priorities and instructions. Only problems and unfamiliar situations not covered by instructions are referred to supervisor.

The supervisor assures that finished work is accurate and in compliance with instructions and established procedures.

Factor 3. Guidelines—Level 3-2—125 points

Administrative instructions and manuals provide specific guidance for duties such as the preparation of time and attendance reports and the maintenance of office files. Also, sample letters and correspondence manuals usually provide detailed guidelines.

The employee uses judgement in selecting the most appropriate guidelines for application to specific cases. For example, the employee selects the most appropriate correspondence format when more than one is authorized, determines subject matter for classification of file materials, and selects procedures for routing correspondence or requests for action by determining nature of correspondence or requests.

Factor 4. Complexity—Level 4-2—75 points

The clerical duties performed include the full range of procedural duties in support of the office. Decisions regarding what needs to be done generally involve choice among established alternatives.

Actions to be taken and responses to be made primarily concern differences in factual situations and awareness of functional specialties of the staff members.

Factor 5. Scope and Effect—Level 5-2—75 points

The purpose of the work is to provide clerical support for the division office. The work has direct effect on the clerical support provided in subordinate units within the division.

Factor 6. Personal Contacts—Level 6-2—25 points

Most contacts are with employees within the immediate organization, vendors, and offices serviced by the division.

Factor 7. Purpose of Contacts—Level 7-2—50 points

The contacts are to exchange information and to plan and coordinate work efforts so that, for example, the staff submits reports and replies to correspondence promptly, and meetings are scheduled at mutually convenient times.

Factor 8. Physical Demands—Level 8-1—5 points

Most of the work is performed while seated. Occasionally the employee must lift computer printouts weighing from 10 to 20 pounds.

Factor 9. Work Environment—Level 9-1—5 points

The work is performed in a typical office setting.

TOTAL POINTS—835

SERIES	GRADE	BMK ≈
GS-318	05	01

SECRETARY (STENOGRAPHY)

Duties

This position is located in the Systems Engineering Branch, an organization which provides guidance, control, and direction to avionic system and subsystem efforts, and which defines requirements for equipment developments to satisfy future subsystem needs.

The incumbent participates actively in the management of the Systems Engineering Branch office by performing routine administrative and miscellaneous clerical work. Based on a good working knowledge of the organization and substantive programs under the supervisor's control, the incumbent resolves problems associated with the administrative and clerical work of the office. Within this basic structure the incumbent performs the following duties:

— Receives calls, greets visitors, and directs to staff members only those contacts needing their attention or action. Takes care of routing matters, and on the basis of knowledge of the programs or operations, refers other inquiries to appropriate personnel. Incumbent personally responds to routine and non-technical requests for information such as status of reports, duty status of engineers and technicians, suspense date for matters requiring compliance, and similar information readily available from the files. Places both local and long distance calls for personnel. Maintains Branch Chief's calendar and schedules appointments based on knowledge of Branch Chief's interest and commitments.

— Composes correspondence on administrative support or clerical functions of the office. Composes routine correspondence on other subjects as outlined in regulations and procedures or specifically requested by Branch Chief. Reads outgoing correspondence for procedural and grammatical accuracy.

— Receives and reviews classified and unclassified mail for the Branch. Determines which items should be brought to the attention of the Branch Chief as opposed to those that should be sent directly to other appropriate personnel for action. Reviews outgoing mail for attachments, dates, signatures, complete addresses, and destinations. Maintains suspense records on all correspondence and action documents and follows up to ensure a timely reply or action.

— Takes and transcribes dictation of correspondence, reports, and telephone conversations involving both technical and specialized terminology. Notes are often typed in final form without rough draft, reviewed for proper arrangement and grammar, and compiled in final form. Types an intermediate draft when requested. Uses reference sources such as technical dictionaries and assures proper arrangement, grammatical accuracy, and spelling of the final copy.

— Prepares in final form all types of documentation and forms incident to Branch personnel administration and office management. Prepares travel requests and all associated actions and documentation. Assembles, prepares, and submits Branch reports of staff time charges, and maintains personnel time cards.

— Reads directives and instructional material pertaining to administrative practices and clerical procedures in order to be aware of new, revised, or amended procedures for such matters as preparation and processing of correspondence, engineering reports, and forms; filing; mail procedures; preparation of travel vouchers; and security procedures.

— From rough draft, notes, or oral instructions, types correspondence, forms, reports, and specifications including a wide variety of technical terminology. Responsible for proper spelling, grammar, format, and arrangement of material.

— Performs periodic inventory of classified documents within the Branch. Arranges for the destruction of classified material.

— Provides guidance and assistance on applicable procedures, instructions, and regulations to other clerical personnel assigned to the Branch.

Factor 1. Knowledge Required—Level 1-3—350 points

Knowledge Type III

— Knowledge of the substantive programs of the Systems Engineering Branch as they relate to the clerical and administrative functions of the Branch.

— Skill in taking and transcribing dictation. A qualified stenographer is required.

— Knowledge of the duties, commitments, goals, and priorities of Branch staff to advise other clerical support personnel on such matters as the application of instructions and regulations and their effect on the work of the staff.

— Knowledge of spelling, arrangement, grammar, and required formats.

— Skill in operating a typewriter. A qualified typist is required.

Situation A

This Branch includes 17 professional engineering and support positions. Internal procedures are simple and informal, and the Branch Chief usually coordinates the work through face-to-face discussions with the staff.

Factor 2. Supervisory Controls—Level 2-3—275 points

Supervisor issues work assignments in terms of general instructions and desired results. The secretary plans and carries out duties independently.

The supervisor gives a spot check review of completed work to ensure compliance with established policies and procedures.

Factor 3. Guidelines—Level 3-2—125 points

Specific guidelines are available as needed for reference purposes. They include technical dictionaries, directives pertaining to administrative practices and clerical procedures, security regulations, correspondence manuals, and prescribed filing systems. Incumbent uses judgement in selecting guidelines for application to individual cases.

Factor 4. Complexity—Level 4-2—75 points

The work consists of duties involving several related sequential steps, processes, and methods.

Decisions made by secretary in performing the work require recognizing the differences among the few easily recognizable situations.

Differences in actions taken and responses made by secretary depend on the source of information, type of transaction, or other factual matters.

Factor 5. Scope and Effect—Level 5-2—75 points

The purpose of the position is to relieve the supervisor of the routine administrative and miscellaneous clerical work. The work affects the accuracy and reliability of further processes.

Factor 6. Personal Contacts—Level 6-2—25 points

Personal contacts include visitors from other offices within the agency.

Factor 7. Purpose of Personal Contacts—Level 7-2—50 points

The incumbent plans and coordinates the work of the office. This includes contacts for purposes such as clarifying or exchanging information, scheduling and arranging meetings, making travel arrangements, and providing other Branch employees with guidance and help on applicable procedures.

Factor 8. Physical Demands—Level 8-1—5 points

The work places no special physical demands on the employee. The work includes some walking, standing, bending, and carrying of light items such as paper and books.

Factor 9. Work Environment—Level 9-1—5 points

The work environment involves the normal risks and discomforts typical of an office.

TOTAL POINTS—985

SERIES GRADE BMK ≈
GS-318 05 02

SECRETARY (TYPING)

Duties

The incumbent assists the Chief of the Executive Personnel Division.

— Controls all incoming correspondence and action documents. Reads all incoming correspondence, screens items to be handled personally, and forwards the remainder to staff for action.

— Maintains files and records such as candidate files, executive inventory files, executive training files, and logs showing the status of recruiting actions and correspondence. Ensures that files include all required documents and that all documents are properly signed.

— Receives requests for information, advises when the information can be furnished, and provides it personally from files and records or follows up with staff to see that it is provided.

— Drafts responses such as routine requests from candidates for supergrade positions for more information concerning arrangements for employment interviews or the proper procedures for applying for a position. Also drafts letters to Department executives notifying them of assignments for training at the Federal Executive Institute or Brookings Institute.

— Receives visitors to the office including all appointments for executive recruiters. This involves setting up appointments, securing building clearance, and arranging for additional appointments with bureau and office senior staff. Occasionally includes arranging airline scheduling and hotel accommodations for out-of-town candidates for positions with the Department.

— Arranges for large meetings or conferences including selecting mutually satisfactory time, reserving meeting rooms, notifying participants, attending the meetings, and preparing reports of the proceedings.

— Arranges travel for staff, including scheduling transportation, making hotel reservations, keeping in touch with staff enroute and preparing travel vouchers.

— Completes forms required for executive recruiting and training actions.

— Types correspondence, reports, and records in final form from rough drafts. Ensures correct punctuation, capitalization, spelling, grammar, and conformance to style.

Factor 1. Knowledge Required by the Position—Level 1-3—350 points

Knowledge Type III

— Knowledge of the work program of the office sufficient to screen requests for information, personally provide authorized information form files and records or advise on established procedures (such as those for employment interviews), and refer non-routine requests to the appropriate staff member.

— Knowledge of the duties, priorities, and commitments of the staff sufficient to independently set up large conferences, arrange travel and accommodations for those attending, and prepare reports of the proceedings.

— Skill in operating a typewriter. A qualified typist is required.

— Knowledge of correct grammar, spelling, punctuation, capitalization, and style.

Work Situation A

The Executive Personnel Division includes from three to five specialists providing executive recruiting and development services for the Department. The supervisors direct the staff through face-to-face meetings. Formal controls are largely limited to records concerning the status of correspondence and recruiting actions.

Factor 2. Supervisory Controls—Level 2-2—275 points

The supervisor defines the major priorities of the office and explains special assignments. The incumbent plans and carries out the day-to-day work of the office independently, referring only very unusual office problems to the supervisor or other staff. Much of the work cannot be reviewed in detail. The supervisory review is to ensure that the work of the office is processed promptly and completely in accordance with established priorities.

Factor 3. Guidelines—Level 3-2—125 points

Guides include office instructions concerning such matters as correspondence format and controls, the format and content of files such as executive inventory files, and processing travel vouchers. Guides also include standing, unwritten instructions concerning such matters as which member of the staff will handle various assignments.

The incumbent is responsible for knowing which guide applies, referring problems to the supervisor when they clearly are not covered by existing guides.

Factor 4. Complexity—Level 4-2—75 points

Employee performs full range of procedural duties in support of the office, including such duties as arranging travel and conferences for staff and providing for following up on requests for information. Decisions regarding what needs to be done involve various choices requiring the secretary to recognize the existence of and differences among clearly recognizable situations.

Actions to be taken or responses to be made differ in such things as the sources of information, the kind of transaction or entries, or other readily verifiable differences.

Factor 5. Scope and Effect—Level 5-2—75 points

The purpose of the work is to carry out specific procedures. The work affects the accuracy and reliability of further processes.

Factor 6. Personal Contacts—Level 6-2—25 points

Contacts are with employees at all levels within the Department and with candidates for Department supergrade positions.

Factor 7. Purpose of Contacts—Level 7-2—50 points

Contacts are to give and obtain information; to set up meetings or arrange travel; and to ensure that correspondence, reports, and recruiting cases are completed within deadlines.

Factor 8. Physical Demands—Level 8-1—5 points

No special physical qualifications are required to perform the work. The work requires the ability to move around the office and carry light items such as the office files.

Factor 9. Work Environment—Level 9-1—5 points

The work is performed in offices and meeting rooms.

TOTAL POINTS—985

Appendix I

SAMPLE APPLICATION PACKETS

GS-0318-05 Secretary Position

The application excerpts in this chapter illustrate ways to complete the more demanding blocks on an application packet. For the secretary application and the social science analyst position, we show how work experiences would be described using the SF 171, the OF 612, and a resume. Some of the information has been changed to avoid mentioning real employers. Notice the importance of specifying in short, clear sentences, the tasks done on the job. Clarity is important.

The secretary application (Lynn Murdock) illustrates the way to specify, in detail, tasks done in earlier jobs. Also see the way skills and accomplishments are reported.

WORK EXPERIENCE *If you have no work experience, write "NONE" in A below and go to 25 on page 3.*

23 May we ask your present employer about your character, qualifications and work record? *A "NO" will not affect our review of your qualifications. If you answer "NO" and we need to contact your present employer before we can offer you a job, we will contact you first.* .... | **YES** | **NO** |
| | | X |

24 READ **WORK EXPERIENCE** IN THE INSTRUCTIONS BEFORE YOU BEGIN.

- Describe your current or most recent job in Block A and work backwards, describing each job you held during the past 10 years. If you were unemployed for longer than 3 months within the past 10 years, list the dates and your address(es) in an experience block.

- You may sum up in one block work that you did more than 10 years ago. But if that work is related to the type of job you are applying for, describe each related job in a separate block.

- INCLUDE VOLUNTEER WORK *(non-paid work)*---If the work *(or a part of the work)* is like the job you are applying for, complete all parts of the experience block just as you would for a paying job. You may receive credit for work experience with religious, community, welfare, service, and other organizations.

- INCLUDE MILITARY SERVICE--You should complete all parts of the experience block just as you would for a non-military job, including all supervisory experience. Describe each major change of duties or responsibilities in a separate experience block.

- IF YOU NEED MORE SPACE TO DESCRIBE A JOB--Use sheets of paper the same size as this page (be sure to include all information we ask for in A and B below). On each sheet show your name, Social Security Number, and the announcement number or job title.

- IF YOU NEED MORE EXPERIENCE BLOCKS, use the SF 171-A or a sheet of paper.

- IF YOU NEED TO UPDATE (ADD MORE RECENT JOBS), use the SF 172 or a sheet of paper as described above.

A Name and address of employer's organization *(include ZIP Code, if known)*

Hunderley Office Systems
2322 Union Avenue
Binghamton, N.Y., 13672

| Dates employed *(give month, day and year)* | Average number of hours per week | Number of employees you supervise |
| From: Jun '90 To: current | 40 | 0 |

Salary or earnings	Your reason for wanting to leave
Starting $ 14,500 per year	Seeking challenging
Ending $ 18,232 per year	work

Your immediate supervisor
Name: Karen Thompson | Area Code: 607 | Telephone No.: 555-1212 | Exact title of your job: Secretary

If Federal employment *(civilian or military)* list series, grade or rank, and, if promoted in this job, the date of your last promotion

Description of work: Describe your specific duties, responsibilities and accomplishments in this job, including the job title(s) of any employees you supervised. *If you describe more than one type of work (for example, carpentry and painting, or personnel and budget), write the approximate percentage of time you spent doing each.*

I am secretary for the Vice President for Operations. I am the only secretary for a group of eight people. I handle all routine correspondence for the office, as well as other tasks assigned by the VP.

DUTIES:

Using an electric typewriter, I am responsible for setting up memo formats and typing memos from handwritten drafts prepared by any of eight professionals. I have to translate the drafts into a standard company memo format. After typing the memo, I have to proofread (and correct any errors if found), and type the memo. After typing the memo, I have to proofread it, again correcting any errors, before submitting a final copy for signature. I am required to work with minimal direction from either my boss or from the professionals in the office.

I also prepare four types of reports: two quarterly, one annual, one as needed by my VP.

The two quarterly reports are an expenditures report and an activities report. Using spreadsheets provided by the accounting office plus worksheets supplied by the people in

(continued on the supplemental information sheet)

For Agency Use (skill codes, etc.)

B Name and address of employer's organization *(include ZIP Code, if known)*

Accurate Systems, Inc.
656 King Street
Elmira, N.Y., 14845

| Dates employed *(give month, day and year)* | Average number of hours per week | Number of employees you supervised |
| From: July 88 To: June 90 | 20 | 0 |

Salary or earnings	Your reason for leaving
Starting $ 2.85 per hour	Wanted a full time
Ending $ 3.50 per hour	job

Your immediate supervisor
Name: Jack Kenton | Area Code: 607 | Telephone No.: 555-2121 | Exact title of your job: Helper

If Federal employment *(civilian or military)* list series, grade or rank, and, if promoted in this job, the date of your last promotion

Description of work: Describe your specific duties, responsibilities and accomplishments in this job, including the job title(s) of any employees you supervised. *If you describe more than one type of work (for example, carpentry and painting, or personnel and budget), write the approximate percentage of time you spent doing each.*

I worked 4 hours a day in a small computer company as helper to both the secretary and the company president.

I used a thermofax machine to make roughly 30 overhead transparencies or briefing slides per month. I had to take material prepared by the secretary and make the transparencies and organize them for presentation. I also used a Xerox to make paper copies of the slides. I collated and stapled them together with a cover page.

During briefings, (two to ten a week) I would work the overhead projector while the president briefed the slides.

About 80 percent of my time was spent preparing correspondence for mailing. I had to match letters with envelopes, and put the letters and attachments into the envelopes, seal them and mail them.

When the secretary was out of the office, I worked as receptionist, answering the phones and taking messages and greeting people who wanted to see the president. I did this one hour a day each week.

For Agency Use (skill codes, etc.)

Page 2 IF YOU NEED MORE EXPERIENCE BLOCKS, USE SF 171-A *(SEE BACK OF INSTRUCTION PAGE).*

SUPPLEMENTAL INFORMATION SHEET FOR SF 171

SUPPLEMENTAL INFORMATION:

1. Name (Last, First, Middle Initial) Murdock, Lynn	2. SSN 555-12-3456
3. Job Title/Announcement Number Ann. # E/NWS93-008A.CFH, Secretary GS-0318-05	4. Date

Continuation of Block 24A

the office. I have to work closely with the other staff to correctly match expenses and projects. The activities report is a typed list of work done by the Division. Everyone contributes a list of work done and time spent on the projects; I use a electric typewriter to compile their reports.

The annual report is prepared in pen by the VP. I type the report for her, proofread it, check for errors, then submit a draft copy to her. If she approves the draft, I type the final copy in a standard company format.

I also prepare, when asked, a report of jobs sent into the division and their due dates. I developed a log sheet to keep track of such correspondence.

I was given a special bonus last Christmas (1992) for a form I made last year. I designed a telephone solicitation form which reduced the average time spent with customers from five to three minutes, saving the company approximately $70 per hour of solicitation.

To simplify the making of quarterly reports, I wrote a three page booklet, "Office Procedures", which tells the Sales Reps what they have to do to order supplies or have me type their correspondence or complete the various reports we do.

We recently obtained a microcomputer in the office. I am taking classes at night to learn how to use it. My VP says that if I can put anything on it to help the office, I can use the computer.

I also maintain central files for the Division; past quarterly reports, travel records, annual reports and so on. I am responsible for organizing four filing cabinets and regularly cleaning out old files. I check with the VP and the Sales Reps before I remove any old files.

I am also the receptionist for the Division. I answer the phone, take messages for people in the Division, and transfer calls. When people come into the office, I am the first person they meet. I direct them to the right place.

I also type about 40 letters a week for the Division. After I type them on the electric typewriter, I have to check for spelling errors and typos. Draft copies go back to the writer; if that person ok's the draft, then I type the final version, get the writer's signature and mail the letter.

When company mail comes into the Division, I screen the material for any due dates; I keep a log of correspondence and due dates. After the VP reads the correspondence and assigns it to a Sales Rep, I log the name of the item, who it's from, who has it, and when it is due. At the beginning of each week, I check the log. If a Rep has something due that week, I remind the Rep when it is due.

I go to an office supply store once a month or so to buy office supplies. I have a signature card at the store. They bill the company directly. I have to make a list of office supplies, needed, then get them at the store.

I handle an appointment book for the VP. When she has to go to a meeting or someone wants to meet with her, I check the schedule book, make appointments, and notify her. I have to coordinate a calendar on her desk with the appointment book so both have the same schedules.

SUPPLEMENTAL INFORMATION SHEET FOR SF 171

SUPPLEMENTAL INFORMATION:

1. Name (Last, First, Middle Initial) Murdock, Lynn	2. SSN 555-12-3456
3. Job Title/Announcement Number Ann. # E/NWS93-008A .CFH, Secretary GS-0318-05	4.Date

Block 32

Special Skills:

I worked on an IBM Selectric since July, 1988. I can change the ribbon and the type ball on it.

I worked on several different copy machines since July, 1988. I know how to collate, change toner, add paper, and fix jammed machines. I've also used several other types of office equipment, including a collator, a hole punch, and a paper cutter.

In my first job, at Accurate Systems, Inc., at least once a month I made about 30 overhead transparencies on a thermofax machine. The secretary typed the masters, I made the transparencies. Then I used the transparencies to Xerox about fifteen paper copies of the briefing slides or transparencies. I had to collate and staple these into a booklet to be handed out at briefings.

Since late January, 1993, I have been studying computers at the junior college. I am taking a course in Word Perfect and another in Lotus. I know how to prepare and print a letter in Word Perfect and how to set up a simple spreadsheet in Lotus.

Accomplishments:

I designed a log sheet at Hunderley Office Systems to keep track of correspondence and requests for help coming into the division.

Last Christmas (1992) I was given a special cash bonus for another form I designed. This one is for telephone solicitations by our Sales Reps. Because of the way it is set up, they save about two minutes when they call customers and the VP said that saves the company about $70 per hour of solicitation per Sales Rep.

Last summer (1992), I wrote a small three page booklet, "Office Procedures" for the Sales Reps. This tells them how to order supplies, the procedure to have me type their letters, and other things to make our work easier.

I was class valedictorian at Millard Filmore High School in 1988.

Form Approved
OMB No. 3206-0219

OPTIONAL APPLICATION FOR FEDERAL EMPLOYMENT - OF 612

You may apply for most jobs with a resume, this form, or other written format. If your resume or application does not provide all the information requested on this form and in the job vacancy announcement, you may lose consideration for a job.

1 Job title in announcement	**2** Grade(s) applying for	**3** Announcement number
Secretary	GS-0318-05	E/NWS93-008A

4 Last name	First and middle names	**5** Social Security Number
MURDOCK	Lynn	555-12-3456

6 Mailing address		**7** Phone numbers (include area code)
324 Grove Street		Daytime 703/555-4231

City	State	ZIP Code	
Binghampton	NY	12333	Evening 703/555-1234

WORK EXPERIENCE

8 Describe your paid and nonpaid work experience related to the job for which you are applying. Do **not** attach job descriptions.

1) Job title (if Federal, include series and grade)

Secretary

From (MM/YY)	To (MM/YY)	Salary	per	Hours per week
June '90	current	$ 18,232	year	40

Employer's name and address	Supervisor's name and phone number
Hunderley Office Systems	Karen Thompson
2322 Union Avenue Binghampton, N.Y., 13672	607 555-1212

Describe your duties and accomplishments

I am secretary for the Vice President for Operations. I am the only secretary for a group of eight people. I handle all routine correspondence for the office, as well as other tasks assigned by the VP.

DUTIES:

Using an electric typewriter, I am responsible for setting up memo formats and typing memos from handwritten drafts prepared by any of eight professionals. I have to translate the drafts into a standard company memo format. After typing the memo, I have to proofread (and correct any errors if found), and type the memo. After typing the memo, I have to proofread it, again correcting any errors, before submitting a final copy for signature.

Continued on a Separate Page

2) Job title (if Federal, include series and grade)

Helper

From (MM/YY)	To (MM/YY)	Salary	per	Hours per week
July 88	June 90	$ 3.50	hour	20

Employer's name and address	Supervisor's name and phone number
Accurate Systems, Inc.	Jack Kenton
656 King Street Elmira, New York, 14845	607 555-2121

Describe your duties and accomplishments

I worked 4 hours a day in a small computer company as helper to both the secretary and the company president.

I used a thermofax machine to make roughly 30 overhead transparencies or briefing slides per month. I had to take material prepared by the secretary and make the transparencies and organize them for presentation. I also used a Xerox to make paper copies of the slides. I collated and stapled them together with a cover page.

During briefings, (two to ten a week) I would work the overhead projector while the president briefed the slides.

About 80 percent of my time was spent preparing correspondence for mailing. I had to match letters with

Continued on a Separate Page

9 May we contact your current supervisor?

YES [X] NO [ ] ▸ If we need to contact your current supervisor before making an offer, we will contact you first.

EDUCATION

10 Mark highest level completed. **Some HS** [ ] **HS/GED** [X] **Associate** [ ] **Bachelor** [ ] **Master** [ ] **Doctoral** [ ]

11 Last high school (HS) or GED school. Give the school's name, city, State, ZIP Code (if known), and year diploma or GED received.

Ottumwa Central High School 06/82

12 Colleges and universities attended. Do **not** attach a copy of your transcript unless requested.

| Name | | | Total Credits Earned | | Major(s) | Degree - Year |
			Semester	Quarter		(if any) Received
1)						
City	State	ZIP Code				
2)						
3)						

OTHER QUALIFICATIONS

13 **Job-related** training courses (give title and year). **Job-related** skills (other languages, computer software/hardware, tools, machinery, typing speed, etc.). **Job-related** certificates and licenses (current only). **Job-related** honors, awards, and special accomplishments (publications, memberships in professional/honor societies, leadership activities, public speaking, and performance awards). Give dates, but do **not** send documents unless requested.

Other Courses or Training

Name: Word Perfect

Location: Cardill Associates, Binghampton, NY

From: 1/ 93 To: 2/93

Classroom Hours: 30

Subjects: Word Perfect

Continued on a Separate Page

GENERAL

14 Are you a U.S. citizen? YES [X] NO [ ] ▸ Give the country of your citizenship.

15 Do you claim veterans' preference? NO [X] YES [ ] ▸ Mark your claim of 5 or 10 points below.

5 points [ ] ▸ Attach your DD 214 or other proof. **10 points** [ ] ▸ Attach an *Application for 10-Point Veterans' Preference* (SF 15) and proof required

16 Were you ever a Federal civilian employee?

		Series	Grade	From (MM/YY)	To (MM/YY)

NO [X] YES [ ] ▸ For highest civilian grade give:

17 Are you eligible for reinstatement based on career or career-conditional Federal status?

NO [X] YES [ ] ▸ If requested, attach SF 50 proof.

APPLICANT CERTIFICATION

18 **I certify** that, to the best of my knowledge and belief, all of the information on and attached to this application is true, correct, complete and made in good faith. **I understand** that false or fraudulent information on or attached to this application may be grounds for not hiring me or for firing me after I begin work, and may be punishable by fine or imprisonment. **I understand** that any information I give may be investigated.

SIGNATURE   **DATE SIGNED**

Work Experience Continuation

MURDOCK, Lynn
Secretary

1) Secretary - Page 1
E/NWS93-008A

555-12-3456

GS-0318-05

I am required to work with minimal direction from either my boss or from the professionals in the office.

I also prepare four types of reports: two quarterly, one annual, one as needed by my VP.

The two quarterly reports are an expenditures report and an activities report. Using spreadsheets provided by the accounting office plus worksheets supplied by the people in the office, I have to work closely with the other staff to correctly match expenses and projects. The activities report is a typed list of work done by the Division. Everyone contributes a list of work done and time spent on the projects; I use a electric typewriter to compile their reports.

The annual report is prepared in pen by the VP. I type the report for her, proofread it, check for errors, then submit a draft copy to her. If she approves the draft, I type the final copy in a standard company format.

I also prepare, when asked, a report of jobs sent into the division and their due dates. I developed a log sheet to keep track of such correspondence.

I was given a special bonus last Christmas (1992) for a form I made last year. I designed a telephone solicitation form which reduced the average time spent with customers from five to three minutes, saving the company approximately $70 per hour of solicitation.

To simplify the making of quarterly reports, I wrote a three page booklet, "Office Procedures", which tells the Sales Reps what they have to do to order supplies or have me type their correspondence or complete the various reports we do.

We recently obtained a microcomputer in the office. I am taking classes at night to learn how to use it. My boss says that if I can put anything on it to help the office, I can use the computer.

I also maintain central files for the Division; past quarterly reports, travel records, annual reports and so on. I am responsible for organizing four filing cabinets and regularly cleaning out old files. I check with the VP and the Sales Reps before I remove any old files.

I am also the receptionist for the Division. I answer the phone, take messages for people in the Division, and transfer calls. When people come into the office, I am the first person they meet. I direct them to the right place.

I also type about 40 letters a week for the Division. After I type them on the electric typewriter, I have to check for spelling errors and typos. Draft copies go back to the writer; if that person ok's the draft, then I type the final version, get the writer's signature and mail the letter.

When company mail comes into the Division, I screen the material for any due dates; I keep a log of correspondence and due dates. After the VP reads the correspondence and assigns it to a Sales Rep, I log the name of the item, who it's from, who has it, and when it is due. At the beginning of each week, I check the log. If a Rep has something due that week, I remind the Rep that it is due.

I go to an office supply store once a month or so to buy office supplies. I have a signature card at the store. They bill the company directly. I have to make a list of office supplies, needed, then get them at the store.

I handle an appointment book for the VP. When she has to go to a meeting or someone wants to meet with her, I check the schedule book, make appointments, and notify her. I have to coordinate a calendar on her desk with the appointment book so both have the same schedules.

Work Experience Continuation

MURDOCK, Lynn
Secretary

2) Helper - Page 1
E/NWS93-008A

555-12-3456
GS-0318-05

envelopes, and put the letters and attachments into the envelopes, seal them and mail them.

When the secretary was out of the office, I worked as a receptionist, answering the phones and taking messages and greeting people who wanted to see the president. I did this one hour a day each week.

OF 612 Continuation Page

MURDOCK, Lynn

Secretary

Page 1

E/NWS93-008A

555-12-3456

GS-0318-05

Question 13 - Other Qualifications

Name: Introduction to LOTUS 1-2-3
Location: Cardill Associates, Binghampton, NY

From: 4/93 To: 4/93

Classroom Hours: 35

Subjects: LOTUS 1-2-3

<u>**Typing Speed**</u>
95 Words Per Minute

<u>**Dictation Speed**</u>
25 Words Per Minute

<u>**SKILLS, ACCOMPLISHMENTS AND AWARDS**</u>

Christmas, 1992, I received a $100 bonus for making a telephone solicitation form which reduced the average time spent with customers from five to three minutes, saving the company approximately $70 per hour of solicitation.

Special Skills:
  I worked on an IBM Selectric since July, 1988. I can change the ribbon and the type ball on it.
  I worked on several different copy machines since July, 1988. I know how to collate, change tone, add paper, and fix jammed machines. I have also used several other types of office equiopment, including a collator, a hole punch, and a paper cutter.
  In my first job, at Accurate Systems, Inc., at least once a month I made about 30 overhead transparencies on a thermofax machine. The secretary typed the masters, I made the slides or transparencies. I had to collate and stapel these into a booklet to be handed out at the briefings.
  Since January, 1993, I have been studying computers at the junior college. I am taking a course in Word Perfect and another in Lotus. I know how to prepare and print a letter in Word Perfect and how to set up a simple spreadsheet in Lotus.

Accomplishments:
  I designed a log sheet at Hunderley Office Systems to keep track of correspondence and requests for help
Continued on Next Page

OF 612 Continuation Page

MURDOCK, Lynn
Secretary

Page 2
E/NWS93-008A

555-12-3456
GS-0318-05

Question 13 - Other Qualifications

coming into the Division.

I got a cash bonus in 1993 for creating a form to help telephone solicitors.

Last summer, 1992, I wrote a small three page booklet, "Office Procedures", for the Sales Reps. This tells them how to order supplies, the procedure to have me type their letters, and other things to make our work easier.

I was class valedictorian at Ottumwa Central High School in 1982.

Continued on Next Page

Lynn MURDOCK

555-12-3456
324 Grove Street
Binghampton, NY 12333
Daytime: 703/555-4231   Evening: 703/555-1234

Objective

Position as Secretary, GS-0318-05, announcement number E/NWS93-008A

Employment

Secretary,   June '90 to current
Hunderley Office Systems
2322 Union Avenue Binghampton, N.Y., 13672
Karen Thompson, 607 555-1212   Permission to Contact

Duties and Accomplishments:
I am secretary for the Vice President for Operations. I am the only secretary for a group of eight people. I handle all routine correspondence for the office, as well as other tasks assigned by the VP.
DUTIES:
  Using an electric typewriter, I am responsible for setting up memo formats and typing memos from handwritten drafts prepared by any of eight professionals. I have to translate the drafts into a standard company memo format. After typing the memo, I have to proofread (and correct any errors if found), and type the memo. After typing the memo, I have to proofread it, again correcting any errors, before submitting a final copy for signature. I am required to work with minimal direction from either my boss or from the professionals in the office.
  I also prepare four types of reports: two quarterly, one annual, one as needed by my VP.
  The two quarterly reports are an expenditures report and an activities report. Using spreadsheets provided by the accounting office plus worksheets supplied by the people in the office, I have to work closely with the other staff to correctly match expenses and projects. The activities report is a typed list of work done by the Division. Everyone contributes a list of work done and time spent on the projects; I use a electric typewriter to compile their reports.
  The annual report is prepared in pen by the VP. I type the report for her, proofread it, check for errors, then submit a draft copy to her. If she approves the draft, I type the final copy in a standard company format.
  I also prepare, when asked, a report of jobs sent into the division and their due dates. I developed a log sheet to keep track of such correspondence.
  I was given a special bonus last Christmas (1992) for a form I made last year. I designed a telephone solicitation form which reduced the average time spent with customers from five to three minutes, saving the company approximately $70 per hour of solicitation.

To simplify the making of quarterly reports, I wrote a three page booklet, "Office Procedures", which tells the Sales Reps what they have to do to order supplies or have me type their correspondence or complete the various reports we do.

We recently obtained a microcomputer in the office. I am taking classes at night to learn how to use it. My boss says that if I can put anything on it to help the office, I can use the computer.

I also maintain central files for the Division; past quarterly reports, travel records, annual reports and so on. I am responsible for organizing four filing cabinets and regularly cleaning out old files. I check with the VP and the Sales Reps before I remove any old files.

I am also the receptionist for the Division. I answer the phone, take messages for people in the Division, and transfer calls. When people come into the office, I am the first person they meet. I direct them to the right place.

I also type about 40 letters a week for the Division. After I type them on the electric typewriter, I have to check for spelling errors and typos. Draft copies go back to the writer; if that person ok's the draft, then I type the final version, get the writer's signature and mail the letter.

When company mail comes into the Division, I screen the material for any due dates; I keep a log of correspondence and due dates. After the VP reads the correspondence and assigns it to a Sales Rep, I log the name of the item, who it's from, who has it, and when it is due. At the beginning of each week, I check the log. If a Rep has something due that week, I remind the Rep that it is due.

I go to an office supply store once a month or so to buy office supplies. I have a signature card at the store. They bill the company directly. I have to make a list of office supplies, needed, then get them at the store.

I handle an appointment book for the VP. When she has to go to a meeting or someone wants to meet with her, I check the schedule book, make appointments, and notify her. I have to coordinate a calendar on her desk with the appointment book so both have the same schedules.

$18,232 per year Hours per week: 40

Helper,   July 88 to June 90

Accurate Systems, Inc.
656 King Street Elmira, New York, 14845
Jack Kenton, 607 555-2121

Duties and Accomplishments:
I worked 4 hours a day in a small computer company as helper to both the secretary and the company president.

I used a thermofax machine to make roughly 30 overhead transparencies or briefing slides per month. I had to take material prepared by the secretary and make the transparencies and organize them for presentation. I also used a Xerox to make paper copies of the slides. I collated and stapled them together with a cover page.

During briefings, (two to ten a week) I would work the overhead projector while the president briefed the slides.

About 80 percent of my time was spent preparing correspondence for mailing. I had to match letters with envelopes, and put the letters and attachments into the envelopes, seal them and mail them.

When the secretary was out of the office, I worked as a receptionist, answering the phones and taking messages and greeting people who wanted to see the president. I did this one hour a day each week.

$3.50 per hour Hours per week: 20

Education

Highest Level Completed: High School/GED

Ottumwa Central High School 06/82

Other Qualifications

Other Courses or Training
Name: Word Perfect
Location: Cardill Associates, Binghampton, NY

From: 1/ 93 To: 2/93

Classroom Hours: 30

Subjects: Word Perfect

Name: Introduction to LOTUS 1-2-3
Location: Cardill Associates, Binghampton, NY

From: 4/93 To: 4/93

Classroom Hours: 35

Subjects: LOTUS 1-2-3

Typing Speed
95 Words Per Minute

Dictation Speed
25 Words Per Minute

SKILLS, ACCOMPLISHMENTS AND AWARDS

Christmas, 1992, I received a $100 bonus for making a telephone solicitation form which reduced the average time spent with customers from five to three minutes, saving the company approximately $70 per hour of solicitation.

Special Skills:
 I worked on an IBM Selectric since July, 1988. I can change the ribbon and the type ball on it.
 I worked on several different copy machines since July, 1988. I know how to collate, change tone, add paper, and fix jammed machines. I have also used several other types of office equiopment, including a collator, a hole punch, and a paper cutter.
 In my first job, at Accurate Systems, Inc., at least once a month I made about 30 overhead transparencies on a thermofax machine. The secretary typed the masters, I made the slides or transparencies. I had to collate and stapel these into a booklet to be handed out at the briefings.
 Since January, 1993, I have been studying computers at the junior college. I am taking a course in Word Perfect and another in Lotus. I know how to prepare and print a letter in Word Perfect and how to set up a simple spreadsheet in Lotus.

Accomplishments:
 I designed a log sheet at Hunderley Office Systems to keep track of correspondence and requests for help coming into the Division.
 I got a cash bonus in 1993 for creating a form to help telephone solicitors.
 Last summer, 1992, I wrote a small three page booklet, "Office Procedures", for the Sales Reps. This tells them how to order supplies, the procedure to have me type their letters, and other things to make our work easier.
 I was class valedictorian at Ottumwa Central High School in 1982.

Personal Information

U.S. citizen
No Veterans' Preference
Never Federally Employed
Not eligible for reinstatement (based on career or career-conditional Federal status).

Applicant Certification

I certify that, to the best of my knowledge and belief, all of the information on and attached to this application is true, correct, complete and made in good faith. I understand that false or fraudulent information on or attached to this application may be grounds for not hiring me or for firing me after I begin work, and may be punishable by fine or imprisonment. I understand that any information I give may be investigated.

SIGNATURE   DATE SIGNED

GS-0101-13 Social Science Analyst Position

This application (Harold M. Ramey) is from a current federal employee seeking to move laterally to a grade 11 position based on work done outside the federal government. Note the use of publications in the three different forms.

(Harold M. Ramey)

WORK EXPERIENCE *If you have no work experience, write "NONE" in A below and go to 25 on page 3.*

23 May we ask your present employer about your character, qualifications and work record? *A "NO" will not affect our review of your qualifications. If you answer "NO" and we need to contact your present employer before we can offer you a job, we will contact you first.* ....

YES	NO
X	

24 READ WORK EXPERIENCE IN THE INSTRUCTIONS BEFORE YOU BEGIN.

- Describe your current or most recent job in Block A and work backwards, describing each job you held during the past 10 years. If you were unemployed for longer than 3 months within the past 10 years, list the dates and your address(es) in an experience block.

- You may sum up in one block work that you did more than 10 years ago. But if that work is related to the type of job you are applying for, describe each related job in a separate block.

- INCLUDE VOLUNTEER WORK *(non-paid work)*---If the work *(or a part of the work)* is like the job you are applying for, complete all parts of the experience block just as you would for a paying job. You may receive credit for work experience with religious, community, welfare, service, and other organizations.

- INCLUDE MILITARY SERVICE--You should complete all parts of the experience block just as you would for a non-military job, including all supervisory experience. Describe each major change of duties or responsibilities in a separate experience block.

- IF YOU NEED MORE SPACE TO DESCRIBE A JOB--Use sheets of paper the same size as this page (be sure to include all information we ask for in A and B below). On each sheet show your name, Social Security Number, and the announcement number or job title.

- IF YOU NEED MORE EXPERIENCE BLOCKS, use the SF 171-A or a sheet of paper.

- IF YOU NEED TO UPDATE (ADD MORE RECENT JOBS), use the SF 172 or a sheet of paper as described above.

A Name and address of employer's organization *(include ZIP Code, if known)*

Office of the Naval Inspector General
Analysis Branch, Inspections Division
XXX Richmond Highway
Crystal City, VA, 22302

Dates employed *(give month, day and year)*	Average number of hours per week	Number of employees you supervise
From: 11/92 To: current	40	0
Salary or earnings	Your reason for wanting to leave	
Starting $ 34,744 per year	Not what I expected	
Ending $ 34,744 per year		

Your immediate supervisor			Exact title of your job	If Federal employment *(civilian or military)* list series, grade or rank, and, if promoted in this job, the date of your last promotion
Name	Area Code	Telephone No.	Management Analyst	
CDR M. Scott	703	555-1212	GS-0343-11, Step 2	newly hired

Description of work: Describe your specific duties, responsibilities and accomplishments in this job, including the job title(s) of any employees you supervised. *If you describe more than one type of work (for example, carpentry and painting, or personnel and budget), write the approximate percentage of time you spent doing each.*

My position requires me to assist officers in inspection general activities. As yet, I have not participated in any activities; all my time has been spent in training activities for my job, including 3 months at IG school and two months at the Defense Systems Management college at Ft. Belvoir, VA.

For Agency Use (skill codes, etc.)

B Name and address of employer's organization *(include ZIP Code, if known)*

Office of Analysis
Illinois Dept. of Commerce & Industry
617 Broad St.
Springfield, IL 62702

Dates employed *(give month, day and year)*	Average number of hours per week	Number of employees you supervised
From: 4/84 To: 9/92	40+	2+
Salary or earnings	Your reason for leaving	
Starting $ 30,000 per year	Wife got a job in	
Ending $ 38,500 per year	the D.C. area	

Your immediate supervisor			Exact title of your job	If Federal employment *(civilian or military)* list series, grade or rank, and, if promoted in this job, the date of your last promotion
Name	Area Code	Telephone No.	Senior Analyst	
Ms. C. Wilson	217	555-1717		

Description of work: Describe your specific duties, responsibilities and accomplishments in this job, including the job title(s) of any employees you supervised. *If you describe more than one type of work (for example, carpentry and painting, or personnel and budget), write the approximate percentage of time you spent doing each.*

(see description on the continuation sheet)

For Agency Use (skill codes, etc.)

Page 2 IF YOU NEED MORE EXPERIENCE BLOCKS, USE SF 171-A *(SEE BACK OF INSTRUCTION PAGE).*

Standard Form 171-A–*Continuation Sheet for SF 171*

Form Approved
OMB No. 3206-0012

● Attach all SF 171-A's to your application at the top of page 3.

1. Name *(Last, First, Middle Initial)*	2. Social Security Number
Ramey, Harold M.	555-12-3456

3. Job Title or Announcement Number You Are Applying For	4. Date Completed
Ann. No. 33-93BB, Social Science Analyst, GS-101-11	

ADDITIONAL WORK EXPERIENCE BLOCKS

C — Name and address of employer's organization *(include ZIP Code, if known)*

Dept. of Sociology
Northern Illinois University
DeKalb, Illinois, 60115

Dates employed *(give month, day and year)*	Average number of hours per week	Number of employees you supervised
From: 9/81 To: 1/84	20	0

Salary or earnings	Your reason for leaving
Starting $ 550 per month	Graduated
Ending $ 550 per month	

Your immediate supervisor			Exact title of your job	If Federal employment *(civilian or military)* list series, grade or rank, and, if promoted in this job, the date of your last promotion
Name	Area Code	Telephone No.	Graduate Research/	
Dr. Thomas M Ladd	817	555-1212	Teaching Assistant	

Description of work: Describe your specific duties, responsibilities and accomplishments in this job, including the job title(s) of any employees you supervised. *If you describe more than one type of work (for example, carpentry and painting, or personnel and budget), write the approximate percentage of time you spent doing each.*

Served as a grad assistant for Dr. Ladd, both in the classroom and during a field research project in Thailand.
Classroom duties included conducting one or more lectures a month in undergraduate sociology courses; I had to make a lesson plan, present the lecture, answer questions from students, and prepare multiple choice questions about my lectures for exams. I also distributed materials in classes for Dr. Ladd, advised students about his class, helped grade some exams, and other duties as assigned by Dr. Ladd.
The three month research project in Thailand, funded by the World Bank, was to study bank officers' knowledge of international commercial agreements. My duties were to interview bank officers throughout Thailand; following a nine page interview guide, I had to ask them questions and record their answers. I interviewed roughly seventy Thai officials during the period. When we returned to Illinois, I assisted Dr. Ladd in transfering the information to a microcomputer for analysis. Under his general guidance, I processed the data using Lotus 1-2-3.

For Agency Use (skill codes, etc.)

Name and address of employer's organization *(include ZIP Code, if known)*	Dates employed *(give month, day and year)*	Average number of hours per week	Number of employees you supervised
	From: To:		
	Salary or earnings	Your reason for leaving	
	Starting $ per		
	Ending $ per		

Your immediate supervisor			Exact title of your job	If Federal employment *(civilian or military)* list series, grade or rank, and, if promoted in this job, the date of your last promotion
Name	Area Code	Telephone No.		

Description of work: Describe your specific duties, responsibilities and accomplishments in this job, including the job title(s) of any employees you supervised. *If you describe more than one type of work (for example, carpentry and painting, or personnel and budget), write the approximate percentage of time you spent doing each.*

For Agency Use (skill codes, etc.)

SUPPLEMENTAL INFORMATION SHEET FOR SF 171

SUPPLEMENTAL INFORMATION:

1. Name (Last, First, Middle Initial) Ramey, Harold M.	2. SSN 555-12-3456
3. Job Title/Announcement Number Ann. No. 33-93BB, Social Science Analyst, GS-101-11	4. Date

Continuation of Block 24 B:

(90% of workload)   I served as a team leader conducting studies and analyses of various business issues for the Illinois Department of Commerce & Industry. The Office Director would normally assign one or more analyst, junior analysts or interns to be on my team. As a team leader, I had to select the methodology to use, develop a study plan, and describe in detail how the data would be collected and analyzed. As team leader, I had to make work assignments for the people on the team, monitor their performance to ensure that their work accomplished the team's project, provide feedback on their performance, and provide guidance on ways to make their efforts more useful to the team. I also had primary responsibility for the final reports which resulted from our research.

After the plan was approved, I was responsible for executing the study plan. I directed and supervised my team member's data collection efforts.

After the data was collected, we would encode the data for analysis on desktop microcomputers. Depending on the nature of the study, analyses were done using SPSS-PC, dBase IV, or Lotus 1-2-3.

As team leader, I was primarily responsible for the final report. Normally, some of the report writing would be done by my team members, then in group discussions we would prepare the gist of the final report which I then would write and sometimes brief to members of the state government.

Approximately 30 percent of our studies consisted of business surveys. We would identify a sample of industries or business activities within the state for our analysis. Another 65 percent of our studies involved studies of business trends, economic indicators, and so forth, which we would then use to make a mathematical model to study and forecast future trends. Around 5 percent of the studies I did involved library research of historical data for other states (e.g., the death of the steel industry in the "rustbelt").

(10% of workload)   An additional duty was to train new staff members in survey research methods used in our office. We had about two new analysts per year, plus two to four summer research interns from the University of Illinois. At the beginning of each summer session, I would spend a week training regular and temporary staff in survey methods, sampling theory, and hypothesis testing so they would understand how we worked. I also taught them the rudiments of using SPSS-PC and Lotus 1-2-3.

I also had to report regularly to the Director about the performance of people working on my teams. This was to assist her in conducting performance appraisals, discipline, and dispensing awards to people in the Office.

SUPPLEMENTAL INFORMATION SHEET FOR SF 171

SUPPLEMENTAL INFORMATION:

1. Name (Last, First, Middle Initial) Ramey, Harold M.	2. SSN 555-12-3456
3. Job Title/Announcement Number Ann. No. 33-93BB, Social Science Analyst, GS-101-11	4. Date

SUPPLEMENTAL EXPERIENCE STATEMENT

KSA#1. <u>Ability to design and execute personnel surveys using state-of-the-art survey techniques.</u> Between September 1981 and January 1984, I completed a Master of Arts degree in Sociology. During that time, I had two graduate courses on Survey Research. Also during that time, as a Graduate Assistant for Dr. Ladd, I assisted him in two survey research projects. In the first project, a study of Muslim entrepreneurs in Malaysia, I took his data collection forms and transferred much of the information to card image for analysis on the university's mainframe computer using the <u>SPSS</u> statistical package. I constructed contingency tables and did rank-order correlations of his data. My second project with him included a trip to Thailand in the summer of 1983 to study banks outside of Bangkok. Using a fifteen page interview guide prepared by Dr. Ladd, I interviewed approximately seventy Thai officials. Upon return to the US, I again transferred much of this data to a computer for analysis using <u>SPSS</u>.

At the Illinois Office of Analysis (1984 through 1992), I was a senior analyst. I worked on, then led numerous teams studying a variety of business and economic issues in the state, or issues affecting the state's economy. Using lists of Illinois businesses, for example, several studies required me to draw a random sample of firms, then send questionnaires to the firms. From 1987 through 1992, I was a team leader and hence, responsible for designing questionnaires, determining sampling methodology, selecting the sample from state lists, supervising the mailing of questionnaires, supervising the encoding of returned questionnaires for analysis, supervising the analysis of data, and preparing the final report.

Three studies concerned personnel issues (one on equal employment opportunities, two on pay); one of the studies on pay was published in <u>Illinois Economics</u>.

KSA#2. <u>Ability to analyze survey data using computer statistical packages such as SAS, SPSS, dBase III and Lotus</u>. I have analyzed survey data using the mainframe and the PC versions of SPSS since early 1982. This included transferring data from questionnaires or interview guides to a computer format (card image on a mainframe or delimited ASCII for the PC), checking the quality of the data, and conducting statistical analyses.

While working for the State of Illinois, our office regularly used all the other packages (except SAS) to process data, prepare graphs, and to maintain databases. We shifted to dBase IV in 1991 but much of that package is compatible with dBase III.

Among the analyses I have done: crosstabulations (SPSS), Spearman and Kendall's tau correlations (SPSS), and single and multiple linear regressions (SPSS and Lotus). We used the data base not for statistical analyses, but as a data base. Lotus was extensively used to make graphs and charts.

(Sheets for other KSAs follow; they are not reproduced here)

SUPPLEMENTAL INFORMATION SHEET FOR SF 171

SUPPLEMENTAL INFORMATION:

1. Name (Last, First, Middle Initial) Ramey, Harold M.	2. SSN 555-12-3456
3. Job Title/Announcement Number Ann. No. 33-93BB, Social Science Analyst, GS-101-11	4. Date

Block 32:

Awards:

Hubert M. Blalock Award for Distinguished Research, Department of Sociology, Northern Illinois University, DeKalb, Illinois, 1983, for research conducted in Thailand.

Exceptional Performance Award, Illinois Department of Commerce and Industry, 1989 and 1991, for research projects conducted in the state of Illinois.

Publications:

"Minority Salary Trends in the Agricultural Sector of Illinois," Illinois Economics, XXV, August 1991, 325-45.

"Steel Industry Retrenchments in Ohio and Indiana", Illinois Economics, XXIII, May, 1989, 110-147.

"Migrant Labor", Illinois Business Trends Newsletter, January 1988.

"Surplus Corn and Export Tariffs", Illinois Business Trends Newsletter, May 1987.

"Intercity Freight Rates and Drayage Costs" Illinois Business Trends Newsletter, February 1986.

Form Approved
OMB No. 3206-0219

OPTIONAL APPLICATION FOR FEDERAL EMPLOYMENT - OF 612

You may apply for most jobs with a resume, this form, or other written format. If your resume or application does not provide all the information requested on this form and in the job vacancy announcement, you may lose consideration for a job.

1 Job title in announcement	2 Grade(s) applying for	3 Announcement number
Social Science Analyst	GS-101-11	33-93BB

4 Last name	First and middle names	5 Social Security Number
RAMEY	Harold M.	555-12-3456

6 Mailing address
4513 Hamilton Drive

City	State	ZIP Code
Dale City	VA	22334-3311

7 Phone numbers (include area code)

Daytime /

Evening 703/555-2233

WORK EXPERIENCE

8 Describe your paid and nonpaid work experience related to the job for which you are applying. Do **not** attach job descriptions.

1) Job title (if Federal, include series and grade)

Management Analyst GS-0343-11, Step 2

From (MM/YY)	To (MM/YY)	Salary	per	Hours per week
11/92	current	$34,744	year	40

Employer's name and address	Supervisor's name and phone number
Office of the Naval Inspector General	CDR M. Scott
Analysis Branch, Inspections Division Crystal City, VA 22302	703 555-1212

Describe your duties and accomplishments

My position requires me to assist officers in inspector general activities. As yet, I have not participated in any activities; all my time has been spent in training activities for my job, including 3 months at IG school and two months at the Defense Systems Management College at Ft. Belvoir, VA.

2) Job title (if Federal, include series and grade)

Senior Analyst

From (MM/YY)	To (MM/YY)	Salary	per	Hours per week
4/84	9/92	$38,500	year	40+

Employer's name and address	Supervisor's name and phone number
Office of Analysis	Ms. C. Wilson
Illinois Dept. of Commerce & Industry Springfield, IL 62702	217 555-3232

Describe your duties and accomplishments

(see description on the continuation sheet)

9 May we contact your current supervisor?

YES [X] NO [   ] ▸ If we need to contact your current supervisor before making an offer, we will contact you first.

EDUCATION

10 Mark highest level completed. **Some HS** [   ] **HS/GED** [X] **Associate** [   ] **Bachelor** [   ] **Master** [   ] **Doctoral** [   ]

11 Last high school (HS) or GED school. Give the school's name, city, State, ZIP Code (if known), and year diploma or GED received.

Joseph P. Kennedy, Boston, MA 6//76

12 Colleges and universities attended. Do **not** attach a copy of your transcript unless requested.

Name				Total Credits Earned		Major(s)	Degree - Year
				Semester	Quarter		(if any) Received
1) Northern Illinois University							
City		State	ZIP Code				
DeKalb		IL	60115	30			MA 1/81
2) Boston College							
Boston		MA		132			BA
3)							

OTHER QUALIFICATIONS

13 **Job-related** training courses (give title and year). **Job-related** skills (other languages, computer software/hardware, tools, machinery, typing speed, etc.). **Job-related** certificates and licenses (current only). **Job-related** honors, awards, and special accomplishments (publications, memberships in professional/honor societies, leadership activities, public speaking, and performance awards). Give dates, but do **not** send documents unless requested.

<u>Chief Undergraduate Subjects</u>
Subject: Economics
Semester: 36
Quarter:

Subject: Sociology
Semester: 12
Quarter:

Subject: Political Science
Semester: 12
Quarter:

Continued on a Separate Page

GENERAL

14 Are you a U.S. citizen? YES [X] NO [   ] ▸ Give the country of your citizenship. _____

15 Do you claim veterans' preference? NO [X] YES [   ] ▸ Mark your claim of 5 or 10 points below.

5 points [   ] ▸ Attach your DD 214 or other proof. **10 points** [   ] ▸ Attach an *Application for 10-Point Veterans' Preference* (SF 15) and proof required

16 Were you ever a Federal civilian employee?

	Series	Grade	From (MM/YY)	To (MM/YY)
NO [ ] YES [X] ▸ For highest civilian grade give:	343	11	11/92	current

17 Are you eligible for reinstatement based on career or career-conditional Federal status?

NO [X] YES [   ] ▸ If requested, attach SF 50 proof.

APPLICANT CERTIFICATION

18 **I certify** that, to the best of my knowledge and belief, all of the information on and attached to this application is true, correct, complete and made in good faith. **I understand** that false or fraudulent information on or attached to this application may be grounds for not hiring me or for firing me after I begin work, and may be punishable by fine or imprisonment. **I understand** that any information I give may be investigated.

SIGNATURE   **DATE SIGNED**

ADDITIONAL WORK EXPERIENCES

RAMEY, Harold M.
Social Science Analyst
33-93BB
555-12-3456
GS-101-11

3) Job title (if Federal, include series and grade)

Graduate Research/Teaching Assistant

From (MM/YY)	To (MM/YY)	Salary	per	Hours per week
9/81	1/84	$ 550	month	20

Employer's name and address	Supervisor's name and phone number
Dept. of Sociology	Dr. Thomas M. Ladd
Northern Illinois University DeKalb, IL 60115	817 555-1122

Describe your duties and accomplishments

Served as a grad assistant for Dr. Ladd, both in the classroom and during a field research project in Thailand.

Classroom duties included conducting one or more lectures a month in undergraduate sociology courses; I had to make a lesson plan, present the lecture, answer questions from students, and prepare multiple choice questions about my lectures for exams. I also distributed materials in classes for Dr. Ladd, advised students about his class, helped grade some exams, and other duties as assigned by Dr. Ladd.

The three month research project in Thailand, funded by the World Bank, was to study bank officers' knowledge of international commercial agreements. My duties were to ask them questions (in Thai) and record their answers. I interviewed roughly seventy Thai officials during the period. When we returned to Illinois, I assisted Dr. Ladd in transfering the information to a microcomputer for analysis. Under his general guidance, I processed the data using Lotus 1-2-3 (I made data summary tables, frequency counts, and some simple correlations and linear regressions).

4) Job title (if Federal, include series and grade)

From (MM/YY)	To (MM/YY)	Salary	per	Hours per week
		$		

Employer's name and address	Supervisor's name and phone number

Describe your duties and accomplishments

Question 13 - Other Qualifications

Chief Graduate Subjects
Subject: Sociology
Semester: 24
Quarter:

Subject: Research Methods
Semester: 9
Quarter:

Other Courses or Training
Name:
Location:

From: / To: /

Classroom Hours:

Subjects:

Name:
Location:

From: / To: /

Classroom Hours:

Subjects:

Language:

Continued on Next Page

OF 612 Continuation Page

RAMEY, Harold M.
Social Science Analyst

Page 1
33-93BB

555-12-3456
GS-101-11

Question 13 - Other Qualifications

Chief Graduate Subjects
Subject: Sociology
Semester: 24
Quarter:

Subject: Research Methods
Semester: 9
Quarter:

Other Courses or Training
Name:
Location:

From: / To: /

Classroom Hours:

Subjects:

Name:
Location:

From: / To: /

Classroom Hours:

Subjects:

Language:

Continued on Next Page

OF 612 Continuation Page
Page 2
33-93BB

RAMEY, Harold M.
Social Science Analyst

555-12-3456
GS-101-11

Question 13 - Other Qualifications

Thai
Can prepare and give lectures fluently.
Can prepare and give lectures with difficulty.
Can speak and understand fluently.
Can speak and understand passably.
Can translate articles into English
Can translate articles from English.
Can read articles for own use easily.
Can read articles for own use with difficulty.

Language:

Can prepare and give lectures fluently.
Can prepare and give lectures with difficulty.
Can speak and understand fluently.
Can speak and understand passably.
Can translate articles into English
Can translate articles from English.
Can read articles for own use easily.
Can read articles for own use with difficulty.

MANUAL CONTINUATION PAGES

(Continuation of Block 8, Part 2)

(90% of workload) I served as a team leader conducting studies and analyses of various business issues for the Illinois Department of Commerce & Industry. The Office Director would normally assign one or more analyst, junior analyst, or interns to be on my team. As team leader, I had to select the methodology to use, develop a study plan, and describe in detail how the data would be collected and analyzed. As a team leader, I had to make work assignments for the people on the team, monitor their performance, and provide guidance on ways to make their efforts more useful for the team. I also had primary responsibility for the final reports which resulted from our research.

After the plan was approved, I was responsible for executing the study plan. I directed and supervised my team members' data collection efforts.

After the data was collected we would encode the data for analysis on desktop microcomputers. Depending on the nature of the study, analyses were done by me using SPSS-PC, dBase IV or Lotus 1-2-3.

As team leader, I was primarily responsible for the final report. Normally some of the report writing would be done by my team members; then in group discussions we would prepare the gist of the final report which I then would write and sometimes brief to members of the state government.

Approximately 30 percent of our studies consisted of business surveys. We would identify a sample of industries or business activities within the state for our analysis. Another 65 percent of our studies involved

Continued on Next Page

OF 612 Continuation Page

RAMEY, Harold M.
Social Science Analyst

Page 3
33-93BB

555-12-3456
GS-101-11

Question 13 - Other Qualifications

studies of business trends, economic indicators and so forth, which we would then use to make a mathmatical model to study and forecast future trends. Around 5 percent of the studies I did involved library research of historical data for other states (e.g., the death of the steel industry in the "rustbelt").

(10% of workload) An additional duty was to train new staff members in survey research methods used in our office. We had about two new analysts per year, plus two to four summer research interns from the University of Illinois. At the beginning of each summer session, I would spend a week training regular and temporary staff in survey methods, samplling theory, and hypothesis testing so they would understand how we worked. I also taught them the rudiments of using SPSS-PC and Lotus 1-2-3.

I also had to report regularly to the Director about the performance of people working on my teams. This was to assist her in conducting performance appraisals, discipline, and dispensing awards to people in the office.

(Continuation of Block 13):

Awards:
Hubert M. Blalock Award for Distinguished Research, Department of Sociology, Northern Illinois university, DeKalb, Ill., 1983, for research conducted in Thailand.
Exceptional Performance Award, Illinois Department of Commerce & Industry, 1989 and 1991, for research projects conducted in the state of Illinois.

Publications:
"Minority Salary Trends in the Agricultural Sector of Illinois," Illinois Economics, XXV, August 1991, 325-45.
"Steel Industry Retrenchments in Ohio and Indiana," Illinois Economics, XXIII, May, 1989, 110-147.
"Migrant Labor," Illinois Business Trends Newsletter, January, 1988.
"Surplus Corn and Export Tariffs," Illinois Business Trends Newsletter, May, 1987.
"Intercity Freight Rates and Drayage Costs," Illinois Business Trends Newsletter, February, 1986.

Continued on Next Page

Harold M. RAMEY

555-12-3456

4513 Hamilton Drive
Dale City, VA 22334-3311
Daytime: / Evening: 703/555-2233

Objective

Position as Social Science Analyst, GS-101-11, announcement number 33-93BB

Employment

Management Analyst GS-0343-11, Step 2,   11/92 to current

Office of the Naval Inspector General
Analysis Branch, Inspections Division   Crystal City, VA 22302
CDR M. Scott, 703 555-1212   Permission to Contact

Duties and Accomplishments:
My position requires me to assist officers in inspector general activities. As yet, I have not participated in any activities; all my time has been spent in training activities for my job, including 3 months at IG school and two months at the Defense Systems Management College at Ft. Belvoir, VA.

$34,744 per year Hours per week: 40

Senior Analyst,   4/84 to 9/92

Office of Analysis
Illinois Dept. of Commerce & Industry   Springfield, IL 62702
Ms. C. Wilson, 217 555-3232

$38,500 per year Hours per week: 40+

Graduate Research/Teaching Assistant,   9/81 to 1/84

Dept. of Sociology
Northern Illinois University DeKalb, IL 60115
Dr. Thomas M. Ladd, 817 555-1122

Duties and Accomplishments:
Served as a grad assistant for Dr. Ladd, both in the classroom and during a field research project in Thailand.

Classroom duties included conducting one or more lectures a month in undergraduate sociology courses; I had to make a lesson plan, present the lecture, answer questions from students, and prepare multiple choice questions about my lectures for exams. I also distributed materials in classes for Dr. Ladd, advised students about his class, helped grade some exams, and other duties as assigned by Dr. Ladd.

The three month research project in Thailand, funded by the World Bank, was to study bank officers' knowledge of international commercial agreements. My duties were to ask them questions (in Thai) and record their answers. I interviewed roughly seventy Thai officials during the period. When we returned to Illinois, I assisted Dr. Ladd in transfering the information to a microcomputer for analysis. Under his general guidance, I processed the data using <u>Lotus 1-2-3</u> (I made data summary tables, frequency counts, and some simple correlations and linear regressions).

$550 per month Hours per week: 20

Education

Highest Level Completed: High School/GED

Northern Illinois University
DeKalb IL, 60115
MA 1/81
Semester Hours: 30

Boston College
Boston MA
BA
Semester Hours: 132

Joseph P. Kennedy, Boston, MA 6//76

Other Qualifications

Chief Undergraduate Subjects
Subject: Economics
Semester: 36
Quarter:

Subject: Sociology
Semester: 12
Quarter:

Subject: Political Science
Semester: 12
Quarter:

Chief Graduate Subjects
Subject: Sociology
Semester: 24
Quarter:

Subject: Research Methods
Semester: 9
Quarter:

Other Courses or Training
Name:
Location:

From: / To: /

Classroom Hours:

Subjects:

Name:
Location:

From: / To: /

Classroom Hours:

Subjects:

Language:
Thai
Can prepare and give lectures fluently.
Can prepare and give lectures with difficulty.
Can speak and understand fluently.
Can speak and understand passably.
Can translate articles into English
Can translate articles from English.
Can read articles for own use easily.
Can read articles for own use with difficulty.

Language:

Can prepare and give lectures fluently.
Can prepare and give lectures with difficulty.
Can speak and understand fluently.
Can speak and understand passably.
Can translate articles into English
Can translate articles from English.
Can read articles for own use easily.
Can read articles for own use with difficulty.

MANUAL CONTINUATION PAGES

(Continuation of Block 24B)

(90% of workload) I served as a team leader conducting studies and analyses of various business issues for the Illinois Department of Commerce & Industry. The Office Director would normally assign one or more analyst, junior analyst, or interns to be on my team. As team leader, I had to select the methodology to use, develop a study plan, and describe in detail how the data would be collected and analyzed. As a team leader, I had to make work assignments for the people on the team, monitor their performance, and provide guidance on ways to make their efforts more useful for the team. I also had primary responsibility for the final reports which resulted from our research.

After the plan was approved, I was responsible for executing the study plan. I directed and supervised my team members' data collection efforts.

After the data was collected we would encode the data for analysis on desktop microcomputers. Depending on the nature of the study, analyses were done by me using SPSS-PC, dBase IV or Lotus 1-2-3.

As team leader, I was primarily responsible for the final report. Normally some of the report writing would be done by my team members; then in group discussions we would prepare the gist of the final report which I then would write and sometimes brief to members of the state government.

Approximately 30 percent of our studies consisted of business surveys. We would identify a sample of industries or business activities within the state for our analysis. Another 65 percent of our studies involved studies of business trends, economic indicators and so forth, which we would then use to make a mathmatical model to study and forecast future trends. Around 5 percent of the studies I did involved library research of historical data for other states (e.g., the death of the steel industry in the "rustbelt").

(10% of workload) An additional duty was to train new staff members in survey research methods used in our office. We had about two new analysts per year, plus two to four summer research interns from the University of Illinois. At the beginning of each summer session, I would spend a week training regular and temporary staff in survey methods, samplling theory, and hypothesis testing so they would understand how we worked. I also taught them the rudiments of using SPSS-PC and Lotus 1-2-3.

I also had to report regularly to the Director about the performance of people working on my teams. This was to assist her in conducting performance appraisals, discipline, and dispensing awards to people in the office.

(Block 32):

Awards:
Hubert M. Blalock Award for Distinguished Research, Department of Sociology, Northern Illinois university, DeKalb, Ill., 1983, for research conducted in Thailand.

Exceptional Performance Award, Illinois Department of Commerce & Industry, 1989 and 1991, for research projects conducted in the state of Illinois.

Publications:
"Minority Salary Trends in the Agricultural Sector of Illinois," Illinois Economics, XXV, August 1991, 325-45.

"Steel Industry Retrenchments in Ohio and Indiana," Illinois Economics, XXIII, May, 1989, 110-147.

"Migrant Labor," Illinois Business Trends Newsletter, January, 1988.

"Surplus Corn and Export Tariffs," <u>Illinois Business Trends Newsletter</u>, May, 1987.
"Intercity Freight Rates and Drayage Costs," <u>Illinois Business Trends Newsletter</u>, February, 1986.

Personal Information

U.S. citizen
No Veterans' Preference
Highest Series: 343   Highest Grade: 11   From: 11/92   To: current
Not eligible for reinstatement (based on career or career-conditional Federal status).

Applicant Certification

I certify that, to the best of my knowledge and belief, all of the information on and attached to this application is true, correct, complete and made in good faith. I understand that false or fraudulent information on or attached to this application may be grounds for not hiring me or for firing me after I begin work, and may be punishable by fine or imprisonment. I understand that any information I give may be investigated.

SIGNATURE   DATE SIGNED

WG-3502-02 Laborer Position

This application package excerpt (Jack K. Cook) shows more detail in completing KSAOs or KSAs for a position. Even though the position has a very low grade, attention to detail makes this application stand out from others.

WORK EXPERIENCE *If you have no work experience, write "NONE" in A below and go to 25 on page 3.*

23 May we ask your present employer about your character, qualifications and work record? *A "NO" will not affect our review of your qualifications. If you answer "NO" and we need to contact your present employer before we can offer you a job, we will contact you first.* ....

	YES	NO
	X	

24 READ **WORK EXPERIENCE** IN THE INSTRUCTIONS BEFORE YOU BEGIN.

- Describe your current or most recent job in Block A and work backwards, describing each job you held during the past 10 years. If you were unemployed for longer than 3 months within the past 10 years, list the dates and your address(es) in an experience block.
- You may sum up in one block work that you did more than 10 years ago. But if that work **is related** to the type of job you are applying for, describe each related job in a separate block.
- INCLUDE VOLUNTEER WORK *(non-paid work)*---If the work *(or a part of the work)* **is like the job** you are applying for, complete all parts of the experience block just as you would for a paying job. You may receive credit for work experience with religious, community, welfare, service, and other organizations.

- INCLUDE MILITARY SERVICE--You should complete all parts of the experience block just as you would for a non-military job, including all supervisory experience. Describe each major change of duties or responsibilities in a separate experience block.
- IF YOU NEED MORE SPACE TO DESCRIBE A JOB--Use sheets of paper the same size as this page (be sure to include all information we ask for in A and B below). On each sheet show your name, Social Security Number, and the announcement number or job title.
- IF YOU NEED MORE EXPERIENCE BLOCKS, use the SF 171-A or a sheet of paper.
- IF YOU NEED TO UPDATE (ADD MORE RECENT JOBS), use the SF 172 or a sheet of paper as described above.

A Name and address of employer's organization *(include ZIP Code, if known)*

7 Sarduccis Moving Company
636 South Pickett Street
Alexandria, VA, 22334

Dates employed *(give month, day and year)*	Average number of hours per week	Number of employees you supervise
From: 11/87 To: now	40	0

Salary or earnings	Your reason for wanting to leave
Starting $ 7.25 per hour	Want better benefits
Ending $ 8.55 per hour	

Your immediate supervisor Name	Area Code	Telephone No.	Exact title of your job	If Federal employment *(civilian or military)* list series, grade or rank, and, if promoted in this job, the date of your last promotion
Mike Cavazos	703	555-1515	Day laborer	

Description of work: Describe your specific duties, responsibilities and accomplishments in this job, **including** the job title(s) of any employees you supervised. *If you describe more than one type of work (for example, carpentry and painting, or personnel and budget), write the approximate percentage of time you spent doing each.*

I have been with the company since 1987 as a day laborer. When I work in the warehouse, I help the forklift driver load pallets on trucks. I sweep the aisles and keep stuff away from the front of the forklift and loading docks. I have to work all day cleaning the work area, removing old packing materials, and helping the driver with pallets.

Sometimes, I have had to open crates for people. I use a wire cutter to snap the wire bands around the crates. I reseal crates if people want that.

Sometimes I go out with a driver. I help unload the trailer. We usually spend all day unloading stuff at peoples houses or we go to a lot of businesses to drop off packages and crates.

The foreman tells all the day laborers where they will work at the start of the shift. Then he checks on us from time to time during the shift to see if we are doing the work.

For Agency Use (skill codes, etc.)

B Name and address of employer's organization *(include ZIP Code, if known)*

St. Elizabeth's Hospital
3255 Jackson Street
Roanoke, VA, 24019

Dates employed *(give month, day and year)*	Average number of hours per week	Number of employees you supervised
From: 4/69 To: 11/87	40	0

Salary or earnings	Your reason for leaving
Starting $ 3.45 per hour	More pay; moved to
Ending $ 4.55 per hour	Alexandria

Your immediate supervisor Name	Area Code	Telephone No.	Exact title of your job	If Federal employment *(civilian or military)* list series, grade or rank, and, if promoted in this job, the date of your last promotion
Clem Higgins	703	992-9999	Janitor	

Description of work: Describe your specific duties, responsibilities and accomplishments in this job, **including** the job title(s) of any employees you supervised. *If you describe more than one type of work (for example, carpentry and painting, or personnel and budget), write the approximate percentage of time you spent doing each.*

I worked nights as janitor. I had to empty trash cans in the offices, mop floors, and sometimes carry medical trash to the medical trash container.

When I begin my shift, I had to load my cart with cleaning materials (cleaners, mop, sponges, clean towels for the bathrooms, other stuff). Then I would go floor by floor, emptying trash cans, cleaning counters and windows, bathrooms, and other public areas. I did not have to go into patient rooms (day shift did that).

After cleaning, I would get the mop and bucket and wash floors in hallways and public areas. Sometimes I would get the buffer and wax floors too.

At the end of shift, I had to take bags of dirty laundry to the laundry room.

I had a beeper. The night head nurse would call me if they needed me. I had a checklist of things to do. As I did things on the list, I checked them off. Once in a while, I had to do things for nurses like move beds.

For Agency Use (skill codes, etc.)

Page 2 IF YOU NEED MORE EXPERIENCE BLOCKS, USE SF 171-A *(SEE BACK OF INSTRUCTION PAGE)*.

SUPPLEMENTAL INFORMATION SHEET FOR SF 171

SUPPLEMENTAL INFORMATION:

1. Name (Last, First, Middle Initial) Cook, Jack K.	2. SSN 123-45-9999
3. Job Title/Announcement Number Announcement 3/93, Laborer, WG-3502-02	4. Date

Qualification Requirements:

1) Ability to do the work without more than normal supervision.

In both jobs I have held since high school I have worked without much supervision. At the hospital, I had a list of things to do each night. I had them completed when the foreman came in at 7 in the morning. I could do them all unless the chief nurse had a lot of lifting and other work for me to do to help the nurses.

At the moving company, the foreman would assign laborers to work at the docks or in the warehouse or to ride the trucks. Again, I worked with limited supervision to complete my tasks.

2) Ability to follow simple oral and written instructions.

At the hospital, I had a clipboard, with four or five pages of things to do. As I did each one, I checked it off. If I saw a problem, I'd write it on one of the sheets and give it to the foreman when he came in. Sometimes the head nurse would beep me. I would help them do big cleanups, move beds and heavy items, mop up accidents and other jobs. Mostly the work was heavy lifting or cleanup.

At the moving company, there were no written instructions. The foreman just gave us jobs and we would complete them. The office would send orders out to the warehouse or dock telling us what we had to do. On the trucks, the driver knew where to go and would tell me what to unload. The last half hour of each shift was cleanup. If I worked in the warehouse, I had to sweep the lanes and clean the shelf areas, and haul trash out to the dumpster.

3) Ability to lift or carry objects weighing 80-85 pounds.

Sometimes the trash bags at the hospital got pretty heavy but I don't know how much they weighed. The laundry bags were also heavy and must have weighed eighty pounds. I would lift them into a cart. The floor buffer was also heavy. I had to drag that around when I buffed the floors.

At the moving company, any box over 100 pounds was left on a pallet and moved by fork lift or hand truck. Smaller packages were put on shelves and the laborers had to move them. Wherever I worked, I usually had to lift these packages. In the warehouse, I'd carry them maybe five feet to a wagon to haul to the dock. If I worked on the dock, I'd have to carry the boxes ten or twenty feet to a truck. When I worked on the trucks and had to take boxes to customers the distance was often greater.

4) Ability to use and maintain tools and equipment such as hand and power saws, drill motors, simple hand tools, etc.

SUPPLEMENTAL INFORMATION SHEET FOR SF 171

SUPPLEMENTAL INFORMATION:

1. Name (Last, First, Middle Initial)	2. SSN
Cook, Jack K.	123-45-9999
3. Job Title/Announcement Number	4. Date
Announcement 3/93, Laborer, WG-3502-02	

At the hospital, I operated and changed cloths on a floor buffer.

At the moving company, I used small pusher type fork lifts to lift heavy boxes.

I also have a lot of tools at home (in Roanoke). I used to do my own car tuneups and would help my dad work on wood for fences or the addition to the house. I had to work with a router and a sander and with several saws. I also worked with other power tools such as drills. I know how to change blades on a saw, how to change drill bits. I worked with small power tools at home from about 1966 until I left Roanoke in 1987.

5) Ability to work safely.

I have never been injured on the job and have never filed for workmen's comp. At the moving company, I got an award twice for no sick days in 1989 and 1991.

Block 32

Special Skills:

I did wood work with my dad for about twenty years, making cabinets for the house as well as building an addition to the house.

I rebuilt the engine on my '57 Chevy in 1970, rebored it, and put on a blower. I did most of this in my garage at home using our own power tools.

Accomplishments:

I got awards at the moving company in 1989 and 1991 for not taking any leave for illness.

At the hospital, in April, 1973, I got employee of the month award.

GS-346-14, Logistics Management Specialist Position

This SF 171 (Holly Davidson) is an individual's "master" form. No KSAO pages are attached until a specific position is sought (the KSAOs will be listed with the position's announcement). The individual wants to remain in this job series with the Department of the Army, therefore the use of jargon should not cause a problem. All the Army 346-series jobs will have KSAOs which address most of the special Army programs she lists in her employment history.

Like many senior federal employees, this person has had a number of very specialized training courses. These are listed as part of her Block 31.

(Holly Davidson)

WORK EXPERIENCE *If you have no work experience, write "NONE" in A below and go to 25 on page 3.*

23 May we ask your present employer about your character, qualifications and work record? A *"NO"* will not affect our review of your qualifications. If you answer *"NO"* and we need to contact your present employer before we can offer you a job, we will contact you first. ....

	YES	NO
	X	

24 READ **WORK EXPERIENCE** IN THE INSTRUCTIONS BEFORE YOU BEGIN.

- Describe your current or most recent job in Block A and work backwards, describing each job you held during the past 10 years. If you were unemployed for longer than 3 months within the past 10 years, list the dates and your address(es) in an experience block.

- You may sum up in one block work that you did more than 10 years ago. But if that work is related to the type of job you are applying for, describe each related job in a separate block.

- INCLUDE VOLUNTEER WORK *(non-paid work)*---If the work *(or a part of the work)* is like the job you are applying for, complete all parts of the experience block just as you would for a paying job. You may receive credit for work experience with religious, community, welfare, service, and other organizations.

- INCLUDE MILITARY SERVICE--You should complete all parts of the experience block just as you would for a non-military job, including all supervisory experience. Describe each major change of duties or responsibilities in a separate experience block.

- IF YOU NEED MORE SPACE TO DESCRIBE A JOB--Use sheets of paper the same size as this page (be sure to include all information we ask for in **A** and **B** below). On each sheet show your name, Social Security Number, and the announcement number or job title.

- IF YOU NEED MORE EXPERIENCE BLOCKS, use the SF 171-A or a sheet of paper.

- IF YOU NEED TO UPDATE (ADD MORE RECENT JOBS), use the SF 172 or a sheet of paper as described above.

A | Name and address of employer's organization *(include ZIP Code, if known)* | Dates employed *(give month, day and year)* | Average number of hours per week | Number of employees you supervise |
|---|---|---|---|

US Army XXX Command
ATTN: XXX-P
5000 Patton Avenue
Alexandria, VA 22333

From: 3 Jun 85 To: current | 40 | 0

Salary or earnings | Your reason for wanting to leave

Starting $ 41,277 per year
Ending $ 61,141 per year | Seeking a supervisor position

Your immediate supervisor Name	Area Code	Telephone No.	Exact title of your job	If Federal employment *(civilian or military)* list series, grade or rank, and, if promoted in this job, the date of your last promotion
Ms. P. Hanks	703	555-2121	Logistics Management Specialist	GS-346-14

Description of work: Describe your specific duties, responsibilities and accomplishments in this job, including the job title(s) of any employees you supervised. *If you describe more than one type of work (for example, carpentry and painting, or personnel and budget), write the approximate percentage of time you spent doing each.*

Principle staff member of the Plans & Projects Div., Deputy Chief of Staff for Management (DCS-M), US Army XXX Command.

Principle staff member of the Concepts and Doctrine Division, Deputy Chief of Staff for Readiness (DCS-R), US Army XXX Command. This position was realigned from the DCS for Readiness to the DCS for Management in Nov, 1987; responsibilities remained the same.

In this position, I serve as a senior logistic management specialist and project leader with responsibility for the development and promulgation of Army-wide logistics concepts, doctrine, and policies involving the functions of supply, maintenance, transportation, procurement, services, and facilities.

(continued on supplement sheet)

For Agency Use (skill codes, etc.)

B | Name and address of employer's organization *(include ZIP Code, if known)* | Dates employed *(give month, day and year)* | Average number of hours per week | Number of employees you supervised |
|---|---|---|---|

US Army XXX Command
ATTN: XXY-PR
5000 Patton Avenue
Alexandria, VA 22333

From: Mar 85 To: Jun 85 | 40 | 13

Salary or earnings | Your reason for leaving

Starting $ 52,262 per year
Ending $ 52,262 per year | Incumbent returned from school

Your immediate supervisor Name	Area Code	Telephone No.	Exact title of your job	If Federal employment *(civilian or military)* list series, grade or rank, and, if promoted in this job, the date of your last promotion
COL W. King	703	555-2112	Supervisory Logistics Management Specialist	GM-346-15

Description of work: Describe your specific duties, responsibilities and accomplishments in this job, including the job title(s) of any employees you supervised. *If you describe more than one type of work (for example, carpentry and painting, or personnel and budget), write the approximate percentage of time you spent doing each.*

Temporary Branch Chief of the Mobilization Reserve Components Support Branch, Military Plans & Operations Division, DCS for Readiness in a position responsible for supervising 3 military officers and ten civilians.

In this position I was responsible for the command's mobilization planning and for the Reserve Components Support Program. Mobilization planning included responsibility for planning, coordinating, directing, supervising and reviewing Command mobilization planning to include implementation of DOD/JCS/DA guidance and directives to meet command mobilization requirements. The Reserve Components Support Program included overall coordination for RC mobilization planning, war planning, logistics assistance, unit training, and in conjunction with DCS for Personnel, reservist individual training.

(see continuation sheet)

For Agency Use (skill codes, etc.)

Page 2 IF YOU NEED MORE EXPERIENCE BLOCKS, USE SF 171-A *(SEE BACK OF INSTRUCTION PAGE)*.

SUPPLEMENTAL INFORMATION SHEET FOR SF 171

SUPPLEMENTAL INFORMATION:

1. Name (Last, First, Middle Initial) Davidson, Holly	2. SSN 334-55-6699
3. Job Title/Announcement Number Ann. # 345-92, Logistics Mgt Specialist, GS-346-14	4. Date

Continuation of Block 24 A:

I serve as project leader for the development and operation of the XXX Logistics 21 (LOG 21) Mission Area Analysis (MAA) study. The LOG 21 MAA is a structured program through which the missions, functions, and capabilities of XXX are compared against the logistics requirements of the Army as it evolves into the 21st century. The thrust of the program is to ensure that changes in logistics requirements are realistically planned for and programmed. I am responsible for the identification of deficiencies/technological opportunities which prohibit XXX from accomplishing its mission of supporting the Army in the field, for the prioritization of these issues, and for the identification of proponents and milestones for corrective actions.

As focal point for the LOG 21, I provide guidance, tasking and policy to the Major Subordinate Commands (MSCs), Separate Reporting Activities (SRAs), and HQ staff in re the biennial Mission Area Development Plan (MADP) submissions. I have full responsibility for administering and coordinating the subject matter expert prioritization process, for overall analysis, and for all other actions required for publication of the MADP.

I develop and implement concepts for the linkage of the LOG program with other similar programs such as the Internal Control/Materiel Weakness Program and the Military Construction, Army program.

I maintain and enhance the LOG 21 data base which consists of approximately 8 megabytes in INFORMIX software. I design and develop automated reports and tracking systems.

I participate in the XXX Military Construction, Army (MCA) Working Group representing LOG issues and the LOG prioritization process. I participate in the HQ prioritization of XXX MCA projects for funding.

I participate in the Logistics Research & Development (LOG R&D) Working Group by presenting logistics issues identified during the LOG process which require LOG R&D funding.

I serve as the DCS for Management representative on the HQ Resource Action Committee (RAC) and am responsible for defending all DCS funding actions. I am also the DCS point of contact for the coordination of all responses to Program Budget Decisions (PBDs) applicable to the DCS of Management. While in the DCS for Readiness I also served as the DCS for Readiness RAC member and was responsible for coordinating and defending all DCS funding actions.

While in the DCS for Readiness, I served as a Team Leader of GS-14 and GS-13 action officers responsible for coordinating the accomplishment of the LOG 21 process. I was responsible for distributing workload, developing workload priorities for the team, and for timely and satisfactory completion. I provided reports to the Division Chief for team members' performance standards, appraisals, awards and training needs.

For my efforts in this position, I received two Performance Awards of $500 ea. from the DCS for Management and an Exceptional and a Sustained Superior Performance Appraisal with a monetary award of $1500 from the DCS for Readiness. I also received Letters of Appreciation/Recognition from the Commanding General, XXX; the Chief of Staff, XXX; the Deputy for Management and Analysis, XXX; and the Inspector General, XXX for my participation in special Task Forces and my work in the LOG 21 program.

Standard Form 171-A–*Continuation Sheet for SF 171*

• Attach all SF 171-A's to your application at the top of page 3.

Form Approved
OMB No. 3206-0012

1. Name *(Last, First, Middle Initial)*

Davidson, Holly

2. Social Security Number

999-88-7654

3. Job Title or Announcement Number You Are Applying For

Ann. # 345-92, Logistics Mgt Specialist, GS-346-14

4. Date Completed

ADDITIONAL WORK EXPERIENCE BLOCKS

C

Name and address of employer's organization *(include ZIP Code, if known)*

US Army XXX Command
5000 Patton Avenue
Alexandria, VA 22333

Dates employed *(give month, day and year)*
From: Nov 82 To: Feb 85

Salary or earnings
Starting $41,277 per year
Ending $47,392 per year

Average number of hours per week 40

Number of employees you supervised 0

Your reason for leaving
Promotion to temporary GM-15

Your immediate supervisor

Name: Mr. J. Reno

Area Code: 703   Telephone No. 555-5555

Exact title of your job
Logistics Management Specialist

If Federal employment *(civilian or military)* list series, grade or rank, and, if promoted in this job, the date of your last promotion
GS-346-14

Description of work: Describe your specific duties, responsibilities and accomplishments in this job, including the job title(s) of any employees you supervised. *If you describe more than one type of work (for example, carpentry and painting, or personnel and budget), write the approximate percentage of time you spent doing each.*

Principle staff member of the Readiness Assistance Division, Deputy Chief of Staff (DCS) for Readiness, US Army XXX Command.

In this position, I served as a Team Leader in the Readiness Analysis Branch and was assigned full responsibility for basic evaluation and analysis of the readiness status of equipment of the Total Army and of the command-managed materiel base. As a team leader, I was responsible for coordinating subordinate technical specialists GS-13 and lower in accomplishment of above activities. This involved distributing workload, making assignments based on abilities, developing workload priorities and setting deadlines. I was responsible for coordinating over all work of the team and reviewed all work for timely and satisfactory completion. I also was required to provide input to the Branch Chief on subordinate employee performance standards, appraisals, and training needs.

(see continuation sheet)

For Agency Use (skill codes, etc.)

D

Name and address of employer's organization *(include ZIP Code, if known)*

US Army YYY Command
5000 Patton Avenue
Alexandria, VA 22333

Dates employed *(give month, day and year)*
From: May 82   To: Jan 83

Salary or earnings
Starting $33,586 per year
Ending $36,094 per year

Average number of hours per week 40

Number of employees you supervised 0

Your reason for leaving
Promotion to GS 14

Your immediate supervisor

Name: Mr. J. Reno

Area Code: 703   Telephone No. 555-5555

Exact title of your job
Logistics Management Specialist

If Federal employment *(civilian or military)* list series, grade or rank, and, if promoted in this job, the date of your last promotion
GS-346-13

Description of work: Describe your specific duties, responsibilities and accomplishments in this job, including the job title(s) of any employees you supervised. *If you describe more than one type of work (for example, carpentry and painting, or personnel and budget), write the approximate percentage of time you spent doing each.*

Principal staff member of the Readiness Analysis Branch, Readiness Assistance Division, Directorate for Readiness, US Army YYY Command.

In this position I served as a technical specialist evaluating and providing analyses of the wholesale logistics readiness of the US Army. I was the HQ focal point for the Total Logistics Readiness/Sustainability (TLR/S) Annual Assessment. I participated in the development of the HQDA TLR/S tasking directives and was the command's coordinator of the TLR/S Planning Conference. I provided guidance and direction to the command Major Subordinate Commands (MSCs)/Standard Report Activities, coordination and resolving critical problem areas impacting on meeting established milestones.

I was also the HQ focal point for the inventory and depot outloading portion of the command Readiness Evaluation System (DRES) and was successful in synchronizing the scenario and the computational methodology of the process with the TLR/S assessments.

(See continuation sheet)

For Agency Use (skill codes, etc.)

SUPPLEMENTAL INFORMATION SHEET FOR SF 171

SUPPLEMENTAL INFORMATION:

1. Name (Last, First, Middle Initial)	2. SSN
Davidson, Holly	334-55-6699
3. Job Title/Announcement Number	4. Date
Ann. # 345-92, Logistics Mgt Specialist, GS-346-14	

Continuation of Block 24 B:

As acting chief of a newly created branch, I organized the group into 3 teams and appointed team leaders to each. I was also successful in getting one GS-12 position upgraded to a GS-13 through a job audit. In coordination with the Division Chief, I interviewed and selected a GS-14 team leader to head up the mobilization team.

I served in the capacity of Division Chief during the chief's absence for conferences, meetings, TDY and leave with full authority to make necessary mission management decisions to accomplish the assigned mission of the division.

I was responsible for developing the planning, programming, budgeting, and execution system (PPBES) resource strategy category of mobilizing/deploying and for coordinating justification of the mobilization and employment management decision increment packages (MDEPs).

I provided direction and developed coordinated command policy and procedures for all command elements which interfaced with the Reserve components. This included coordinating the meetings of the Army Reserve Force Policy Committee and coordinating the resolutions and milestones directed by the Committee.

I provided direction and coordinated the efforts of the newly added analysis team. These efforts included developing a standardized automated process for developing the Class IX repair parts analyses in support of the OMNIBUS and Army Logistic Assessment scenarios and developing a concept for merging the XXX Readiness Evaluation System and the LOG 21 program.

Continuation of Block 24 C:

I also personally performed work similar to the subordinate technical specialists. I served as the XXX focal point of the DA sponsored Total Logistics Readiness Sustainability (TLR/S) assessment (also known as the Omnibus Army Logistics Assessment [ALA]). In this duty, I was responsible for ensuring that XXX's role in the assessment of the US Army's capability to deploy logistically ready forces and sustain the force in combat was consistent with HQDA defined scenarios. I coordinated and developed impact statements concerning the shortfall of critical repair parts and ammunition for major weapon systems for the purpose of influencing the annual Program Objective Memorandum (POM). As the HQ XXX representative to the annual TLR/S Planners Conference, I developed and provided guidance and direction to subordinate commands/activities with regard to tasking directives and milestone schedules.

I performed continuing analyses of logistic readiness data to determine progress against established objectives, isolating and identifying areas of potential and existing logistic shortfalls. These assessments included performing analyses of unit readiness and equipment operational readiness trend reports to determine equipment and repair parts shortages and other problems degrading logistics readiness. One such analysis was used to brief the new CINC USAREUR prior to his assignment to Europe.

I was the XXX focal point for the XXX portion of the DA sponsored Army Logistics Assessment (ALA). (The ALA was a Vice Chief of Staff of the Army approved annual assessment of the Army's capability to enter and sustain in multiple global scenarios.) It identified warfighting constraints in all logistical functional areas by scenario by timeframe in support of DOD warfighting guidance. The XXX portion provided a detailed analysis of the XXX materiel base readiness to go to war. I provided detailed assessment signed by the XXX Commander addressing what had been done in these areas, what was ongoing, and what remained to be done to fix logistic problems through the budget process of the ALA. This assessment was then integrated into the Army PPBES by HQDA for policy changes and corrective procurement action.

For my efforts during my assignment to this position, I received two Exceptional performance ratings.

Standard Form 171-A–*Continuation Sheet for SF 171*

Form Approved:
OMB No. 3206-0012

• Attach all SF 171-A's to your application at the top of page 3.

1. Name (Last, First, Middle Initial)	2. Social Security Number
Davidson, Holly	999-88-7654

3. Job Title or Announcement Number You Are Applying For	4. Date Completed
Ann. # 345-92, Logistics Mgt Specialist, GS-346-14	

ADDITIONAL WORK EXPERIENCE BLOCKS

E

Name and address of employer's organization (include ZIP Code, if known)	Dates employed (give month, day and year)	Average number of hours per week	Number of employees you supervised
US Army XXY Command 5000 Patton Avenue Alexandria, VA 22333	From: May 81 To: Jan 82	40	0
	Salary or earnings Starting $ 32,048 per year Ending $ 33,586 per year	Your reason for leaving Desired US Army Logistics position	

Your immediate supervisor Name	Area Code	Telephone No.	Exact title of your job	If Federal employment (civilian or military) list series, grade or rank, and, if promoted in this job, the date of your last promotion
Mr. R. Paulson	703	555-1122	Logistics Management Specialist	GS-346-13

Description of work: Describe your specific duties, responsibilities and accomplishments in this job, including the job title(s) of any employees you supervised. *If you describe more than one type of work (for example, carpentry and painting, or personnel and budget), write the approximate percentage of time you spent doing each.*

Principle staff member of the Plans Division, Plans and Systems Analysis Directorate, US Army WWW Center, US Army XXY Command.

In this position I was responsible for developing, staffing and implementing new and revised policy and procedures for the Army's total Security Assistance Program (Foreign Military Sales (FMS) and Military Assistance Program (MAP)). I developed, staffed and implemented new and revised policy and procedure guidance, both generated internally and directed by higher headquarters, to appropriate subordinate security assistance organizational elements. Guidance generated by higher headquarters often required interpretation and application to my Command's regulations and policy. I prepared implementing documents via regulations, letters of instruction, and memos or notices. Also, tasks included reviewing and evaluating recommendations and suggestions offered by users of the guidance developed by the command.

I reviewed and participated in discussions on matters relating to security assistance policies, systems, procedures, and practices, reports, letters, etc. impacting on security assistance mid/long-range planning.

For Agency Use (skill codes, etc.)

Name and address of employer's organization (include ZIP Code, if known)	Dates employed (give month, day and year)	Average number of hours per week	Number of employees you supervised
	From: To:		
	Salary or earnings Starting $ per Ending $ per	Your reason for leaving	

Your immediate supervisor Name	Area Code	Telephone No.	Exact title of your job	If Federal employment (civilian or military) list series, grade or rank, and, if promoted in this job, the date of your last promotion

Description of work: Describe your specific duties, responsibilities and accomplishments in this job, including the job title(s) of any employees you supervised. *If you describe more than one type of work (for example, carpentry and painting, or personnel and budget), write the approximate percentage of time you spent doing each.*

For Agency Use (skill codes, etc.)

SUPPLEMENTAL INFORMATION SHEET FOR SF 171

SUPPLEMENTAL INFORMATION:

1. Name (Last, First, Middle Initial) Davidson, Holly	2. SSN 334-55-6699
3. Job Title/Announcement Number Ann. # 345-92, Logistics Mgt Specialist, GS-346-14	4. Date

Continuation of Block 24 D:

I analyzed and evaluated unit and materiel readiness reports and reviewed combat and round-out unit logistics readiness reports to identify units which failed to achieve readiness goals. I determined Army logistics conditions and trends with respect to materiel and other associated readiness resources available for Theater War Reserves and identified actions required to resolve problems.

I conducted periodic visits to high, adjacent, and subordinate commands/activities to coordinate staff actions and provide consultants services to subordinate elements on policies and procedures regarding Army-wide logistic readiness.

For my performance in this position, I received an Exceptional Performance rating with a Quality Step Increase. I also received a Letter of Appreciation from the Chief, Logistic Plans and Analysis Division, Logistics Evaluation Agency, for my efforts in managing the command's portion of the TLR/S analysis.

Continuation of Block 24 E:

I participated in mobilization exercises, assessing required levels of war reserve assets and provided planning guidance to materiel subordinate commands.

I was the Army Security Assistance representative to a joint committee formed to study and resolve problems concerning Reports of Discrepancies (RODs).

Block 31 (Other schools or training):

Computer-Aided Acquisition & Logistics Support (CALS) training	Mar 91 (1 day)
Personnel Management for Supervisors	Mar 90 (5 days)
Introduction to Lotus 1/2/3	Dec 89 (2 days)
Introduction to Harvard Graphics	Jan 89 (2 days)
Expert Systems Overview	Sep 88 (3 days)
Human Behavior in Organizations	Mar 88 (5 days)
Force Integration Training	Oct 86 (4 days)
XXX HQ Weapons System Staff Management	Jun 84
Accounting 101/102	Sep 80-Jun 81
Presenting Statistics	Jul 80

Appendix J

SAMPLE APPLICATION CHECKLIST

I. LIST ASSETS

    A. Identify, in general terms, your:

        1. Educational background

        2. Previous paid and unpaid work/efforts

    B. Identify, in general terms, where you want to work

    C. What federal organizations appeal to you?

II. Identify jobs AND grades for which you are eligible by:

    A. Using FOCIS

    B. Get advice from OPM or state employment counselors

C. Scan appendices in this book (job series and, for GS jobs, the general qualification standards)

III. Focus on the requirements for target jobs:

    A. Identify any required exams

        1. Call nearest OPM for test dates and sites

        2. Check libraries for hints, sample questions, or copies of old exams

    B. Review X-118/X118C standards and agency-made standards

        1. Determine whether your assets qualify you for the target job

        2. Does the target series/grade appeal to you?

        3. Are you almost qualified for other series or grades?

IV. Get current job announcements from:

    A. OPM's FEICs or the *Career America Connection*

    B. Agency personnel offices

    C. State employment offices

    D. *Federal Career Opportunities/Federal Jobs Digest*

    E. Federal Job Opportunities Bulletin Boards

V. Begin preparing the application packet

    A. Get *X-118* or *X-118C Qualification Standards* for the target job

    B. If more information is needed, get *Position Classification Standards* for the target job

    C. Examine announcement; are additional forms needed?

    D. If not already prepared, make a "master" SF 171/OF 612 for the target series and grade

E. Call for more information about the vacancy

VI. Prepare a "Mail-in" packet

A. Make a **clear** copy of the master SF 171 or OF 612 and fill in unfilled blocks, including block 1 and your signature and date

B. Prepare the supplemental forms (race and sex surveys, SF 15, KSAO sheets, etc.)

C. Make a photo copy of the completed packet

D. Mail the application packet and complete a log record

VII. Follow-through

A. Call the POC a few days later and ask:

1. Whether the packet arrived

2. Has anything changed regarding that vacancy?

3. What timetable will be followed in rating the applications and sending ratings to hiring officials?

B. Based on the timetable given by the POC, call later to find out if you were rated

1. If you were not rated, ask why not

2. If your application was misread, ask to appeal the rating

3. Again ask for timetable and other information about this vacancy

C. If rated, call back every two weeks and ask:

1. Has the application gone to the hiring activity?

2. Has anything changed regarding the vacancy?

D. If not selected, call the POC and ask why

E. Update the log records

Appendix K

STANDARD FORMS

Several standard U.S. government forms are reproduced here, including

- *SF 171, Application for Federal Employment* used to apply for federal jobs

- *SF 171-A, Continuation Sheet for SF 171* used to describe additional work experience

- *Supplemental Information Sheet for SF 171* a form to use when the information will not fit a block on the SF 171 (this is not a government form)

- *SF 172, Amendment to Application for Federal Employment* used by current federal employees to update their records or to amend an SF 171 (conditions having changed since it was submitted for a vacancy)

- *OF 612, Optional Application for Federal Employment* used in place of the SF 171 as the heart of an application packet.

- *Work Experience Continuation Sheet for OF 612* used with OF 612 to list more jobs, or provide more details about jobs and work experience.

- *OF 306, Declaration for Federal Employment* is a form that may be requested by the hiring agency from applicants who use OF 612 or a resume as the core of their application packet. This is not used with an SF 171.

- *OPM Form 1170/17, List of College Courses* a form to use to record your college background if a course listing is required.

- *SF 15, Application for 10-Point Veteran Preference* used by veterans and certain relatives of veterans to claim the ten point veterans' preferential treatment when being rated for a federal job. Also includes additional information on eligibility for veterans preference and the special program for Vietnam Era vets.

- *Application Package Log Sheet* is a way to keep track of an SF 171 application packet.

SF 171, APPLICATION FOR FEDERAL EMPLOYMENT

The SF 171 will be the centerpiece in any application package. See Chapter Five for guidance on how to write a strong SF 171. The copies of the form on the following pages may be reproduced and submitted as part of an application.

Application for Federal Employment–SF 171

Read the instructions before you complete this application. *Type or print clearly in dark ink.*

Form Approved:
OMB No. 3206-0012

GENERAL INFORMATION

1 What kind of job are you applying for? *Give title and announcement no. (if any)*

2 Social Security Number

3 Sex ☐ Male ☐ Female

4 Birth date *(Month, Day, Year)*

5 Birthplace *(City and State or Country)*

6 Name *(Last, First, Middle)*

Mailing address *(include apartment number, if any)*

City   State   ZIP Code

7 Other names ever used *(e.g., maiden name, nickname, etc.)*

8 Home Phone   Area Code | Number

9 Work Phone   Area Code | Number   Extension

10 Were you ever employed as a civilian by the Federal Government? If **"NO"**, go to **Item 11.** If **"YES"**, mark each type of job you held with an **"X"**.

☐ Temporary ☐ Career-Conditional ☐ Career ☐ Excepted

What is your **highest** grade, classification series and job title?

Dates at **highest** grade: FROM   TO

DO NOT WRITE IN THIS AREA

FOR USE OF EXAMINING OFFICE ONLY

Date entered register

Form reviewed:
Form approved:

Option	Grade	Earned Rating	Veteran Preference	Augmented Rating
			☐ No Preference Claimed	
			☐ 5 Points *(Tentative)*	
			☐ 10 Pts. *(30% Or More Comp. Dis.)*	
			☐ 10 Pts. *(Less Than 30% Comp. Dis.)*	
			☐ Other 10 Points	

Initials and Date

☐ Disallowed   ☐ Being Investigated

FOR USE OF APPOINTING OFFICE ONLY

Preference has been verified through proof that the separation was under honorable conditions, and other proof as required.

☐ 5-Point   ☐ 10-Point--*30% or More Compensable Disability*   ☐ 10-Point--*Less Than 30% Compensable Disability*   ☐ 10-Point--*Other*

Signature and Title

Agency   Date

AVAILABILITY

11 When can you start work? *(Month and Year)*

12 What is the **lowest** pay you will accept? *(You will not be considered for jobs which pay less than you indicate.)*

Pay $ _____ per _____ **OR** Grade _____

13 In what geographic area(s) are you willing to work?

14 Are you willing to work:

	YES	NO
A. 40 hours per week *(full-time)?*		
B. 25-32 hours per week *(part-time)?*		
C. 17-24 hours per week *(part-time)?*		
D. 16 or fewer hours per week *(part-time)?*		
E. An intermittent job *(on-call/seasonal)?*		
F. Weekends, shifts, or rotating shifts?		

15 Are you willing to take a temporary job lasting:

A. 5 to 12 months *(sometimes longer)?*		
B. 1 to 4 months?		
C. Less than 1 month?		

16 Are you willing to travel away from home for:

A. 1 to 5 nights each month?		
B. 6 to 10 nights each month?		
C. 11 or more nights each month?		

MILITARY SERVICE AND VETERAN PREFERENCE

17 Have you served in the United States Military Service? *If your only active duty was training in the Reserves or National Guard, answer "NO".* If **"NO"**, go to item 22.   YES NO

18 Did you or will you retire at or above the rank of major or lieutenant commander?

MILITARY SERVICE AND VETERAN PREFERENCE *(Cont.)*

19 Were you discharged from the military service under honorable conditions? *(If your discharge was changed to "honorable" or "general" by a Discharge Review Board, answer "YES". If you received a clemency discharge, answer "NO".)* If **"NO"**, provide below the date and type of discharge you received.   YES NO

Discharge Date *(Month, Day, Year)*	Type of Discharge

20 List the dates *(Month, Day, Year)*, and branch for all **active duty** military service.

From	To	Branch of Service

21 If all your active military duty was after October 14, 1976, list the full names and dates of all campaign badges or expeditionary medals you received or were entitled to receive.

22 **Read the instructions that came with this form before completing this item.** When you have determined your eligibility for veteran preference from the instructions, place an **"X"** in the box next to your veteran preference claim.

☐ NO PREFERENCE

☐ 5-POINT PREFERENCE -- You must show proof when you are hired.

☐ 10-POINT PREFERENCE -- If you claim 10-point preference, place an **"X"** in the box below next to the basis for your claim. **To receive 10-point preference you must also complete a Standard Form 15, Application for 10-Point Veteran Preference,** which is available from any **Federal Job Information Center. ATTACH THE COMPLETED SF 15 AND REQUESTED PROOF TO THIS APPLICATION.**

☐ Non-compensably disabled or Purple Heart recipient.

☐ Compensably disabled, less than 30 percent.

☐ Spouse, widow(er), or mother of a deceased or disabled veteran.

☐ Compensably disabled, 30 percent or more.

THE FEDERAL GOVERNMENT IS AN EQUAL OPPORTUNITY EMPLOYER

PREVIOUS EDITION USABLE UNTIL 12-31-90

NSN 7540-00-935-7150   171-110

Standard Form 171 (Rev. 6-88)
U.S. Office of Personnel Management
FPM Chapter 295

Page 1

WORK EXPERIENCE *If you have no work experience, write "NONE" in A below and go to 25 on page 3.*

23 May we ask your present employer about your character, qualifications, and work record? *A "NO" will not affect our review of your qualifications. If you answer "NO" and we need to contact your present employer before we can offer you a job, we will contact you first.* . . . . | YES | NO |

24 READ **WORK EXPERIENCE** IN THE INSTRUCTIONS BEFORE YOU BEGIN.

- Describe your current or most recent job in Block **A** and work backwards, describing each job you held **during the past 10 years.** If you were **unemployed** for longer than **3 months** within the past 10 years, list the dates and your address(es) in an experience block.

- You may sum up in one block work that you did **more than 10 years ago.** But if that work **is related** to the type of job you are applying for, describe each related job in a separate block.

- INCLUDE VOLUNTEER WORK *(non-paid work)*--**If the work** *(or a part of the work)* **is like the job you are applying for,** complete **all** parts of the experience block just as you would for a paying job. You may receive credit for work experience with religious, community, welfare, service, and other organizations.

- INCLUDE MILITARY SERVICE--You should complete **all** parts of the experience block just as you would for a non-military job, including all supervisory experience. Describe each major change of duties or responsibilities in a separate experience block.

- IF YOU NEED MORE SPACE TO DESCRIBE A JOB--Use sheets of paper the same size as this page (be sure to include **all** information we ask for in **A** and **B** below). On **each** sheet show your name, Social Security Number, and the announcement number or job title.

- IF YOU NEED MORE EXPERIENCE BLOCKS, use the SF 171-A or a sheet of paper.

- IF YOU NEED TO UPDATE (ADD MORE RECENT JOBS), use the SF 172 or a sheet of paper as described above.

A | Name and address of employer's organization *(include ZIP Code, if known)* | Dates employed *(give month, day and year)* | Average number of hours per week | Number of employees you supervise |

From: To:

Salary or earnings | Your reason for wanting to leave

Starting $ per

Ending $ per

Your immediate supervisor
Name | Area Code | Telephone No. | Exact title of your job | If Federal employment *(civilian or military)* list series, grade or rank, and, if promoted in this job, the date of your last promotion

Description of work: Describe your specific duties, responsibilities and accomplishments in this job, **including** the job title(s) of any employees you supervise. *If you describe more than one type of work (for example, carpentry and painting, or personnel and budget), write the approximate percentage of time you spent doing each.*

For Agency Use (skill codes, etc.)

B | Name and address of employer's organization *(include ZIP Code, if known)* | Dates employed *(give month, day and year)* | Average number of hours per week | Number of employees you supervised |

From: To:

Salary or earnings | Your reason for leaving

Starting $ per

Ending $ per

Your immediate supervisor
Name | Area Code | Telephone No. | Exact title of your job | If Federal employment *(civilian or military)* list series, grade or rank, and, if promoted in this job, the date of your last promotion

Description of work: Describe your specific duties, responsibilities and accomplishments in this job, **including** the job title(s) of any employees you supervised. *If you describe more than one type of work (for example, carpentry and painting, or personnel and budget), write the approximate percentage of time you spent doing each.*

For Agency Use (skill codes, etc.)

Page 2   IF YOU NEED MORE EXPERIENCE BLOCKS, USE SF 171-A *(SEE BACK OF INSTRUCTION PAGE).*

← ATTACH ANY ADDITIONAL FORMS AND SHEETS HERE

EDUCATION

25 Did you graduate from high school? *If you have a GED high school equivalency or will graduate within the next nine months, answer "YES".*

26 Write the name and location *(city and state)* of the last high school you attended or where you obtained your GED high school equivalency.

YES | If **"YES"**, give month and year graduated or received GED equivalency: .... _____
NO | If **NO"**, give the highest grade you completed: . _____

27 Have you ever attended college or graduate school? YES / NO
| If **"YES"**, continue with 28.
| If **NO"**, go to 31.

28 NAME AND LOCATION *(city, state and ZIP Code)* OF COLLEGE OR UNIVERSITY.. *If you expect to graduate within nine months, give the **month** and **year** you expect to receive your degree:*

Name	City	State	ZIP Code	MONTH AND YEAR ATTENDED From	To	NUMBER OF CREDIT HOURS COMPLETED Semester	Quarter	TYPE OF DEGREE *(e.g. B.A., M.A.)*	MONTH AND YEAR OF DEGREE
1)									
2)									
3)									

29 CHIEF UNDERGRADUATE SUBJECTS *Show major on the first line*

	NUMBER OF CREDIT HOURS COMPLETED Semester	Quarter
1)		
2)		
3)		

30 CHIEF GRADUATE SUBJECTS *Show major on the first line*

	NUMBER OF CREDIT HOURS COMPLETED Semester	Quarter
1)		
2)		
3)		

31 If you have completed any **other courses or training related to the kind of jobs you are applying for** *(trade, vocational, Armed Forces, business)* give information below.

NAME AND LOCATION *(city, state and ZIP Code)* OF SCHOOL	MONTH AND YEAR ATTENDED From	To	CLASS-ROOM HOURS	SUBJECT(S)	TRAINING COMPLETED YES	NO
School Name 1)						
City _____ State ___ ZIP Code						
School Name 2)						
City _____ State ___ ZIP Code						

SPECIAL SKILLS, ACCOMPLISHMENTS AND AWARDS

32 Give the title and year of any honors, awards or fellowships you have received. List your special qualifications, skills or accomplishments that may help you get a job. *Some examples are: skills with computers or other machines; most important publications (do not submit copies); public speaking and writing experience; membership in professional or scientific societies; patents or inventions; etc.*

33 How many words per minute can you: TYPE? TAKE DICTATION?

Agencies may test your skills before hiring you.

34 List **job-related** licenses or certificates that you have, such as: *registered nurse; lawyer; radio operator; driver's; pilot's; etc.*

LICENSE OR CERTIFICATE	DATE OF LATEST LICENSE OR CERTIFICATE	STATE OR OTHER LICENSING AGENCY
1)		
2)		

35 Do you speak or read a language other than English *(include sign language)*? *Applicants for jobs that require a language other than English may be given an interview conducted solely in that language.* YES / NO
| If **"YES"**, list each language and place an **"X"** in each column that applies to you.
| If **"NO"**, go to 36.

LANGUAGE(S)	CAN PREPARE AND GIVE LECTURES Fluently	With Difficulty	CAN SPEAK AND UNDERSTAND Fluently	Passably	CAN TRANSLATE ARTICLES Into English	From English	CAN READ ARTICLES FOR OWN USE Easily	With Difficulty
1)								
2)								

REFERENCES

36 List three people who are not related to you and are not supervisors you listed under **24** who know your qualifications and fitness for the kind of job for which you are applying. At least **one** should know you well on a personal basis.

FULL NAME OF REFERENCE	TELEPHONE NUMBER(S) *(Include Area Code)*	PRESENT BUSINESS OR HOME ADDRESS *(Number, street and city)*	STATE	ZIP CODE
1)				
2)				
3)				

Page 3

BACKGROUND INFORMATION-- *You must answer each question in this section before we can process your application.*

		YES	NO
37	Are you a citizen of the United States? *(In most cases you must be a U.S. citizen to be hired. You will be required to submit proof of identity and citizenship at the time you are hired.)* If **"NO"**, give the country or countries you are a citizen of: _____		

NOTE: It is important that you give complete and truthful answers to questions 38 through 44. If you answer **"YES"** to any of them, provide your explanation(s) in **Item 45. Include** convictions resulting from a plea of nolo contendere *(no contest)*. **Omit:** 1) traffic fines of $100.00 or less; 2) any violation of law committed before your 16th birthday; 3) any violation of law committed before your 18th birthday, if finally decided in juvenile court or under a Youth Offender law; 4) any conviction set aside under the Federal Youth Corrections Act or similar State law; 5) any conviction whose record was expunged under Federal or State law. We will consider the date, facts, and circumstances of each event you list. In most cases you can still be considered for Federal jobs. However, **if you fail to tell the truth or fail to list all relevant** events or circumstances, this may be grounds for not hiring you, for firing you after you begin work, or for criminal prosecution (18 USC 1001).

		YES	NO
38	During the last **10 years**, were you **fired from any job** for any reason, did you **quit after being told that you would be fired**, or did you leave by mutual agreement because of specific problems?.		
39	Have you **ever** been convicted of, or forfeited collateral for **any felony violation?** *(Generally, a felony is defined as any violation of law punishable by imprisonment of longer than one year, except for violations called misdemeanors under State law which are punishable by imprisonment of two years or less.)*		
40	Have you **ever** been convicted of, or forfeited collateral for **any firearms or explosives violation**?		
41	Are you **now** under charges for **any** violation of law?		
42	During the **last 10 years** have you forfeited collateral, been convicted, been imprisoned, been on probation, or been on parole? Do **not** include violations reported in 39, 40, or 41, above.		
43	Have you **ever** been convicted by a military **court-martial**? If no military service, answer **"NO"**.		
44	Are you **delinquent** on any Federal debt? *(Include delinquencies arising from Federal taxes, loans, overpayment of benefits, and other debts to the U.S. Government **plus** defaults on Federally guaranteed or insured loans such as student and home mortgage loans.)*		

45 If **"YES" in: 38** - Explain for each job the problem(s) and your reason(s) for leaving. Give the employer's name and address.

        39 through 43 - Explain each violation. Give place of occurrence and name/address of police or court involved.

        44 - Explain the type, length and amount of the delinquency or default, and steps you are taking to correct errors or repay the debt. Give any identification number associated with the debt and the address of the Federal agency involved.

    NOTE: If you need more space, use a sheet of paper, and include the item number.

Item No.	Date (Mo./Yr.)	Explanation	Mailing Address
			Name of Employer, Police, Court, or Federal Agency
			City State ZIP Code
			Name of Employer, Police, Court, or Federal Agency
			City State ZIP Code

		YES	NO
46	Do you receive, or have you ever applied for retirement pay, pension, or other pay based on military, Federal civilian, or District of Columbia Government service?		
47	Do any of your relatives work for the United States Government or the United States Armed Forces? Include: *father; mother; husband; wife; son; daughter; brother; sister; uncle; aunt; first cousin; nephew; niece; father-in-law; mother-in-law; son-in-law; daughter-in-law; brother-in-law; sister-in-law; stepfather; stepmother; stepson; stepdaughter; stepbrother; stepsister; half brother; and half sister.*		

If **"YES"**, provide details below. If you need more space, use a sheet of paper.

Name	Relationship	Department, Agency or Branch of Armed Forces

SIGNATURE, CERTIFICATION, AND RELEASE OF INFORMATION

YOU MUST SIGN THIS APPLICATION.   Read the following carefully before you sign.

- A false statement on any part of your application may be grounds for not hiring you, or for firing you after you begin work. Also, you may be punished by fine or imprisonment (U.S. Code, title 18, section 1001).
- If you are a male born after December 31, 1959 you must be registered with the Selective Service System or have a valid exemption in order to be eligible for Federal employment. You will be required to certify as to your status at the time of appointment.
- **I understand** that any information I give may be investigated as allowed by law or Presidential order.
- **I consent** to the release of information about my ability and fitness for Federal employment **by** *employers, schools, law enforcement agencies and other individuals and organizations,* **to** *investigators, personnel staffing specialists, and other authorized employees of the Federal Government.*
- **I certify** that, to the best of my knowledge and belief, **all** of my statements are true, correct, complete, and made in good faith.

48 SIGNATURE *(Sign each application in dark ink)*	49 DATE SIGNED *(Month, day, year)*

Page 4

SF 171-A, CONTINUATION SHEET FOR SF 171

This form is used to list additional jobs and other work experiences. As explained in Chapter Five, use one block for each job or work experience which is relevant to the target job, starting with your current job and working back roughly ten years. The first job listed on a continuation sheet should be put into the top half of the page and the block should be labeled "C."

The copies of the form on the following page may be reproduced and submitted as part of an application.

Standard Form 171-A— *Continuation Sheet for SF 171*

• Attach all SF 171-A's to your application at the top of page 3.

Form Approved:
OMB No. 3206-0012

1. Name *(Last, First, Middle Initial)*

2. Social Security Number

3. Job Title or Announcement Number You Are Applying For

4. Date Completed

ADDITIONAL WORK EXPERIENCE BLOCKS

☐ Name and address of employer's organization *(include ZIP Code, if known)*

Dates employed *(give month, day and year)*

From: To:

Salary or earnings

Starting $ per

Ending $ per

Average number of hours per week

Number of employees you supervised

Your reason for leaving

Your immediate supervisor

Name   Area Code   Telephone No.

Exact title of your job

If Federal employment *(civilian or military)* list series, grade or rank, and, if promoted in this job, the date of your last promotion

Description of work: Describe your specific duties, responsibilities and accomplishments in this job, **including** the job title(s) of any employees you supervised. *If you describe more than one type of work (for example, carpentry and painting, or personnel and budget), write the approximate percentage of time you spent doing each.*

For Agency Use (skill codes, etc.)

☐ Name and address of employer's organization *(include ZIP Code, if known)*

Dates employed *(give month, day and year)*

From: To:

Salary or earnings

Starting $ per

Ending $ per

Average number of hours per week

Number of employees you supervised

Your reason for leaving

Your immediate supervisor

Name   Area Code   Telephone No.

Exact title of your job

If Federal employment *(civilian or military)* list series, grade or rank, and, if promoted in this job, the date of your last promotion

Description of work: Describe your specific duties, responsibilities and accomplishments in this job, **including** the job title(s) of any employees you supervised. *If you describe more than one type of work (for example, carpentry and painting, or personnel and budget), write the approximate percentage of time you spent doing each.*

For Agency Use (skill codes, etc.)

THE FEDERAL GOVERNMENT IS AN EQUAL OPPORTUNITY EMPLOYER

PREVIOUS EDITION USABLE

Standard Form **171-A** (Rev. 6-88)
U.S. Office of Personnel Management
FPM Chapter 295

SUPPLEMENTAL INFORMATION SHEET FOR SF 171

Some of the blocks on the SF 171 and the SF 171-A Continuation Sheet do not provide enough space for adequate descriptions. Make copies of the form on the next page and use it to provide additional information. Each block you describe on this form should be clearly marked (see the examples) so the reviewer will know which blocks are being given more space. Be sure to review the examples in Appendix J.

SUPPLEMENTAL INFORMATION SHEET FOR SF 171

SUPPLEMENTAL INFORMATION:

1. Name (Last, First, Middle Initial)	2. SSN
3. Job Title/Announcement Number	4. Date

SF 172, AMENDMENT TO APPLICATION FOR FEDERAL EMPLOYMENT

This form can be used by current federal employees to update their personnel records. The form can also be used if you have applied for a position, no decision has yet been made about your application, and things in your life have changed since you submitted your application package. You may complete this form and send it to the same place your sent your application and request that the new information be added to your application. The information that has to be put into the blocks on this form is identical to the information required on comparable blocks of the SF 171.

Copies of the form on the next two pages may be made and submitted.

Standard Form 172—Amendment to
Application for Federal Employment—SF 171

Form Approved:
OMB No. 3206-0002
Approval Expires 10-31-87

Read the following instructions before you complete this application. Type or print clearly in dark ink.

- You may use this form to update your Application for Federal Employment (SF 171) if you have had 2 or fewer new jobs since you completed your last SF 171.
- You must submit a new SF 171 if you have previously updated your application or have three or more new jobs.
- Federal agencies must accept your previously completed SF 171 as current when this form or a signed photocopy is attached.

GENERAL INFORMATION

1 Reason for updating SF 171 *(Check one:)*
☐ To update my SF 171 for _____
   (Indicate position title or announcement number)
☐ To update SF 171 in my Official Personnel Folder.
☐ To update attached SF 171. ☐ As requested.

3 Birth date *(Month, Day, Year)*

4 Social Security Number

5 What is the lowest pay or grade you will accept?

Pay $ _____ per _____   OR Grade _____

2 Name *(Last, First, Middle)*

Street address or RFD number *(include apartment number, if any)*

City _____   State _____   ZIP Code _____

6 Name on SF 171 being amended, if different from 2

7 May we ask your present employer about your character, qualifications and work record? A "NO" will not affect our review of your qualifications. If you answer "NO" and we need to contact your present employer before we can offer you a job, we will contact you first . . . . | YES | NO |

WORK EXPERIENCE   *If you have no new work experience, write "NONE" in A below and go to 9 on page 2*

8 ○ Describe your current or most recent job or volunteer experience in Block A and work backwards, describing up to 2 periods of experience not on your SF 171.
   ○ If you were unemployed for longer than 3 months, list the dates and your address(es) at that time in 10.

A Name and address of employer's organization *(include ZIP Code, if known)*

Dates employed *(give month and year)*
From: _____   To: _____

Average number of hours per week

Salary or earnings
Starting $ _____ per
Ending $ _____ per

Place of employment
City
State

Exact title of your job

Name of immediate supervisor

Area Code   Telephone Number

Number and titles of employees you supervised

Kind of business or organization *(manufacturing, accounting, social service, etc.)*

If Federal employment *(civilian or military)*, list: series, grade or rank, and the date of your last promotion

Your reason for wanting to leave

Description of work: Describe your specific duties, responsibilities and accomplishments in this job. *If you describe more than one type of work (for example, carpentry and painting or personnel and budget), write the approximate percentage of time you spent doing each.*

For Agency Use (skill codes, etc.)

THE FEDERAL GOVERNMENT IS AN EQUAL OPPORTUNITY EMPLOYER
PREVIOUS EDITION USABLE

NSN 7540-00-142-8756

172-105

Standard Form 172 (Rev. 3/84)
Office of Personnel Management
FPM Chapter 295

B Name and address of employer's organization *(include ZIP Code, if known)*

Dates employed *(give month and year)*	
From:	To:

Average number of hours per week

Salary or earnings	
Starting $	per
Ending $	per

Place of employment
City
State

Exact title of your job	Name of immediate supervisor	Area Code Telephone Number	Number and titles of employees you supervised

Kind of business or organization *(manufacturing, accounting, social service, etc.)*	If Federal employment *(civilian or military)*, list: series, grade or rank, and the date of your last promotion	Reason for leaving

Description of work: Describe your specific duties, responsibilities and accomplishments in this job. *If you describe more than one type of work (for example, carpentry and painting or personnel and budget), write the approximate percentage of time you spent doing each.*

For Agency Use (skill codes, etc.)

OTHER CHANGES OR ADDITIONS AND ADDITIONAL SPACE

9 Does **any other information** on your SF 171 need updating *(for example, telephone number, education, or special skills)?* ....

YES ☐ Provide updated information in **10**.
NO ☐ Go to **11** and **12**.

10 Write the number to which each answer applies. **If you need more space**, use sheets of paper the same size as this page. On each sheet write your name and Social Security Number. Attach all sheets to this form.

SIGNATURE, CERTIFICATION, AND RELEASE OF INFORMATION *For Privacy Act Statement See SF 171*

YOU MUST SIGN THIS APPLICATION. Read the following carefully before you sign.

A false statement on any part of your application or this amendment may be grounds for not hiring you, or for firing you after you begin work. Also, you may be punished by fine or imprisonment (U.S. Code, Title 18, Section 1001).

I **understand** that any information I give may be investigated as allowed by law or Presidential order;

I **consent** to the release of information about my ability and fitness for Federal employment by *employers, schools, law enforcement agencies and other individuals and organizations, to investigators, personnel staffing specialists, and other authorized employees of the Federal Government.*

I **certify** that, to the best of my knowledge and belief, all statements on my SF 171 and SF 172 are correct, complete, and made in good faith.

11 Signature *(Sign in dark ink)*	12 Date Signed *(Month, day, year)*

OPM Form 1170/17, LIST OF COLLEGE COURSES

The form on the next few pages can be used to submit copies of your educational transcript(s) if you are applying for a position which has positive educational requirements (for example, if the announcement says you must have a certain number of college semester hours in mathematics or other subjects). For your application, you can tape a copy of your educational transcript to copies of the form. If accepted for the position, the personnel office will require an official copy of all transcripts.

The forms on the next few pages may be reproduced as needed.

Form Approved
OMB No. 3206-0038

SUPPLEMENTAL QUALIFICATIONS STATEMENT
LIST OF COLLEGE COURSES AND CERTIFICATE OF SCHOLASTIC ACHIEVEMENT
Complete and submit this Form with your Application for Federal Employment or as instructed.

1. Name (Last, First, M.I.)	2. Birth date (Month, day, year)	3. Social Security Number

4. Position for which you are applying (Include options, if any)

5. List the undergraduate and/or graduate college degrees you have received or expect to receive (Give name of degree, name of college or university granting degree, and date received or to be received)

6. State your major undergraduate course(s) of study	6a. State your major graduate course(s) of study

PART I — COLLEGE COURSES

List below by appropriate academic field (e.g., biology, mechanical engineering, economics, sociology, etc.) all courses you have taken (including those failed) which appear to satisfy the qualification requirements of positions for which you are applying. List graduate and undergraduate courses separately. Credits for each category should be totaled to determine if you meet the minimum course requirements.

Indicate academic field: _____

Indicate academic field: _____

DESCRIPTIVE TITLE	COMPLE- TION DATE	GRADE	CREDIT HOURS SEM.	QTR	CLASS ROOM	DESCRIPTIVE TITLE	COMPLE- TION DATE	GRADE	CREDIT HOURS SEM	QTR	CLASS ROOM
TOTAL						TOTAL					

Indicate academic field:

DESCRIPTIVE TITLE	COMPLE-TION DATE	GRADE	CREDIT HOURS		
			SEM	QTR	CLASS ROOM
TOTAL					

Indicate academic field:

DESCRIPTIVE TITLE	COMPLE-TION DATE	GRADE	CREDIT HOURS		
			SEM	QTR	CLASS ROOM
TOTAL					

Indicate academic field:

DESCRIPTIVE TITLE	COMPLE-TION DATE	GRADE	CREDIT HOURS		
			SEM.	QTR.	CLASS ROOM
TOTAL					

Indicate academic field:

DESCRIPTIVE TITLE	COMPLE-TION DATE	GRADE	CREDIT HOURS		
			SEM	QTR	CLASS ROOM
TOTAL					

MISCELLANEOUS COURSES

DESCRIPTIVE TITLE	COMPLE-TION DATE	GRADE	CREDIT HOURS			DESCRIPTIVE TITLE	COMPLE-TION DATE	GRADE	CREDIT HOURS		
			SEM	QTR	CLASS ROOM				SEM	QTR	CLASS ROOM
TOTAL						TOTAL					

PART II – PRIVACY ACT STATEMENT AND CERTIFICATION

The Office of Personnel Management is authorized by section 1302 of Chapter 13 (Special Authority) and sections 3301 and 3304 of Chapter 33 (Examination, Certification, and Appointment) of Title 5 of the U.S. Code to collect the information on this form.

Executive Order 9397 (Numbering System for Federal Accounts Relating to Individual Persons) authorizes the collection of your Social Security Number (SSN). Your SSN is used to identify this form with your basic application. It may be used for the same purposes as stated on the application.

The information you provide will be used primarily to determine your qualifications for Federal employment. Other possible uses or disclosures of the information are:

1. To make requests for information about you from any source; (e.g., former employers or schools), that would assist an agency in determining whether to hire you;

2. To refer your application to prospective Federal employers and, with your consent, to others (e.g., State and local governments) for possible employment;

3. To a Federal, State, or local agency for checking on violations of law or other lawful purposes in connection with hiring or retaining you on the job, or issuing you a security clearance;

4. To the courts when the Government is party to a suit; and

5. When lawfully required by Congress, the Office of Management and Budget, or the General Services Administration.

Providing the information requested on this form, including your SSN, is voluntary. However, failure to do so may result in your not receiving an accurate rating, which may hinder your chances for obtaining Federal employment.

ATTENTION – THIS STATEMENT MUST BE SIGNED
Read the following paragraph carefully before signing this Statement

A false answer to any question in this Statement may be grounds for not employing you, or for dismissing you after you begin work, and may be punishable by fine or imprisonment (U.S. Code, Title 18, Sec. 1001). All statements are subject to investigation, including a check of your fingerprints, police records, and former employers. All the information you give will be considered in reviewing your Statement and is subject to investigation.

CERTIFICATION	Signature (Sign in ink)	Date Signed
I CERTIFY that all of the statements made in this Statement are true, complete, and correct to the best of my knowledge and belief, and are made in good faith.		

COMPLETE PART III ON THE NEXT PAGE IF YOU
CLAIM SUPERIOR ACADEMIC ACHIEVEMENT

PART III - SCHOLASTIC ACHIEVEMENT

NOTE: This part is for the use of college students and graduates who may qualify for some GS-7 positions on the basis of undergraduate scholastic achievement, as provided in an open job announcement. *See the appropriate job announcement for complete requirements.* Proof of scholastic achievement under one of these provisions should not be submitted with your application, but will be required by the hiring agency at the time of appointment. If you do not wish to qualify on this basis or if you do not meet the scholastic requirements for the position, do not complete this part. In any case, YOU MUST SIGN YOUR NAME AFTER THE CERTIFICATION STATEMENT AT THE BOTTOM OF PAGE 3.

A. **COLLEGE OR CLASS STANDING.** Must be in upper third of your graduating class in the college or university, or major subdivision such as School of Engineering, School of Business Administration, etc.

NUMBER IN CLASS _____ YOUR STANDING _____

Proof of class standing should be in the form of a statement in writing from the institution's registrar, the dean of your course of study, or other appropriate official. This statement of class standing must be based on a suitable measure of your academic performance, such as the results of a comprehensive examination or an overall faculty assessment, and must indicate the basis of the judgment. Class standing must be based on your standing in your college or university or the first major subdivision (e.g., the School of Business Administration, the College of Arts and Sciences, etc.). Subdivisions below this level, i.e., a single academic department within a large university, such as the English Department or the Accounting Department, are not recognized as major subdivisions for this purpose.

B. **COLLEGE-GRADE POINT AVERAGE.** Your grade-point average (GPA) should be recorded in the manner that is most beneficial to you, using one of methods below. Your grade-point average must be expressed in terms of a value on a 4.0 scale based on 4 years, the last 2 years, or courses completed in the major field of study.* If computing your GPA, indicate the method used and period covered by checking the appropriate boxes in item 2 *and* in item 3 below, and compute your average in the space provided below on this page.

1. GPA as recorded on final transcript _____ (Transcript must cover *at least* the last 2 years)

2. (Check One) ☐ Average of undergraduate courses ☐ Average in major field of study

3. (Check One) ☐ At time of filing * ☐ All 4 years ☐ Last 2 years

* You may be rated provisionally eligible if you are a senior student, provided you have the required average in the junior year. You will be required to submit evidence at the time of appointment that you maintained the required average during your senior year.

In computing your grade-point average, round to the first decimal place, (e.g., 2.95 = 3.0 , 2.94 = 2.9, 3.45 = 3.5, etc.). If your college uses a different system, explain below, or on an attachment, how it compares with the grade-point average on a 4.0 scale:

If more than 10 percent of your courses were graded on a pass/fail or similar system rather than on a traditional grading system, you can usually claim credit under the scholastic achievement provision based only on class standing or membership in a national honor society. The exception is if you can document that only your freshman-year courses (25 percent or less of your total credit) were credited on a pass/fail or similar system.

NO. OF SEMESTER OR QUARTER HOURS AT 4.0 ("A") _____ X 4 = _____

NO. OF SEMESTER OR QUARTER HOURS AT 3.0 ("B") _____ X 3 = _____

NO. OF SEMESTER OR QUARTER HOURS AT 2.0 ("C") _____ X 2 = _____

NO. OF SEMESTER OR QUARTER HOURS AT 1.0 ("D") _____ X 1 = _____

NO. OF SEMESTER OR QUARTER HOURS AT 0.0 ("F") _____ X 0 = _____

TOTAL (1) _____ TOTAL (2) _____

COMPUTED GRADE-POINT AVERAGE _____
Total (2) divided by Total (1)

C. **HONOR SOCIETY MEMBERSHIP.** Must be one of the national scholastic honor societies meeting the minimum requirements of the Association of College Honor Societies (other than freshman scholarship honor societies).

Name of honor society and date you were elected to membership. _____

SF 15, APPLICATION FOR
10-POINT VETERAN PREFERENCE

The form on the next two pages may be reproduced and submitted with your application if you qualify for a veteran preference. The two-page form lists which people are eligible for the preference, but the following three pages, which come from Chapter 211 of the *Federal Personnel Manual,* **define** the terms in clearer detail. A veteran of the Armed Forces does not necessarily qualify for the ten point preference, while some employees of the Public Health Service and the National Oceanic and Atmospheric Administration (NOAA) **do** qualify! Also, under certain circumstances, the spouse of a living veteran, the widow or widower of a veteran, and the natural mother of some disabled or deceased veterans are eligible for veterans preference points.

Next, there is a page which describes eligibility for Veterans Readjustment Appointment, a special hiring program for some veterans who served during the Vietnam era (5 August, 1964 through 7 May, 1975). The last page in this appendix has a list of points of contact for questions about veterans' preferences.

Note that if you intend to apply for a disabled (or deceased) veteran's ten point preference, you will need to complete an SF 15 **plus** provide official documentation verifying the disability or death. See the SF 15, page two, for further details.

Standard Form 15 (Rev. 7/83)
U.S. Office of Personnel
Management
FPM Supplement 296–33
FPM Chapter 211

APPLICATION FOR 10-POINT VETERAN PREFERENCE
(TO BE USED BY VETERANS & RELATIVES OF VETERANS)

Form Approved
OMB No. 3206–0001

PERSON APPLYING FOR PREFERENCE

1. Name (Last, First, Middle)

2. Name and Announcement Number of Civil Service or Postal Service Exam You Have Applied For or Position Which You Currently Occupy

3. Home Address (Street Number, City, State and ZIP Code)

4. Social Security Number

5. Date Exam was Held or Application Submitted

VETERAN INFORMATION (TO BE PROVIDED BY PERSON APPLYING FOR PREFERENCE)

6. Veteran's Name (Last, First, Middle) Exactly As It Appears on Service Records

7. Veteran's Periods of Service

Branch of Service	From	To	Service Number

8. Veteran's Social Security Number

9. VA Claim Number, If Any

TYPE OF 10-POINT PREFERENCE CLAIMED

INSTRUCTIONS: Check the block which indicates the type of preference you are claiming. Answer all questions associated with that block. The "DOCUMENTATION REQUIRED" column refers you to the back of this form for the documents you must submit to support your application. [PLEASE NOTE: Eligibility for veterans' preference is governed by 5 U.S.C. §2108, 5 CFR Part 211, and FPM chapter 211. All conditions are not fully described in this form because of space restrictions. The office to which you apply can provide additional information. Instructions on how to apply for five point preference are on SF 171, Personal Qualifications Statement, or PS Form 2591, Application for Employment (U.S. Postal Service Application).]

DOCUMENTATION REQUIRED
(See reverse of this form.)

☐ 10. VETERAN'S CLAIM FOR PREFERENCE based on non-compensable service-connected disability; award of the Purple Heart; or receipt of disability pension under public laws administered by the VA.

.... A and B

☐ 11. VETERAN'S CLAIM FOR PREFERENCE based on eligibility for or receipt of compensation from the VA or disability retirement from a Service Department for a service-connected disability.

.... A and C

☐ 12. PREFERENCE FOR SPOUSE of a living veteran based on the fact that the veteran, because of a service-connected disability, has been unable to qualify for a Federal or D.C. Government job, or any other position along the lines of his/her usual occupation. (If your answer to item "a" is "NO", you are ineligible for preference and need not submit this form.)

a. Are you presently married to the veteran?   ☐ YES ☐ NO

C and H

☐ 13. PREFERENCE FOR WIDOW OR WIDOWER of a veteran.
(If your answer is "NO" to item "a" or "YES" to item "b", you are ineligible for preference and need not submit this form.)

a. Were you married to the veteran when he or she died?   ☐ YES ☐ NO

b. Have you remarried? (Do not count marriages that were annulled.)   ☐ YES ☐ NO

A, D, E, and G
(Submit G when applicable.)

☐ 14. PREFERENCE FOR (NATURAL) MOTHER of a service-connected permanently and totally disabled, or deceased veteran provided you are or were married to the father of the veteran, *and*
—your husband (either the veteran's father or the husband of a remarriage) is totally and permanently disabled, *or*
—you are now widowed, divorced, or separated from the veteran's father and have not remarried, *or*
—you are widowed or divorced from the veteran's father and have remarried, but are now widowed, divorced, or separated from the husband of your remarriage.
(If your answer is "NO" to item "c" or "d", you are ineligible for preference and need not submit this form.)

a. Are you married?   ☐ YES ☐ NO

b. Are you separated? If "YES," do not complete "c." Go to "d."   ☐ YES ☐ NO

c. If married now, is your husband totally and permanently disabled?   ☐ YES ☐ NO

d. If the veteran is dead, did he/she die in active service?   ☐ YES ☐ NO

DISABLED VETERAN:
C, F, and H
(Submit F when applicable.)

DECEASED VETERAN:
A, D, E, and F
(Submit F when applicable.)

PRIVACY ACT STATEMENT

The Veterans' Preference Act of 1944 authorizes the collection of this information. The information will be used, along with any accompanying documentation, to determine whether you are entitled to 10-point veterans' preference. This information may be disclosed to: (1) the Veterans' Administration, or the appropriate branch of the Armed Forces to verify your claim; (2) a court, or a Federal, State, or local agency for checking on law violations or for other related authorized purposes; (3) a Federal, State, or local government agency, if you are participating in a special employment assistance program; or (4) other Federal, State, or local government agencies, congressional offices, and international organizations for purposes of employment consideration, e.g., if you are on an Office of Personnel Management list of eligibles.

Executive Order 9397 authorizes Federal agencies to use the Social Security Number (SSN) to identify individual records in Federal personnel records systems. Your SSN will be used to ensure accurate retention of records pertaining to you and may also be used to identify you to others from whom information about you is sought. Furnishing your SSN and the other information sought is voluntary. However, failure to provide any part of the information may result in a ruling that you are not eligible for 10-point veterans' preference or in delaying the processing of your application for employment.

I certify that all of the statements made in this claim are true, complete, and correct to the best of my knowledge and belief and are made in good faith. [A false answer to any question may be grounds for not employing you, or for dismissing you after you begin work, and may be punishable by fine or imprisonment (U.S. Code, Title 18, Section 1001).]

This Form Must Be Signed By All Persons Claiming 10-Point Preference

Signature of Person Claiming Preference

Date Signed (Month, Day, Year)

FOR USE BY APPOINTING OFFICER ONLY
Signature and Title of Appointing Officer

☐ Preference Entitlement Was Verified

Name of Agency

Date Signed (Month, Day, Year)

PREVIOUS EDITIONS UNUSABLE

15–109

NSN: 7540-00-634-3972

DOCUMENTATION REQUIRED—READ CAREFULLY

(PLEASE SUBMIT PHOTOCOPIES OF DOCUMENTS BECAUSE THEY WILL *NOT* BE RETURNED)

A. DOCUMENTATION OF SERVICE AND SEPARATION UNDER HONORABLE CONDITIONS

Submit any of the documents listed below as documentation, provided they are dated on or after the day of separation from active duty military service.
1. Honorable or general discharge certificate.
2. Certificate of transfer to Navy Fleet Reserve, Marine Corps Fleet Reserve, or Enlisted Reserve Corps.
3. Orders of Transfer to Retired List.
4. Report of Separation from a branch of the Armed Forces.
5. Certificate of Service or release from active duty, provided honorable separation is shown.
6. Official Statement from a branch of the Armed Forces showing that honorable separation took place.
7. Notation by the Veterans' Administration or a branch of the Armed Forces on official statement, described in B or C below, that the veteran was honorably separated from military service.
8. Official statement from the Military Personnel Records Center that official service records show that honorable separation took place.

B. DOCUMENTATION OF SERVICE-CONNECTED DISABILITY (NON-COMPENSABLE, I.E., LESS THAN 10%); PURPLE HEART; AND NONSERVICE-CONNECTED DISABILITY PENSION

Submit one of the following documents:
1. An official statement, *dated within the last 12 months,* from the Veterans' Administration or from a branch of the Armed Forces, certifying to the present existence of the veteran's service-connected disability of less than 10%.
2. An official citation, document, or discharge certificate, issued by a branch of the Armed Forces, showing the award to the veteran of the Purple Heart for wound or injuries received in action.
3. An official statement, *dated within the last 12 months,* from the Veterans Administration, certifying that the veteran is receiving a nonservice-connected disability pension.

C. DOCUMENTATION OF SERVICE-CONNECTED DISABILITY (COMPENSABLE, I.E., 10% OR MORE)

Submit one of the following documents, if you checked Item 11 on the front of this form:
1. An official statement, *dated within the last 12 months,* from the Veterans' Administration or from a branch of the Armed Forces, certifying to the veteran's present receipt of compensation for service-connected disability or disability retired pay.
2. An official statement, *dated within the last 12 months,* from the Veterans' Administration or from a branch of the Armed Forces, certifying that the veteran has a service-connected disability of 10% or more.

3. An official statement or retirement orders from a branch of the Armed Forces, showing that the retired serviceman was retired because of permanent service-connected disability or was transferred to the permanent disability retirement list. The statement or retirement orders must indicate that the disability is 10% or more.

For spouses and mothers of disabled veterans checking Items 12 or 14, submit the following:

An official statement, *dated within the last 12 months,* from the Veterans' Administration or from a branch of the Armed Forces, certifying: 1) the present existence of the veteran's service-connected disability, 2) the percentage and nature of the service-connected disability or disabilities (including the combined percentage), 3) a notation as to whether or not the veteran is currently rated as "unemployable" due to the service-connected disability, and 4) a notation as to whether or not the service-connected disability is rated as permanent and total.

D. DOCUMENTATION OF VETERAN'S DEATH

1. If on active military duty at time of death, *submit* official notice, from a branch of the Armed Forces, of death occurring under honorable conditions.
2. If death occurred while not on active military duty, *submit* death certificate.

E. DOCUMENTATION OF SERVICE OR DEATH DURING A WAR, IN A CAMPAIGN OR EXPEDITION FOR WHICH A CAMPAIGN BADGE IS AUTHORIZED, OR DURING THE PERIOD OF APRIL 28, 1952, THROUGH JULY 1, 1955

Submit documentation of service or death during a war or during the period April 28, 1952, through July 1, 1955, or during a campaign or expedition for which a campaign badge is authorized.

F. DOCUMENTATION OF DECEASED OR DISABLED VETERAN'S MOTHER'S CLAIM FOR PREFERENCE BECAUSE OF HER HUSBAND'S TOTAL AND PERMANENT DISABILITY

Submit a statement from husband's physician showing the prognosis of his disease and percentage of his disability.

G. DOCUMENTATION OF ANNULMENT OF REMARRIAGE BY WIDOW OR WIDOWER OF VETERAN

Submit either:
1. Certification from the Veterans' Administration that entitlement to pension or compensation was restored due to annulment.
2. A certified copy of the court decree of annulment.

H. DOCUMENTATION OF VETERAN'S INABILITY TO WORK BECAUSE OF A SERVICE-CONNECTED DISABILITY

Answer questions 1–7 below:

1. Is the veteran currently working? ☐ YES ☐ NO If "NO", go to Item 3	2. If currently working, what is the veteran's present occupation?
3. What was the veteran's occupation, if any, before military service?	4. What was the veteran's military occupation at time of separation?

5. Has the veteran been employed, or is he/she now employed, by the Federal civil service or D.C. Government? ☐ YES ☐ NO
If "YES", provide the following:

A. Title and Grade of Position Most Recently, or Currently, Held	B. Name and Address of Agency	C. Dates of Employment From / To

6. Has the veteran resigned from, been disqualified for, or separated from a position in the Federal civil service or D.C. Government along the lines of his/her usual occupation because of service-connected disability? ☐ YES ☐ NO
If "YES", submit documentation of the resignation, disqualification, or separation.

7. Is the veteran receiving a civil service retirement pension? ☐ YES ☐ NO
If "YES", give the Civil Service retirement annuity number _ _ _ _ _ _ _ _ CSA NUMBER—

STANDARD FORM 15 (REV. 7/83) BACK

SUBCHAPTER 2. ENTITLEMENT TO PREFERENCE

2—1. DEFINITIONS

The following definitions are used for the purposes of preference in Federal employment.

(1) "Veteran" means a person who was separated with an honorable discharge or under honorable conditions from active duty in the armed forces performed
   (a)   in a war;
   (b)   in a campaign or expedition for which a campaign badge has been authorized; *or,*
   ©   during the period beginning April 28, 1952, and ending July 1, 1955; *or,*
   (d)   for more than 180 consecutive days, other than for training, any part of which occurred during the period beginning February 1, 1955 and ending October 14, 1976.[1]

Persons who lost their lives under honorable conditions while serving in the armed forces during a period named in (1)(a) through (d) are also referred to as veterans for the purposes of this chapter only. (Refer to FPM Supplement 296-33 for a list of recognized wars, campaigns, and expeditions).

(2) "Active duty," or "active military duty," means full-time duty with military pay and allowances in the armed forces, except for training or for determining physical fitness and except for service in the Reserves or National Guards.

(3) "Armed Forces" means the United States Army, Navy, Air Force, Marine Corps, and Coast Guard.

(4) "Uniformed services" means the armed forces, the commissioned corps of the Public Health Service, and the commissioned corps of the National Oceanic and Atmospheric Administration (formerly the Environmental Science Services Administration, Coast and Geodetic Survey).

(5) "Discharge under honorable conditions" means either an honorable or a general discharge from the armed forces. The Department of Defense has responsibility for administering and defining military discharges. (An amnesty or clemency discharge does not meet the Veterans' Preference Act requirement for discharge under honorable conditions. Accordingly, no preference may be granted to applicants with such discharges.)

(6) "Disabled veteran" means a person who was separated under honorable conditions from active duty in the armed forces performed at any time and who has established the present existence of a service-connected disability or is receiving compensation, disability retire-

ment benefits, or pension because of a public statute administered by the Veterans Administration or a military department.[2] (Refer to FPM Supplement 296-33 for a list of acceptable evidence.)

(7) "Ex-serviceperson" means a person who was separated from active duty performed in peace or war. (A person on active duty may be an ex-serviceperson because of separation from previous active duty.)

(8) "Spouse" means legal husband or wife. Common law marriages is recognized for preference, if valid under the laws of the place where the parties lived at the time of the marriage.

(9) "Separation" from a spouse means living apart. A separation need not be approved by a court of law but must be bona fide and permanent.

(10) "Legal separation" from a spouse means a separation a *mensa et thoro* (from bed and board) by court decree, which frees the parties but does not dissolve the marriage tie.

2—2. TYPES OF PREFERENCE

There are 7 different types of preference, each with a separate set of requirements. when used for competitive civil service examination purposes, the applicant must first make a passing grade before preference points may be added to the rating score.

(1) Five-point. Every veteran as defined in subchapter 2-1(1) of this chapter is entitled to a 5-point preference.[3] However, veterans who are eligible for and take advantage of 10-point preference are not entitled to an additional 5-point preference.

(2) Ten-point (disability). Every disabled veteran as defined in subchapter 2-1(6) of this chapter is entitled to 10-point (disability) preference.

---

[1]Section 702 of Public Law 94-502, enacted October 15, 1976 abolishes peacetime preference for those entering active duty after October 14, 1976, *unless* they serve in a campaign or war or meet the definition of "disabled veteran" described in subchapter 2-1(6) of this chapter.

[2]If the Veterans Administration recognizes the existence of a service-connected disability arising from an injury or disease incurred while en route to, at, or returning from, a place of induction or entry into duty, the person is considered to be a disabled veteran. However, even an individual who is receiving compensation, disability retirement benefits, or pension by reason of laws administered by the Veterans Administration is not eligible for preference, unless he or she has met the requirement of having served on active duty, other than for training, as defined in 2-1(2) of this section. Furthermore, the spouse, widow, widower, or mother of such a disabled veteran is not entitled to preference.

An individual who is disabled while undergoing training with a military reserve unit is *not* considered to be a disabled veteran and is not entitled to preference.

(3) Ten-point (compensable disability). A disabled veteran who was separated under honorable conditions from active duty in the armed forces performed at any time and who has a compensable service-connected disability rating of 10 percent or more is entitled to 10-point (compensable disability) preference rather than 10-point (disability) preference.

Because of certain provisions of the Civil Service Reform Act of 1978, employing offices must distinguish between:

(a) those veterans entitled to 10-point preference due to a compensable service-connected disability of less than 30 percent; and

(b) those veterans entitled to 10-point preference due to a compensable service-connected disability of 30 percent or more. (These persons are given additional passover and retention rights. They may also be appointed noncompetitively to positions for which they qualified.)

The following types of preference are referred to as derivative preference, because they are derived from the military service of a veteran who is not using the preference:

(4) Ten-point (spouse). The spouse of a disabled veteran is entitled to 10-point (spouse) preference provided that the veteran is disqualified by reason of a service-connected disability for a Federal civil service position along the general lines of his or her usual occupation.

(5) Ten-point (widow or widower). The widow or widower of a veteran is entitled to 10-point (widow or widower) preference under the following conditions:

(a) he or she was not divorced from the veteran;

(b) he or she as not remarried, or the remarriage was annulled; and,

© the veteran
— served during a war; or,
— served during the period April 28, 1952 through July 1, 1955; or,
— served in a campaign or expedition for which a campaign badge has been authorized; or,
— died while on active duty that included service specified above provided that the conditions surrounding the death would not have been cause for other than honorable separation.

(6) Ten-point (mother, deceased veteran). The mother of a deceased veteran is entitled to 10-point (mother) preference under the following conditions:

(a) she is the mother of the veteran who died under honorable conditions when on active duty—during a war; or,
— during the period April 28, 1952 through July 1, 1955; or,
— in a campaign or expedition for which a campaign badge is authorized; and,

---

[3]Under section 307 of Public Law 95-454, signed October 13, 1978, as of October 1, 1980 "preference eligible" will no longer include a retired member of the armed forces, unless the individual is a disabled veteran as defined in subchapter 2-1(6) of this chapter of the individual retired below the rank of major or its equivalent.

(b) she is, or was, married to the father of the veteran; and,

© she—lives with her totally and permanently disabled husband (either the veteran's father or her husband through remarriage); or,
— is widowed, divorced, or separated from the veteran's father but has not remarried; or,
— remarried but is now widowed, divorced, or legally separated from her husband.

(7) Ten-point (mother, disabled veteran). The mother of a living disabled veteran is entitled to 10-point (mother) preference under the following conditions:

(a) She is the mother of the veteran who was separated under honorable conditions from active duty performed at any time; and

➡ (b) the veteran is permanently and totally disabled from a service-connected injury or illness; and ⬅

© she is, or was, married to the father of the veteran; and

(d) she
— lives with her totally and permanently disabled husband (either the veteran's father or husband through remarriage); or,
— is widowed, divorced, or separated from the veteran's father and has not remarried; or,
— did remarry but is now widowed, divorced, or legally separated from her husband.

2—3. DUAL PREFERENCE

Both a mother and a spouse (including widow or widower) may be entitled to preference on the basis of one veteran's service if they both meet the requirements. However, no derivative preference is available if the veteran is living and is qualified for Federal employment.

2—4. PREFERENCE PRESERVED

(1) Service before June 27, 1944. Preference authorized by any law, Executive Order, rule or regulations in effect on June 27, 1944 (the date of the Veterans' Preference Act of 1944) and based on peacetime military service is preserved. However, such peacetime ex-servicepersons (or their spouses or unmarried widows/widowers) have preference only for reduction-in-force purposes. Preserved preference eligibility depends upon the following:

(a) the ex-serviceperson (or spouse or widow/widower) was a Federal employee on June 27, 1944, and has been a Federal employee continuously—since that date without a break in service of more than one workday; or

(b) the ex-serviceperson (or the spouse or widow/widower) was on a register or eligible on June 27, 1944, was appointed from that register, and has been a Federal employee continuously since that appointment without a break in service of more than one workday.

(2) Break in service. For preservation of preference based on peacetime service before June 27, 1944, the time between an employee's separation by reduction-in-force and reemployment from the reemployment priority list is not a break in service.

2—5. MINIMUM SERVICE REQUIREMENT FOR PREFERENCE

a.➜Persons who entered on active duty in the armed forces after October 14, 1976—the closing date for performing peacetime service which qualifies for veterans' preference—do not qualify for preference unless they are disabled veterans under 5 U.S.C. 2108, or serve during a war or in a campaign or expedition for which a campaign badge has been authorized. The statutory minimum length of service requirement described in this section only applies to those ex-servicepersons who may be entitled to preference based on service in a war, campaign, or expedition. It is an additional requirement to be met before an agency or OPM may award preference. A list of campaigns and expeditions appears in FPM supplement 296-33, subchapter 7.

b. Section 408 of Public Law 97-306, enacted October 14, 1982, amended 38 U.S.C. 3103A to clarify the application of the general minimum-service requirement established by Public Law 96-342 enacted September 8, 1980, for Veterans Administration and other veterans' benefits, to the definition of preference eligible under the civil service laws.←

c. Accordingly, to qualify for veterans' preference in Federal employment, *a person who enlists after September 7, 1980, or* ➜ *enters on active duty*[1] ← *on or after October 14, 1982, and has not previously completed 24 months of continuous active duty* must:

(1) perform active duty in the armed forces during a war or in a campaign or expedition for which a campaign badge has been authorized, (the long-standing requirement for preference) *and*

(2) serve continuously for 24 months or the full period called or ordered for active duty.

d. Exclusions. The law excepts a person who:

(1) is discharged or released from active duty (a) for a disability incurred or aggravated in line of duty, or (b) under 10 U.S.C. 1171 or 1173 for hardship or other reasons, or

(2) has a service-connected disability which the Veterans Administration determines is compensable.

e. The service requirement does not affect eligibility for veteran's readjustment appointment or for veterans' preference based on peacetime service exceeding 180 days from 1955 to 1976, or other qualifying service prior to September 8, 1980.

➜ The "enters on active duty" language was added by statutory amendment to make clear that officers and others who may begin active duty through means other than enlistment are subject to the minimum-service requirement. The original 1980 law only covered persons who enlist. ←

Veterans Readjustment Appointments
Expanded Job Opportunities in the Federal Service

Public Law 102-16, effective March 23, 1991, makes it even easier for Federal agencies to hire Armed Forces veterans who served during and after the Vietnam era.

The VRA (Veterans Readjustment Appointment) authority is a special hiring program. Eligible veterans do not have to take examinations or compete with nonveteran candidates. VRA appointees are initially hired for a 2-year period. Successful completion of the 2-year VRA appointment leads to a permanent civil service appointment.

⇒ Who is eligible for a VRA appointment?
Veterans who served more than 180 days active duty, any part of which occurred during the Vietnam era (August 5, 1964 to May 7, 1975), and have other than a dishonorable discharge, are eligible if they have (1) a service-connected disability or (2) a campaign badge (for example, the Vietnam Service Medal).

Post-Vietnam-era veterans, who entered the service after May 7, 1975 are eligible if they served on active duty for more than 180 days and have other than a dishonorable discharge.

The 180-day service requirement does not apply to veterans discharged from active duty for service-connected disability.

⇒ How long are veterans eligible for VRA appointments after they leave the service?
Vietnam-era veterans qualify for a VRA appointment until 10 years after discharge or until December 31, 1993, whichever date is later.

Post-Vietnam-era veterans are eligible for 10 years after the date of their last discharge or until December 17, 1999, whichever date is later.

Eligible veterans with a service-connected disability of 30% or more can be hired without time limit.

⇒ Are there any other restrictions on eligibility for a VRA appointment?
No. Under the new VRA law, all veterans described above are eligible. (The law eliminated a previous requirement that VRA appointees have fewer than 16 years of education.)

⇒ What jobs can be filled under the VRA authority?
Federal agencies now can use the VRA authority to fill any white collar position up through GS 11, blue collar jobs up through WG 11, and equivalent jobs under other Federal pay systems.

⇒ How do veterans apply for VRA authority?
Veterans should contact the agency personnel office where they want to work. Agencies recruit candidates and make VRA appointments directly without getting a list of candidates from OPM. Veterans can get a list of local agency personnel offices from the Veterans Representative at the OPM offices listed on the back of this sheet.

⇒ Are disabled veterans entitled to special consideration?
Agencies must give preference to disabled veterans over other veterans.

⇒ Is training available after appointment?
In some cases, agencies provide special training programs for VRA appointees. A program could include on-the-job assignments or classroom training.

⇒ Can VRA appointees work part-time?
Agencies may be able to set up part-time work schedules for individuals who want to attend school or handle family or other responsibilities.

(over)

United States Office of Personnel Management   Career Entry Group Staffing Policy Division   1900 E Street, NW Washington, DC 20415-0001   CE-100 June 1991

U.S. Office of Personnel Management
Area Office Veterans Representatives for Employment Inquiries

Alabama
Lee Hockenberry
Huntsville Area Office
(205) 544-5130

Alaska
John Busteed
Anchorage Area Office
(907) 271-3617

Arizona
Jack Mallin
Phoenix Area Office
(602) 640-5809

California
John Andre
Los Angeles Area Office
(818)575-6507

Susan Fong Young
Sacramento Area Office
(916) 551-3275

Mark Gunby
San Francisco Area Office
(415) 744-7216

Colorado
Doris Veden
Denver Area Office
(303) 969-7036

Connecticut
A.J. Dubois
Hartford Area Office
(203) 240-3607

Delaware
(See Philadelphia, PA)

District of Columbia
William Robinson
Washington Area Service
 Center
(202) 606-1848

Florida
R.C. McFadyen
Orlando Area Office
(407) 648-6150

Georgia
Ruth Walker
Atlanta Area Office
(404) 221-4588

Hawaii
Charles Tamabayashi
Honolulu Area Office
(808) 541-2790

June 1991

Idaho
(See Washington State)

Illinois
Victoria Jones
Chicago Area Office
(312) 353-8799

Indiana
Sharon Ellet
Indianapolis Area Office
(317) 226-6245

Iowa
(See Kansas City, MO)

Kansas
Veria Davis
Wichita Area Office
(316) 269-6797

Kentucky
(See Ohio)

Louisiana
Melody Silvey
New Orleans Area Office
(504) 589-2768

Maine
(see New Hampshire)

Maryland
Thomas Platt
Baltimore Area Office
(301) 962-3222

Massachusetts
Donald MacGee
Boston Area Office
(617) 565-5926

Michigan
Thomas Bixler
Detroit Area Office
(313) 226-2095

Minnesota
Paul McMahon
Twin Cities Area Office
(612) 725-3633

Mississippi
(See Alabama)

Missouri
Richard Krueger
Kansas City Area Office
(816) 426-5705

Kirk Hawkins
St. Louis Area Office
(314) 539-2341

Montana
(See Colorado)

Nebraska
(See Kansas)

Nevada
(See Sacramento, CA)

New Hampshire
Gloria Dunn
Portsmouth Area Office
(603) 433-0744

New Jersey
Don Hodge
Newark Area Office
(201) 645-2376

New Mexico
Rosa Benavidez
Albuquerque Area Office
(505) 766-1099

New York
Walter Chasin
New York Area Office
(212) 264-0442

Larry Burkett
Syracuse Area Office
(315) 423-5650

North Carolina
Ayn Clayborne
Raleigh Area Office
(919) 790-2817

North Dakota
(See Minnesota)

Ohio
John McConnell
Dayton Area Office
(513) 225-2529

Oklahoma
Dan Henderson
Oklahoma City Area
 Office
(405) 231-4613

Oregon
(See Washington State)

Pennsylvania
John Glooch
Harrisburg Field Office
(717) 782-4546

Gene Hyden
Philadelphia Area Office
(215) 597-7670

Pennsylvania (continued)
George Horn
Pittsburgh Area Office
(412) 644-4355

Puerto Rico
Viven Fernandez
San Juan Area Office
(809) 765-5620

Rhode Island
(See Connecticut)

South Carolina
(See North Carolina)

South Dakota
(See Minnesota)

Tennessee
Ralph Bunten
Memphis Area Office
(901) 544-3958

Texas
Frank McLemore
Dallas Area Office
(214) 767-9133

Jose Borrero
San Antonio Area Office
(512) 229-6613

Utah
(See Colorado)

Vermont
(See new Hampshire)

Virgin Islands
(See Puerto Rico)

Virginia
Valerie DeMeis
Norfolk Area Office
(804) 441-3362

Washington (State)
Robert Coleman
Seattle Area Office
(206) 553-4691

West Virginia
(See Ohio)

Wisconsin
(See Illinois)

Wyoming
(See Colorado)

APPLICATION PACKAGE LOG SHEET

Job Series, Grade and Title:_____

Target Agency:_____**Closing Date:**_____

Point of Contact:_____**Phone#:**_____

Date Package Was Sent:_____

Follow-up Action   **Date**   **Remarks**

OPTIONAL APPLICATION FOR FEDERAL EMPLOYMENT
(OF 612 -- Form Approved: OMB No. 3206-021)

You may apply for most jobs with a resume, this form, or other written format. If your resume or application does not provide all the information requested on this form and in the job vacancy announcement, you may lose consideration for a job.

===

1. JOB TITLE IN ANNOUNCEMENT: ------------------------------------

2. GRADE(S) APPLYING FOR: ----------------

3. ANNOUNCEMENT NUMBER: ----------------------

4. LAST NAME: --------------------- FIRST, MIDDLE: -------------------------

5. SOCIAL SECURITY NUMBER: - -
   ------- ---- -------

6. MAILING ADDRESS: --

   CITY/STATE/ZIP: --

7. PHONE NUMBERS (include area code) DAYTIME: -----------------------

                                      EVENING: -----------------------

===

8. WORK EXPERIENCE: Describe your paid and nonpaid work experience related to the job for which you are applying. (Do not attach job descriptions)

1) JOB TITLE (If Federal, include series and grade): --

   FROM (MM/YY): ------------   TO (MM/YY): ------------

   SALARY: $ ------------ per -------- HOURS PER WEEK: --------

   EMPLOYER'S NAME: ---

       AND ADDRESS: ---

   SUPERVISOR'S NAME: -----------------------------------

       AND PHONE: -------------------------------

DESCRIBE YOUR DUTIES AND ACCOMPLISHMENTS:

DUTIES AND ACCOMPLISHMENTS: (CONTINUED)

2) JOB TITLE (If Federal,
   include series and grade): --

   FROM (MM/YY): _____   TO (MM/YY): _____

   SALARY: $ _____ per _____   HOURS PER WEEK: _____

   EMPLOYER'S NAME:

   AND ADDRESS:

   SUPERVISOR'S NAME:

   AND PHONE:

   DESCRIBE YOUR DUTIES AND ACCOMPLISHMENTS:

9. MAY WE CONTACT YOUR CURRENT SUPERVISOR? (If we need to   YES [   ]
    contact your current supervisor before making an offer,
    we will contact you first.)   NO [   ]

EDUCATION

10. MARK HIGHEST LEVEL COMPLETED:
Some HS   [   ]   Bachelor [   ]
HS/GED   [   ]   Master   [   ]
Associate [   ]   Doctoral [   ]

11. LAST HIGH SCHOOL or GED SCHOOL:

CITY/STATE/ZIP(if ZIP known):

YEAR DIPLOMA or GED RECEIVED:
----

12. COLLEGES AND UNIVERSITIES ATTENDED (Do not attach a copy of your transcript unless requested.)

1) NAME:

CITY/STATE/ZIP:

SEMESTER CREDITS EARNED: MAJOR(S):
        (or)   ------   -------------------
QUARTER CREDITS EARNED:
                         ------   -------------------
DEGREE (If any):   YEAR RECEIVED:
         --------------------------   -------

2) NAME:

CITY/STATE/ZIP:

SEMESTER CREDITS EARNED: MAJOR(S):
        (or)   ------   -------------------
QUARTER CREDITS EARNED:
                         ------   -------------------
DEGREE (If any):   YEAR RECEIVED:
         --------------------------   -------

3) NAME:

CITY/STATE/ZIP:

SEMESTER CREDITS EARNED: MAJOR(S):
        (or)   ------   -------------------
QUARTER CREDITS EARNED:
                         ------   -------------------
DEGREE (If any):   YEAR RECEIVED:
         --------------------------   -------

==

OTHER QUALIFICATIONS

13. Job-related training courses (give title and year). Job-related skills (other languages, computer software/hardware, tools, machinery, typing speed, etc.). Job-related certificates and licenses (current only). Job-related honors, awards, and special accomplishments (publications, memberships in professional/honor societies, leadership activities, public speaking, and performance awards). Give dates, but do not send documents unless requested.

OTHER QUALIFICATIONS (CONTINUED)

==
GENERAL:

14. ARE YOU A U.S. CITIZEN? .... YES [　] NO [　]

    If NO, give the country of your citizenship:
    ----

15. DO YOU CLAIM VETERANS' PREFERENCE? .... YES [　] NO [　]

    If YES, mark your claim of 5 or 10 points below:

        5 POINTS [　] -- Attach your DD 214 or other proof.

        10 POINTS [　] -- Attach an Application for 10-Point Veterans'
                         Preference (SF 15) and proof required.

16. WERE YOU EVER A FEDERAL CIVILIAN EMPLOYEE? ..... YES [　] NO [　]

    If YES, for Highest Civilian Grade give:

    SERIES: _____   GRADE: _____   FROM (MM/YY): _____   TO (MM/YY): _____

17. ARE YOU ELIGIBLE FOR REINSTATEMENT BASED ON
    CAREER OR CAREER-CONDITIONAL FEDERAL STATUS? ... YES [　] NO [　]

    If requested, attach SF 50 proof.

APPLICANT CERTIFICATION

18. I certify that, to the best of my knowledge and belief, all of the
    information on and attached to this application is true, correct,
    complete and made in good faith. I understand that false or fraud-
    ulent information on or attached to this application may be grounds
    for not hiring me or for firing me after I begin work, and may be
    punishable by fine or imprisonment. I understand that any informa-
    tion I give may be investigated.

    SIGNATURE: DATE SIGNED:
    --------------------------------   ------------

(Alternate) Work Experience Continuation for OF-612

1 Job title in announcement

2 Grade(s) applying for

3 Announcement number

4 Last name

First and middle names

5 Social Security Number

WORK EXPERIENCE continued

Job title (if Federal, include series and grade)

From (MM/YY)

To (MM/YY)

Salary
$

per

Hours per week

Employer's name and address

Supervisor's name and phone number
(   )

Describe your duties and accomplishments

(Alternate) Work Experience Continuation for OF-612

1 Job title in announcement		2 Grade(s) applying for	3 Announcement number
4 Last name	First and middle names		5 Social Security Number

WORK EXPERIENCE continued

Job title (if Federal, include series and grade)

From (MM/YY)	To (MM/YY)	Salary $	per	Hours per week
Employer's name and address				Supervisor's name and phone number ( )

Describe your duties and accomplishments

Job title (if Federal, include series and grade)

From (MM/YY)	To (MM/YY)	Salary $	per	Hours per week
Employer's name and address				Supervisor's name and phone number ( )

Describe your duties and accomplishments

General Purpose Continuation for OF-612

1 Job title in announcement		2 Grade(s) applying for	3 Announcement number
4 Last name	First and middle names		5 Social Security Number

ADDITIONAL SPACE FOR OF-612 ANSWERS

ITEM NO.	RESPONSE

Optional Form 306
September 1994
U.S. Office of Personnel Management

Declaration for Federal Employment

Form Approved:
O.M.B. No. 3206-0182
NSN 7540-01-368-7775
50306-101

GENERAL INFORMATION

1 FULL NAME
▶

2 SOCIAL SECURITY NUMBER
▶

3 PLACE OF BIRTH (Include City and State or Country)
▶

4 DATE OF BIRTH (MM/DD/YY)
▶

5 OTHER NAMES EVER USED (For example, maiden name, nickname, etc.)
▶
▶

6 PHONE NUMBERS (Include Area Codes)

DAY ▶

NIGHT ▶

MILITARY SERVICE

	Yes	No
7 Have you served in the United States Military Service? *If your only active duty was training in the Reserves or National Guard, answer "NO".*		

If you answered "YES", list the branch, dates (MM/DD/YY), and type of discharge for all active duty military service.

BRANCH	FROM	TO	TYPE OF DISCHARGE

BACKGROUND INFORMATION

For all questions, provide all additional requested information under item 15 or on attached sheets. The circumstances of each event you list will be considered. However, in most cases you can still be considered for Federal jobs.

For questions 8, 9, and 10, your answers should include convictions resulting from a plea of nolo contendere *(no contest)*, but omit (1) traffic fines of $300 or less, (2) any violation of law committed before your 16th birthday, (3) any violation of law committed before your 18th birthday if finally decided in juvenile court or under a Youth Offender law, (4) any conviction set aside under the Federal Youth Corrections Act or similar State law, and (5) any conviction whose record was expunged under Federal or State law.

	Yes	No
8 During the last 10 years, have you been convicted, been imprisoned, been on probation, or been on parole? (Includes felonies, firearms or explosives violations, misdemeanors, and all other offenses.) *If "Yes", use item 15 to provide the date, explanation of the violation, place of occurrence, and the name and address of the police department or court involved.*		
9 Have you been convicted by a military court-martial in the past 10 years? (If no military service, answer "NO".) *If "Yes", use item 15 to provide the date, explanation of the violation, place of occurrence, and the name and address of the military authority or court involved.*		
10 Are you now under charges for any violation of law? *If "Yes", use item 15 to provide the date, explanation of the violation, place of occurrence, and the name and address of the police department or court involved.*		
11 During the last 5 years, were you fired from any job for any reason, did you quit after being told that you would be fired, did you leave any job by mutual agreement because of specific problems, or were you debarred from Federal employment by the Office of Personnel Management? *If "Yes", use item 15 to provide the date, an explanation of the problem and reason for leaving, and the employer's name and address.*		
12 Are you delinquent on any Federal debt? (Includes delinquencies arising from Federal taxes, loans, overpayment of benefits, and other debts to the U.S. Government, plus defaults of Federally guaranteed or insured loans such as student and home mortgage loans.) *If "Yes", use item 15 to provide the type, length, and amount of the delinquency or default, and steps that you are taking to correct the error or repay the debt.*		

ADDITIONAL QUESTIONS

	Yes	No
13 Do any of your relatives work for the agency or organization to which you are submitting this form? (Includes father, mother, husband, wife, son, daughter, brother, sister, uncle, aunt, first cousin, nephew, niece, father-in-law, mother-in-law, son-in-law, daughter-in-law, brother-in-law, sister-in-law, stepfather, stepmother, stepson, stepdaughter, stepbrother, stepsister, half brother, and half sister.) *If "Yes", use item 15 to provide the name, relationship, and the Department, Agency, or Branch of the Armed Forces for which your relative works.*		
14 Do you receive, or have you ever applied for, retirement pay, pension, or other pay based on military, Federal civilian, or District of Columbia Government service?		

CONTINUATION SPACE / AGENCY OPTIONAL QUESTIONS

15 Provide details requested in items 8 through 13 and 17c in the continuation space below or on attached sheets. Be sure to identify attached sheets with your name, Social Security Number, and item number, and to include ZIP Codes in all addresses. If any questions are printed below, please answer as instructed (these questions are specific to your position, and your agency is authorized to ask them).

CERTIFICATIONS / ADDITIONAL QUESTION

APPLICANT: If you are applying for a position and have not yet been selected, Carefully review your answers on this form and any attached sheets. When this form and all attached materials are accurate, complete item 16/16a.

APPOINTEE: If you are being appointed, Carefully review your answers on this form and any attached sheets, including any other application materials that your agency has attached to this form. If any information requires correction to be accurate as of the date you are signing, make changes on this form or the attachments and/or provide updated information on additional sheets, initialing and dating all changes and additions. When this form and all attached materials are accurate, complete item 16/16b and answer item 17.

16 **I certify** that, to the best of my knowledge and belief, all of the information on and attached to this Declaration for Federal Employment, including any attached application materials, is true, correct, complete, and made in good faith. **I understand** that a false or fraudulent answer to any question on any part of this declaration or its attachments may be grounds for not hiring me, or for firing me after I begin work, and may be punishable by fine or imprisonment. **I understand** that any information I give may be investigated for purposes of determining eligibility for Federal employment as allowed by law or Presidential order. **I consent** to the release of information about my ability and fitness for Federal employment by *employers, schools, law enforcement agencies,* and *other individuals and organizations* to *investigators, personnel specialists,* and *other authorized employees of the Federal Government.* **I understand** that for financial or lending institutions, medical institutions, hospitals, health care professionals, and some other sources of information, a separate specific release may be needed, and I may be contacted for such a release at a later date.

16a Applicant's Signature ▶
  (Sign in ink)   Date ▶

16b Appointee's Signature ▶
  (Sign in ink)   Date ▶   APPOINTING OFFICER: Enter Date of Appointment or Conversion ▶

17 **Appointee Only** *(Respond only if you have been employed by the Federal Government before):* Your elections of life insurance during previous Federal employment may affect your eligibility for life insurance during your new appointment. These questions are asked to help your personnel office make a correct determination.

Date *(MM/DD/YY)*

17a When did you leave your last Federal job? -

	Yes	No	Don't Know

17b When you worked for the Federal Government the last time, did you waive Basic Life Insurance or any type of optional life insurance? - - - - - - - - -

17c If you answered "Yes" to item 17b, did you later cancel the waiver(s)? *If your answer to item 17c is "No," use item 15 to identify the type(s) of insurance for which waivers were not cancelled.* - - - - - - - - - - - - - -

INDEX

A

Action plan, 60-69
Agencies, 61
Application(s):
    changes, 1, 15
    checklist, 195-197
    completing, 11
    knowledge, 7-8
    packets, 11, 43-59, 150-194
    updating, 11-12
Assets, 60-61
Awards, 50

B

Blocks, 46-51
Blue collar:
    jobs, 9-10, 31
    qualification standards, 39-40
Bumping rights, 24

C

Career America Connection, 26
Checklist, 195-197
Civilian Personnel Law Manual, 26
Classification standards program, 32
College:
    courses, 13, 212-214
    degrees, 8-9, 13
    majors, 12
    students, 12
Computer program, 5
Congress, 20
Continuation sheets, 57
Copies, 44, 46

D

Deaf, 108
Department of Defense, 28
Department of State, 15
Department of Veterans Affairs, 15
Description of work, 52-56

E

Education, 8-9, 32-33, 44, 48-49, 60-61
Employment, 22-25
Equivalency, 36
Evaluation, 3-4, 30
Examinations, 12-13
Excepted Service, 16
Executive schedule, 19, 93
Experience, 37-38

F

Failure, 65
Federal agencies, 27-28
Federal Career Opportunities, 29

Federal employment, 21-22, 47
Federal government, 20-21
Federal Employment Information Centers,
    27, 102-107
Federal Job Opportunities Bulletin Board,
    26-27, 108
Federal Jobs Digest, 29
*Federal Occupational and Career
    Information System (FOCIS),* 27, 52
Follow-through, 65
Foreign Service, 16
Forms (see Standard Forms)

G
General Schedule:
    jobs, 16-18
    occupations, 76-89
Grade level, 46

H
*Handbook of Occupational Groups
    and Series,* 26
Handbook X-118, 28
Handbook X-118C, 28
Honors, 50

I
In service placement, 35

J
Job announcements, 109-118
Job hotlines, 66

K
KSAs (see KSAOs)
KSAOs, 2, 40-41, 58-59, 115

L
Language, 11, 54-56
Law enforcement pay, 91
Libraries, 29
Locality pay differentials, 94

M
Military experience, 13-14

Minimum requirements, 49
Myths, 7-14

O
Occupations, 76-89
Occupational groups, 16
OF 612, 2, 57
Office of Personnel Management,
    1, 25-27
One Stop Job Shops, 28
OPM Form 1170/17, 211-215

P
Pay:
    comparable, 17
    competitive, 16
    Executive Schedule, 19
    law enforcement, 91
    locality, 16
    Metro D.C. clerical, 91
    schedule, 90-94
Personal information, 44
Personnel specialists, 1, 16, 30
Position(s):
    defining, 29
    management, 4, 15-16, 19-20
    requirements, 29
    standards, 30-42
Position Classification Standards,
    37, 141-149
Position Qualification Standards,
    119-140
Positions, 3, 29, 30-42
Professional services, 10
Publications, 66-67

R
Ratings, 65
Realities, 7-14
Reduction-in-force (RIF), 10, 22-24
References, 50
Regions, 102-107
Reproductions, 46
Resources, 26
Resumes, 2, 178-183
Retreat rights, 24

S

Salaries, 47, 90-94
Schedules, 90-93
Senior Executive Service (SES), 19
SF 15, 216
SF 171, 2, 10 199-203
SF 171 package, 44-59
SF 171-A, 204-205
SF 172, 12, 25, 208-210
Skills, 50, 55
Standard forms, 198-233
Standards:
  agency, 35
  general, 35
State employment offices, 28-29
Status, 40-41
Subscriptions, 67
Supplemental sheets, 57, 206-209

T

Target jobs, 45, 62
Terminology, 70-75
Timetable, 65
Turnover, 22-25

U

Updates, 12

V

Vacancies, 66
Veterans, 14
Veterans Health Administration, 92
Veterans Preference, 48, 216
Veterans Readjustment Appointment
  applicants, 35

W

Wage Grade:
  jobs, 9, 18, 38
  positions, 95-101
  qualification standards, 38
Wage Grade positions, 95-101
Washington Area Service Center, 27
White collar, 9, 31
Work:
  experience, 44

history, 32-33
Workforce reductions, 22-25

X

X-118 Handbook (see *Handbook
  X-118*)
X-118C Handbook (see *Handbook
  X-118C*)
X-118 Qualification Standards Handbook,
  32, 34, 70
X-118 Qualifications Standards, 32-33
X-118C Qualification Standards, 38-40

CAREER RESOURCES

Call or write Impact Publications to receive a free copy of their latest comprehensive and annotated catalog of over 2,000 career resources (books, subscriptions, training programs, videos, audiocassettes, computer software, CD-ROM).

The following career resources are available directly from Impact Publications. Complete this form or list the titles, include postage (see formula at the end), enclose payment, specify your name and address, and send your order to:

IMPACT PUBLICATIONS
9104-N Manassas Drive
Manassas Park, VA 22111
Tel. 703/361-7300
Fax 703/335-9486

Orders from individuals must be prepaid by check, moneyorder, Visa or MasterCard number. We accept telephone and fax orders with a Visa or MasterCard number.

Qty.	Titles	Price	TOTAL
GOVERNMENT JOBS			
___	Book of American Government Jobs	15.95	_____
___	Book of U.S. Postal Exams	17.95	_____
___	Civil Service Handbook	9.95	_____
___	Complete Guide to Public Employment	19.95	_____
___	Complete Guide to U.S. Civil Service Jobs	9.95	_____
___	Directory of Federal Jobs and Employers	21.95	_____
___	Federal Applications That Get Results	23.95	_____
___	Federal Jobs for College Grads	14.95	_____
___	Federal Jobs in Computers	14.95	_____
___	Federal Jobs in Finance and Accounting	14.95	_____
___	Federal Jobs in Law Enforcement	14.95	_____
___	Federal Jobs in Nursing and Health Sciences	14.95	_____

239

___ Federal Jobs in Office Administration   14.95   _____
___ Federal Jobs in Secret Operations   14.95   _____
___ Federal Resumes Guidebook (with diskette)   34.95   _____
___ Find a Federal Job Fast!   13.95   _____
___ General Test Practice For 101 U.S. Jobs   9.95   _____
___ Government Directory of Addresses and Telephone Numbers   149.95   _____
___ Government Job Finder   16.95   _____
___ How to Get a Federal Job   15.00   _____
___ How to Get an Overseas Job With the Federal Government   28.95   _____
___ Law Enforcement Careers   12.95   _____
___ Law Enforcement Employment   19.95   _____

FEDERAL JOB LISTINGS/SUBSCRIPTIONS

___ Federal Career Opportunities (6 issues)   39.00   _____
___ Federal Career Opportunities (25 issues)   175.00   _____
___ Federal Jobs Digest (6 issues)   35.00   _____
___ Federal Jobs Digest (25 issues)   125.00   _____

COMPUTER SOFTWARE FOR FEDERAL JOBS (IBM only)

___ USJOBS Database (annual subscription for 1 user)   375.00   _____
___ FOCIS: Federal Occupational and Career Information System   69.95   _____
___ Quick & Easy Federal Application Kit (individual—1 user)   49.95   _____
___ Quick & Easy Federal Application Kit (organization—unlimited)   399.95   _____

CONSULTANTS AND GOVERNMENT CONTRACTORS

___ Consultants and Consulting Organizations Directory   835.00   _____
___ Consultant's Proposal, Fee, and Contract Problem-Solver   19.95   _____
___ How to Succeed as an Independent Consultant   27.95   _____
___ Winning Government Contracts   19.95   _____

JOBS WITH NONPROFIT ORGANIZATIONS

___ Finding a Job in the Nonprofit Sector   95.00   _____
___ Good Works   24.00   _____
___ Jobs and Careers With Nonprofit Organizations   15.95   _____
___ Non-Profits' Job Finder   16.95   _____

LETTERS AND RESUMES

___ 175 High-Impact Cover Letters   10.95   _____
___ 200 Letters For Job Hunters   19.95   _____
___ Adams Resume Almanac   10.95   _____
___ Conquer Resume Objections   10.95   _____
___ Cover Letters That Knock 'Em Dead   9.95   _____
___ Damn Good Resume Guide   6.95   _____
___ Dynamite Cover Letters   11.95   _____
___ Dynamite Resumes   11.95   _____
___ Electronic Resumes for the New Job Market   11.95   _____
___ Encyclopedia of Job-Winning Resumes   16.95   _____
___ Gallery of Best Resumes   16.95   _____
___ High Impact Resumes and Letters   14.95   _____
___ Job Search Letters That Get Results   15.95   _____
___ Just Resumes   9.95   _____
___ No-Pain Resume Workbook   14.95   _____

___ Perfect Cover Letter   9.95   _____
___ Perfect Resume   12.00   _____
___ Ready -to-Go Resumes (with diskette)   29.95   _____
___ Resume Catalog   15.95   _____
___ Resume Writing Made Easy   10.95   _____
___ Resumes That Knock 'Em Dead   9.95   _____
___ Revising Your Resume   13.95   _____
___ Sure-Hire Resumes   10.95   _____
___ Your First Resume   8.95   _____

COMPUTER SOFTWARE (all IBM; some Apple available)

___ Building Your Job Search Foundation   69.95   _____
___ Creative Resume   139.95   _____
___ INSTANT™ Job Winning Letters System   39.95   _____
___ JOBHUNT™ Quick & Easy Employer Contacts   59.95   _____
___ Jumpstart Your Job Skills   69.95   _____
___ Perfect Resume Computer Kit (Personal)   49.95   _____
___ ResumeMaker™   49.95   _____
___ Right Resume Writer I   59.95   _____
___ Right Resume Writer II   102.95   _____
___ Right Resume Writer III   102.95   _____
___ You're Hired   59.95   _____

JOB SEARCH STRATEGIES AND TACTICS

___ Change Your Job, Change Your Life!   15.95   _____
___ Complete Job Finder's Guide For the 90s   13.95   _____
___ Discover the Best Jobs For You   11.95   _____
___ Five Secrets to Finding a Job   12.95   _____
___ What Color Is Your Parachute?   14.95   _____

ALTERNATIVE JOBS, CAREERS, AND EMPLOYERS

___ 101 Careers   16.95   _____
___ Adams Jobs Almanac (annual)   15.00   _____
___ America's 50 Fastest Growing Jobs   15.95   _____
___ American Almanac of Jobs and Salaries   17.00   _____
___ Best Jobs for the 1990s and Into the 21st Century   19.95   _____
___ Dictionary of Occupational Titles (1991 ed.)   39.95   _____
___ Directory of Executive Recruiters (annual)   39.95   _____
___ Directory of Outplacement Firms (annual)   74.95   _____
___ Educator's Guide to Alternative Jobs and Careers   13.95   _____
___ Encyclopedia of Careers and Vocational Guidance   129.95   _____
___ Environmental Career Guide   14.95   _____
___ Flying High in Travel   19.95   _____
___ Jobs 1996   15.95   _____
___ Jobs For People Who Love Travel   15.95   _____
___ Jobs Rated Almanac   16.95   _____
___ New Emerging Careers   14.95   _____
___ Occupational Outlook Handbook (biannual)   21.95   _____
___ Professional's Private Sector Job Finder   18.95   _____
___ Rites of Passage at $100,000+   29.95   _____
___ Where the Jobs Are   15.95   _____

SELF-ASSESSMENT AND GOAL SETTING

___ Career Discovery Project	12.95	_____
___ Discover What You're Best At	10.95	_____
___ New Quick Job Hunting Map	3.95	_____
___ Three Boxes of Life	14.95	_____
___ Truth About You	11.95	_____
___ Where Do I Go From Here With My Life?	11.95	_____
___ Wishcraft	10.95	_____

SELF-ESTEEM, PROBLEM SOLVING, MANAGING CHANGE

___ 7 Habits of Highly Effective People	12.00	_____
___ Do What You Love, and the Money Will Follow	11.95	_____
___ First Things First	22.00	_____
___ Getting Unstuck	9.95	_____
___ Re-Inventing Your Life	11.95	_____
___ Stop Postponing the Rest of Your Life	9.95	_____
___ Unlimited Power	12.00	_____

INTERVIEWS, NETWORKING, AND SALARIES

___ 60 Seconds and You're Hired	9.95	_____
___ Conquer Interview Objections	10.95	_____
___ Dynamite Answers to Interview Questions	11.95	_____
___ Dynamite Salary Negotiations	13.95	_____
___ Dynamite Tele-Search	12.95	_____
___ Great Connections: Small Talk & Networking for Businesspeople	11.95	_____
___ How to Get Interviews From Classified Job Ads	14.95	_____
___ Interview for Success	13.95	_____
___ *New* Network Your Way To Job and Career Success	12.95	_____
___ Perfect Follow-up to Win the Job	9.95	_____
___ Power Networking	14.95	_____
___ Sweaty Palms	8.95	_____

DRESS, APPEARANCE, AND IMAGE

___ 110 Mistakes Working Women Make and How to Avoid Them: Dressing Smart in the '90s	9.95	_____
___ Amy Vanderbilt Complete Book of Etiquette	27.50	_____
___ Dress for Success	10.95	_____
___ How to Present a Professional Image Video (2 tapes)	149.95	_____
___ Mistakes Men Make That Women Hate	6.95	_____
___ Red Socks Don't Work! Messages From the Real World About Men's Clothing	14.95	_____
___ Winning Image	17.95	_____

INTERNATIONAL AND OVERSEAS JOBS

___ Almanac of International Jobs and Careers	19.95	_____
___ Complete Guide to International Jobs and Careers	13.95	_____
___ How to Get a Job In Europe	17.95	_____
___ How to Get a Job In the Pacific Rim	17.95	_____
___ International Jobs	14.95	_____
___ Jobs Worldwide	17.95	_____
___ Passport to Overseas Employment	14.95	_____
___ Teaching English Abroad	15.95	_____

___ Work Your Way Around the World   17.95   _____
___ Work, Study, Travel Abroad   13.95

MILITARY AND SPOUSES

___ Beyond the Uniform   12.95
___ From Air Force Blue to Corporate Gray   17.95   _____
___ From Army Green to Corporate Gray   15.95   _____
___ From Navy Blue to Corporate Gray   17.95   _____
___ Job Search: Marketing Your Military Experience   16.95   _____
___ *New* Relocating Spouse's Guide To Employment   14.95   _____
___ Re-Entry   13.95   _____
___ Resumes and Cover Letters for Transitioning
     Military Personnel   17.95   _____
___ Retiring From the Military   24.95   _____

WOMEN

___ Every Woman's Essential Job Hunting and Resume Book   11.95
___ More Power to You   10.95   _____
___ Resumes for Re-Entry   10.95   _____
___ Smart Woman's Guide to Resumes and Job Hunting   9.95   _____
___ Survival Guide for Women   16.95   _____

MINORITIES AND DISABLED

___ The Big Book of Minority Opportunities   39.95
___ Financial Aid for Minority Students   29.95   _____
___ Job Strategies for People With Disabilities   14.95   _____
___ Minority Organizations   49.95   _____
___ Successful Job Search Strategies for the Disabled   14.95   _____

STUDENTS AND RECENT GRADUATES

___ College Majors and Careers   15.95
___ Graduating To the 9-5 World   11.95   _____

CD-ROM

___ Encyclopedia of Associations   595.95
___ Ultimate Job Source   49.95   _____
___ Ultimate Job Source (institutional version)   199.95   _____
___ WinWay Resume 3.0 (single user)   69.95   _____
___ WinWay Resume 3.0 (10-user labpak)   469.95   _____

SUBTOTAL   _____

Virginia residents add
4½% sales tax   _____

POSTAGE/HANDLING
($4.00 for first title and 1.00 $4.00
for each additional book)   _____

TOTAL ENCLOSED -------------------------- _____

SHIP TO:

NAME _____

ADDRESS _____

_____

_____

CITY _____ STATE _____ ZIP _____

PAYMENT METHOD:

❑   I enclose check/money order for $ _____ made payable
to IMPACT PUBLICATIONS

❑   Please charge $ _____ to my credit card:

    ❑ Visa   ❑ MasterCard   ❑ American Express

Card # _____

Expiration date _____/_____

Signature _____

SEND TO:

IMPACT PUBLICATIONS
9104-N Manassas Drive
Manassas Park, VA 22111-5211
Tel. 703/371-7300
Fax 703/335-9486

Find a Federal Job Fast Kit

 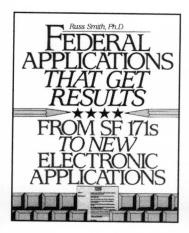 

- **FIND A FEDERAL JOB FAST! How to Cut the Red Tape and Get Hired.** (3rd Edition). *Drs. Ron & Caryl Krannich.* The first book all federal job hunters need to read *prior to* targeting agencies and completing applications. Provides a sound overview of the federal hiring process. Reveals the inside story on locating job vacancies, completing a winning application, marketing oneself among agencies, and getting quickly hired for many jobs. 240 pages. 1995. $13.95

- **THE DIRECTORY OF FEDERAL JOBS AND EMPLOYERS.** *Drs. Ron & Caryl Krannich.* This directory provides the critical contact information on thousands of federal government agencies. Identifies job opportunities with executive, legislative, and judicial branches of government. Includes names, addresses, and phone numbers of personnel offices and job hotlines. Describes the work of specific agencies. 289 pages. 1996. $21.95

- **FEDERAL APPLICATIONS THAT GET RESULTS: From SF 171s to Federal-Style Resumes.** *Dr. Russ Smith.* A comprehensive guide to completing critical federal application forms—SF 171, OF-612, OF-306, and federal-style resumes. Outlines what federal employers look for on applications, major writing principles, the best language to use (KSA's), how to customize your application, and much more. Includes examples of completed applications and special chapters on distribution and resources. Useful appendices include sample forms, critical sections from the all-important *X-118 Handbook*, and addresses of the FEICs. 210 pages. 1996. $23.95

- **THE FEDERAL RESUME GUIDEBOOK (With PC Diskette).** *Kathryn K. Troutman.* The first guide to focus exclusively on the new Federal-style resume. Provides step-by-step guidance on how to write a job-winning Federal resume that meets OPM guidelines and is technically scannable. Includes numerous examples of resumes and letters. Comes complete with a computer diskette. Includes a sample resume and template for creating a Federal-style resume. 1995. $34.95

- **QUICK AND EASY FEDERAL APPLICATIONS KIT.** *DataTech.* Here's the most advanced computerized federal application program available today. If you plan to apply for a federal job, it's best to produce your SF-171, OF-612, or federal-style resume with this powerful software program. Turns blank paper into a completed application using most printers on the market. Prints the form. Approved by the U.S. Office of Personnel Management. Available in 4 versions: **Personal** (single user only): $49.95; **Family** (2 users only): $59.95; **Office** (8 users only): $129.95; **Organization** (unlimited users): $399.95. For IBM or compatible systems only. Available for Windows only.

- **FOCIS: FEDERAL OCCUPATIONAL & CAREER INFORMATION SYSTEM.** *U.S. Office of Personnel Management.* This interactive program helps federal employees and job seekers obtain information about federal careers, occupations, agencies, current job openings, and training. Contains database on nearly 600 federal occupations and 300 federal organizations. Users with modems can dial into an OPM bulletin board, electronically transfer current job vacancy listings to their computer, and search for job openings using FOCIS. Federal employees can access information on more than 1,000 nationwide training courses. Software: three 3½" diskettes, 1.44 M high density. Documentation included. System: IBM-PC or compatible, PC-DOS 3.0 or higher operating system, 400K. Hard disk requires 2.5 to 12.7 Mb depending on the combination of modules installed. Language: dBase II plus compiled in Clipper. Drive should be a 286 or higher processor. An incredible buy at only $69.95!

- **FEDERAL CAREER OPPORTUNITIES.** The best and most comprehensive listing of current federal job vacancies. Includes 3,400 positions from grades GS-5 through SES. Organized by GS series within each agency. Published biweekly as a 64-90 page directory. Subscription rates: 6 issues, $39; 1 year (25 issues), $175.

SPECIAL SAVINGS ON TOTAL PACKAGE: Individuals can purchase the complete package (4 books, 2 software programs, and a 6 issue subscription) for $239.95. Institutions requiring organizational version (unlimited users) of *Quick and Easy Federal Applications Kit* and a 1-year subscription to *Federal Career Opportunities* can purchase this complete package for $1,099.95. Please add $10.00 shipping for complete package. If ordering individual titles, add $4.00 for first item and $1.00 for each additional item. Send your order to:

IMPACT PUBLICATIONS
9104-N Manassas Drive
Manassas Park, VA 22111-5211
Tel. 703/361-7300 (Visa/MasterCard/Amex)
Fax 703/335-9486 (Visa/MasterCard/Amex).
